I0127015

ODYSSEUS & THE OAR

HEALING AFTER WAR AND MILITARY SERVICE

ADAM MAGERS, MA, LPC

DEAD RECKONING

20 17

COLLECTIVE

Publisher: Dead Reckoning Collective
Editor: Arnie Kotler
Book Cover Artwork: Ben Cantwell

Printed in the United States of America

ISBN-13: *978-1-963803-05-1* (paperback)

For more information, please visit:

odyseeusandtheoar.com

and

deadreckoningco.com

For Brittany, Theo, and Willow—thank you
for encouraging and inspiring my post-war adventure.
You were the beacons that brought me home.

For everyone who has worn a military uniform, and
for those who've carried the sounds, memories, and pain of battle
in their hearts:
This book is for you.

PRAISE FOR ODYSSEUS & THE OAR

"I urge all veterans struggling with the wounds of military service, and all those trying to help them, to read this wise and profound book. Despite decades of effort by good sincere therapists working with veterans suffering with Post Traumatic Stress, the record level of veteran suicides and continued toll of addiction, failed marriages, and joblessness, should tell us that current methods of therapy are failing. Some methods may even be doing more harm than good. Magers offers an alternative. I wish Adam Magers could be every veteran's therapist and every therapist's supervisor. Since that's impossible, this book offers the next best thing: a roadmap to help guide our veterans home."

— Karl Marlantes, author of *What It Is Like to Go to War* and *Matterhorn*

"Adam's book is a step-by-step guide that helps readers develop a broad understanding of the journey military veterans must make to 'return home,'; or for anyone trying to come back home after a traumatic event. His exploration of Homer's Odyssey through the lens of Jungian psychology helped me reframe my own 13-year journey home, and to ask, and answer, questions I needed to examine to better understand my life since leaving the military. If the point of therapy isn't just about feeling better, but really to help understand how to better feel—and then let those feelings help guide us—this book is therapy."

— Stacy Bare, Iraq War Veteran, Former US Infantry Officer, Co-Founder of Veterans Expeditions, Director of Adventure Not War, 2014 National Geographic Adventurer of the Year

"Adam's book provides inspiration for veterans suffering from PTSD, as he shines a light on the shadows of the human psyche while exploring the long 'journey home' after war and military service. Through stories and dreams, personal and shared, Odysseus and the Oar presents a new perspective on veterans' experiences that leads to a deeper connection with the soul, creating spiritual and mental awareness. This is a must-read for any veteran seeking a deeper understanding of the wounds that still exist after returning from war."

— Chris Mendoza, Iraq War Veteran, Former US Army Officer and Drill Sergeant

"Our well-intended treatments for warriors coming home with PTSD, involving brief therapy and often medications, has generally failed our fellow citizens. The reason is because cognitive and behavioral treatments affect only mental and behavioral issues. Adam Magers's Odyssey & the Oar convincingly asserts that the deepest wounds are to the soul, one's core sense of self and relation to others. Only when the deeper zones of trauma are reached can healing move forward. Part of the brilliance of this book is seeing how this problem is not new, but was intuitively embodied in the work of The Odyssey, the story of a warrior trying to come home to daily life. In exploring these archetypal parallels, Magers provides profound insights, both archetypal and personal, toward the reintegration of a shattered psyche which must transpire before the warrior can finally leave combat and come home."

— Dr. James Hollis, Senior Jungian Analyst and author

"This heartfelt book by Adam Magers offers more than tepid sympathy to veterans of foreign wars coming home with PTSD. It lays out a vision for a future life of meaning and purpose. Odysseus comes home with a mission given in his descent into the Underworld. The light that shines in the darkness guides the way forward."

— Dr. Murray Stein, Senior Jungian Analyst, author of *Jung's Map of the Soul*

"In Odysseus & the Oar, Adam Magers has proven himself to be a master of classical Jungian thought. In fact, this work could be used by candidates becoming Jungian analysts as important supplemental reading to prepare for theoretical exams. Adam shows a real mastery of mythology, and he uses its metaphors to move toward psychological breakthroughs for people suffering from combat trauma of various sorts. More works like this are needed to show the value of depth psychology in the world of practical problems."

— Dr. Francis J. Manley, Senior Jungian Analyst

"Adam Magers digs deep to harvest all he has learned from his long journey through the traumas of war and beyond, and offers the fruits to all war veterans, that they may heal, transform, and discover the gifts they have to share with the world."

— Joseph Bobrow, Psychoanalyst, Zen Master, & Founder of Veterans Coming Home and Author of *Waking Up from War*

"The mind and heart of trained healer and Iraq war veteran Adam Magers taps into his own experiences, into the thoughts and images of Homer's great myth of a soldier's homecoming, and into Carl Jung's deep understanding of how human souls are affected by trauma. He then invites us to think and feel about what war trauma is, why it persists, why there can be no quick fix, and how veterans can undertake the natural process of rebalancing their own souls. He sets out to guide their explorations through the longest-surviving manual for treating the psychic wounds and scars of war, the Odyssey of Homer. In this profound book, Magers de-demonizes what all returning soldiers go through. He gives his readers, both veterans and those who love and respect them, a way of accepting with heartfelt honesty what veterans are going through. He also gives them confidence that they can and will rebalance their very souls, something soldiers have had to do long before they came back from the plains of Troy."

— Thomas G. Palaima, Professor of Classics, University of Texas at Austin

"In Odysseus and the Oar, Adam Magers offers veterans a map for the journey home, interpreting Homer, Jung, and his own experiences with dreams, symptoms, mindfulness, and art to show how we can make use of every wound to reconnect with Self and Soul. I highly recommend Adam's creative reading of the Odyssey and his effective work with veterans."

— Maxine Hong Kingston, National Book Award-winning author of *The Woman Warrior* and editor of Veterans of War, Veterans of Peace

CONTENTS

FOREWORD

When I first read *Odysseus & the Oar*, I wished that a book like this had been written fifty years earlier, when I was struggling both psychologically and spiritually to return to my family and community from the war in Vietnam. I wished it had been written 100 years earlier to help my grandfather's and my father's generations return home from their wars. Then, it occurred to me that this wished-for book *had been written*—nearly 3,000 years ago by a poet named Homer. It is called the *Odyssey*.

A great mythopoetic work of art like the *Odyssey* is a cultural dream. Few of us, however, have the wisdom and insight to interpret our own dreams. This is where writers, artists, musicians—and psychotherapists such as Adam Magers—come to our aid.

Any veterans who are about to read this book should envision themselves as privileged to sit in Adam Magers's office on a rainy day by a fire, working with him on this dream of coming home. And for any psychoanalysts who work with veterans, think of yourselves as lucky enough to be in the room listening in, learning as Magers works.

Through this book, Magers makes explicit the cultural dream shared by many veterans who are on their individual journeys home. The specifics of those journeys differ. Magers, however, shows us how Odysseus, a mythic warrior and fellow flawed human, stands as an example of what—and what not—to do to shed one's warrior identity in order to finally be reunited with family, community, and a fractured soul.

Soul has become a forbidden four-letter word in the lexicon of most scientifically trained psychotherapists. It is indeed a word that seeks to denote what is undefinable. Souls are not concrete. I, like many, believe they exist, but can't prove it. My understanding of a soul is what makes a Picasso painting more than globs of paint or *Anna Karenina* more than ink splotches.

Native American shamans were convinced of the soul's existence and that many warriors had lost theirs in battle. These shamans went into the spirit world to retrieve those lost souls on behalf of these warriors, to help them heal and return to family and tribe. Today, this loss of soul in veterans is often an unrecognized aspect of "moral injury," a concept that has only recently been added to our understanding of posttraumatic stress

Modern psychotherapy has been ignoring the soul in large part because we live in an age whose zeitgeist is what I would call "the religion of science." Psychologists are taught to distrust anything that can't be proven with rats and pigeons and that our psyches are epiphenomena of complex brain circuitry. Similarly, bureaucrats distrust anything that can't be measured and justified with a number in a budget document. We end up with what is referred to as "evidence-based therapy."

There is nothing wrong with holding psychologists' and veterans' feet to the fire to monitor progress and make sure tax dollars are well-spent. When I was undergoing therapy for my own post-traumatic stress, I had several therapists whom I gladly would have spent an hour a week with for the rest of my life, if it was all paid for by the government. But so-called "evidence-based" and "trauma-focused" therapies, as Magers's book demonstrates, asks too much of both veterans and therapists. This is because these therapies are not so much looking for results, such as healthy humans reintegrated with their communities, they are looking for *speed*. Get it done in twelve sessions.

Clearly, using the current, dominant treatment approach alone is falling short. Our appallingly high veteran suicide rate has hardly been dented in three decades, despite the efforts of thousands of well-meaning therapists and a lot of money. A recent study showed about two-thirds of veteran-patients don't end up with what researchers would call clinical success after receiving these "first-line" therapies.[1] Magers makes a case that these therapies sometimes fail because the totality of the treatment approach is too narrow, as they zero in on a small sliver of potential problems, and that a broader, more soulful approach is appropriate, and maybe even necessary. I am not arguing that current techniques are necessarily wrong, and neither is Magers. Indeed, many are effective for certain aspects of certain veterans' problems. They just aren't enough. Attention must also be given to *soul*, however we understand it, and this is why Magers has written this book.

Soul work takes time. Souls communicate in images, music, stories, and dreams. Any journey to heal the soul must go beyond talk. Talking is good, it's necessary, but it's not sufficient. Souls don't own clocks. Soul time is beyond time. Magers is arguing that we need to let these souls heal with whatever time it takes, and it is likely to take a lot more than twelve one-hour sessions, the standard often used by the VA or DoD. He is also arguing that we need to let the rich symbolism of the *Odyssey* speak to veterans *through the language of the soul*.

There is no clock running here. Odysseus spent twenty years coming home—many of them in apparent drug and sex-induced oblivion. You, the reader, have time to retrace Odysseus's journey with a master tour guide who will help you understand how to apply the wisdom of this ancient tale to your life today. Savor, under the skillful guidance of this book, the symbols, the story, and the insights that will help you savor your life.

Karl Marlantes
Woodinville, Washington
June, 2020

ACKNOWLEDGMENTS

This book would not have been possible if not for the support of countless individuals who touched my life throughout my own odyssey and journey home from the Iraq War, including my endlessly loving and optimistic wife, Brittany; our family and friends; and my fellow classmates and former professors at Pacifica Graduate Institute. I owe thanks to Jake Clark and Dr. Michael Salonius, who offered me my first glimpse into the benefits of adopting a depth psychological perspective as it relates to veterans' challenges. It was Dr. Mike who initially introduced me to Carl Jung's work, which changed the course of my life.

I owe more thanks than I can express to my first Jungian analyst, Dr. Frank Manley, who I worked with for over five years and who was my primary guide through the most intense and transformative years of my life; and my second analyst, Dr. Charles Zeltzer, who helped me explore many of the questions in this book more deeply. I also want to acknowledge my former supervisor and mentor, David Strabala, for his kindness and encouragement over the years.

I'm also thankful for my thoughtful editor, Arnie Kotler, who polished the manuscript and who patiently nurtured the life within it, as well as Keith Dow and Tyler Carroll at Dead Reckoning Collective who believed in this book and offered to publish it. I also owe a special thanks to several individuals who offered their time and expertise to review this manuscript and offer their impressions, insights, and support, especially Karl Marlantes, Dr. James Hollis, Dr. Murray Stein, Dr. Thomas Palaima, Maxine Hong Kingston, Dr. Joseph Bobrow, and Dr. Jennifer Leigh Selig. I must express my thanks and appreciation for Dr. Ifat Peled, a former professor who has been a wonderful teacher and guide, who encouraged me to respect and remain loyal to my own experiences, ideas, and insights as I navigated the editing process. Last, but certainly not least, I want to thank Whitney Logan, who is now completing her training to become a Jungian Analyst. Whitney has been one of my most important teachers and friends, and I feel lucky to have worked with her the past six years. Her influence on me and this book has been significant, as I've been able to sort through many of these ideas in my discussions with her.

Additionally, I owe a tremendous debt to my fellow combat veterans—including close friends who I have shared the most difficult and intimate moments with, as we have taken turns holding one another through hellish challenges; and also the hundreds of warriors I have worked with in a professional capacity through both individual psychotherapy and intensive therapeutic programs for groups of veterans. Without my personal inner journey, and without having the privilege of being so close to so many veterans who have shared their inner journeys with me, the insights within this book would have been impossible. I must express my profound gratitude to my comrades Stacy Bare and Chris Mendoza—fellow combat veterans who studied this book and who gave me the confidence that others, like them, might find it worthwhile.

I am especially thankful to *The Battle Within* community, as these folks rescued the program I designed for veterans from an organization I founded, which sadly lost its way. Long after I had walked away, I had a dream one night that it was time to *"return to my old home with warriors."* When I awoke I asked myself if I was really meant to go back to working with veterans. I thought to myself, "Hell no. Not going down that road again." That same day, I got a call out of the blue from Justin Hoover, my friend and the Executive Director at *The Battle Within*, and he asked me if I could come back to help them out. I knew the psyche was calling me back, and that saying no wasn't an option. It was in the course of producing their curriculum that I re-read several veteran-specific books I had read years earlier, and that I read the *Odyssey* for the first time. Immediately thereafter, this book became my focus, that it might help other veterans heal and transform after war and military service, while also helping my fellow therapists develop a greater understanding of the archetypal dimensions of coming home from war or transitioning out of the military.

I am indebted to a number of individuals whose ideas and work have influenced me and made this book possible, including Carl Jung, James Hillman, Christine Downing, Edward Tick, Karl Marlantes, Jonathan Shay, and Donald Kalsched. I owe Karl a great deal of gratitude because his book, *What it is Like to Go to War,* was what began my journey into the realm of depth psychology. His thoughtful and in-depth review of this book was instrumental in helping me to shape it. I must also offer a special thanks to a former professor, Dr. Matthew Bennett, who taught my classmates and me a great deal about the functioning of the psyche, the role of defenses, and the meaning of suffering. Without a nuanced understanding of the many roots of suffering and how it manifests, my work with veterans and my ideas in this book would have been much more limited.

I also offer enormous gratitude to an individual I've never known, and will never have the opportunity to thank properly—at least not in this world. On August 6, 2011, Spencer C. Duncan was serving as the door gunner on Extortion 17 when it was shot down in Afghanistan. The chinook was carrying 31 US military personnel, including a number of members of SEAL Team 6 who were part of a larger special operations mission. I remember feeling heartbroken when I saw the news report. I thought of the event, imagined what might have happened, and thought of the families. I could not have known that Spencer's parents, Dale and Megan Duncan, were less than 30 minutes away from where I was, crippled by the crushing grief of their son's death—and I could not have guessed what an important role they were to play in my own homecoming and recovery.

Out of the wreckage of Spencer's death, Dale and Megan started the Spencer C. Make It Count Foundation, which has become the backbone of funding for a number of veterans organizations in the greater Kansas City area. In 2013, out of my own helplessness and frustration with not being able to find the support I felt I needed, and knowing countless others were in the same boat, I started a therapeutic program with the intent to bridge the gap. Today the program I designed continues at *The Battle Within*, and Dale and Megan have stayed with it, nurtured it, and ensured its success.

I first met Dale and Megan at their annual fundraising five-kilometer race in Spencer's name back in 2014. I remember being at the 5K that day, walking through a Chinook helicopter (like Extortion 17), and in each seat sat a large portrait of each warrior with a bio telling about their lives. That was the first time I saw Spencer's face. A tear rolled down my cheek, though I still didn't know how much his life would bless mine. Two months later, they fully funded our first ever therapeutic retreat for veterans, and they've been a steadfast partner ever since. Their foundation has largely carried our organization and program through a variety of hardships, never giving up and never ceasing to believe in the work we were doing.

Like the loving parents they are, the Duncans have always sought to understand, hold, support, challenge, and inspire not only me, but the entire community at *The Battle Within*. If it weren't for them standing beside me, I would never have had the opportunity to begin my professional work with other veterans. Our program would never have developed or been able to continue through the hardships it has faced. Because of the Duncans and Spencer, my journey deeper into this work has become possible.

Without my role in these programs, I would not have entered Pacifica Graduate Institute's counseling psychology program, and I would not have become a therapist myself. They didn't just support me professionally, but personally. In some of the darkest hours of my life, Dale and Megan were there for me. My own inner process and development—out of which my understanding of the *Odyssey* grew—was supported by Dale and Megan. And when I told them I saw a gaping hole in the way our society supports veterans after their time in the service or after coming home from war and that I wanted to write a book to help folks understand how we might fill it, Dale and Megan supported me. Without the support of their foundation, it would have been even more financially difficult than it was for me to commit myself to writing this book.

Every year, when I go back to Spencer's 5K and walk through the helicopter, I am touched by the faces of those warriors—but I am most especially touched by Spencer, a man I never knew, who died at age 21 on a special operations mission in Afghanistan. He didn't know me, and I don't know what he would think of this book. I don't know what he would think of me or if we'd be friends if he were still here. If he had come home, would I still be here today? I don't know. There is a chance my suffering might have consumed me. I'm not sure who I would be today if I hadn't fallen into doing this work with veterans, because without that I wouldn't have stumbled into the study of depth psychology, and I wouldn't have ended up in Jungian analysis—and it is without a doubt that the process that has unfolded through these experiences has completely transformed me from the inside out. My life is far more beautiful because of my *odyssey*, a journey home that was helped along by Spencer's spirit. I am not the same person today that I was in 2014, when I first laid eyes on Spencer's picture, sitting in his door gunner's seat in that Chinook. I'm not sure this book would exist if not for Spencer, and his parents, Dale and Megan Duncan—to them I owe a tremendous debt of thanks and gratitude.

Preface

It's no secret that when a war ends, the journey isn't over for those who fight it. As Plato said, "*Only the dead have seen the end of war.*" The *Odyssey* is a symbolic testament to the harsh realities of post-war life that countless warriors have had to contend with, and in this book, my intention is to uncover its deeper meanings so that we can better understand the soul's journey after war and military service. My hope is that it will be useful and supportive for veterans, their therapists, and others who have a desire to understand and support them.

This book was born out of a completely different manuscript. In 2019, over the course of just a few months, I produced a much longer and more technical manuscript that was for clinicians who work with veterans, as well as those with an academic interest in *The Odyssey* or analytical psychology. My highly skilled and experienced editor, Arnie Kotler, encouraged me to write a simpler version for veterans and to pursue the other version later, and I felt that was the right thing to do. Over the course of a month, I whittled down and transformed the original manuscript into something that would just be for veterans—but as I circled through various rounds of editing over the next year, I felt something was unresolved. The book needed a makeover, but life—or the unconscious—had its way with me.

I've had two children since the original manuscript was completed (now my kiddos are almost four and almost two), and moved into a 100-year-old house that I've been renovating and remodeling on my own—while balancing a private practice and working as a Clinical Manager at *The Battle Within*—and all of these things brought progress on the manuscript to a halt. Ultimately, I believe the manuscript's extended pause had significant meaning—as it seems other events needed to transpire to redirect this book's focus. Over the last few years, in the course of my work with veterans, therapists, and others who support veterans, I've been repeatedly reminded why I wrote the professional manuscript in the first place.

I believe that many, if not most, clinicians have not had access to adequate resources or training that would allow them to provide well-rounded therapeutic support for veterans. On one hand, there is a widespread lack of cultural competency among therapists as it relates to veterans, without enough appreciation for the way military culture transforms the individual's personality. I don't think most therapists have a clue about the world many veterans have lived in, or what that world has done to them. How then can therapists hope to help veterans sort that out, or to lead them out of a forest or down a path they don't even realize exists? And how can anyone expect therapists to know these things about veterans when they have been denied a broad enough vantage point to take in these lessons?

On a related note, and on the other hand, theoretical biases in the field lead to a rather narrow training of therapists, which leads to problematic biases that cause therapists to misunderstand and misinterpret veterans' experiences. I think the former problem is largely a result of the latter one—without an adequate theoretical framework or reference, the deeper psycho-cultural aspects of veterans' challenges aren't adequately appreciated or understood. I don't want to be too critical of therapists—I have a great deal of compassion for my colleagues who have expressed feeling lost and unsure about how to best support their veteran clients. I don't feel that therapists have failed, but that our field has gotten lost due to biases that have not been responsibly explored, and due to "research" that is sometimes flawed from the start.[2, 3]

I believe I have a unique vantage point to provide both therapists and veterans with new insights into the challenges that we collectively face. I am a combat veteran who has undergone years of Jungian analysis and other therapies, and I am a therapist who (I believe) received a very well-rounded education in psychology and counseling—to include a master's degree with an emphasis in depth psychology. I've worked with veterans professionally since 2014, and I've spent the last three-plus years doing hundreds of clinical interviews with veterans, first responders, and frontline medical professionals, as well as doing other clinical work with veterans through individual and group therapy. The veterans I've worked with express problems that are distinct from others who've experienced trauma in the line of their work.

Again and again, I hear from veterans (*hundreds of them*) who are disappointed that their therapists attempt trauma-specific therapies on them, without an appreciation for how their all their experiences (not just traumas) have caused them to lose touch with themselves and how that leaves them not knowing where to go, or what to do. Many veterans are just trying to find their way in the world and discover a new sense of self and identity—and dragging veterans through a therapy where they're asked to revisit the horrors they've survived isn't as productive as some therapists think it is. And, again and again, I come across therapists who either aren't sure what to do, or who express their opinion that trauma-focused therapies are the best therapies for veterans—because they have made what I believe is a faulty assumption that acute trauma is the primary source of veterans' challenges.

At one point in time, a lack of sufficient understanding about psychological trauma *was* a serious problem for both veterans and therapists. I don't think that is the primary problem today as it relates to quality of care for veterans. Despite all of the leaps and bounds we've made in improving trauma treatments, many veterans remain disappointed in their experiences in therapy. I think this is because most therapists lack training in theories and therapies that allow us to understand the soul itself—to appreciate the legion of forces that distort the personality, causing us to lose touch with ourselves; and to understand how to work with individuals in a way that can help us reconnect with our souls and to rediscover a sense of meaning and vitality. I believe all theories and all therapies have a place, and that all can be meaningfully employed to help clients, depending on where they're at. I also believe that Jungian theory (which most therapists know little to nothing about) offers unique and extremely valuable insights that can help us understand and navigate the challenges many veterans face. Moreover, I hope to show the reader that a symbolic reading of *The Odyssey*, from a Jungian point of view, can help us not only better understand veterans and their challenges, but also the deeper workings of the psyche as a whole.

I hope *Odysseus & the Oar* will have an impact on psychotherapists who work with veterans, but in the end, I've written it *for* veterans, and so most of the time, I am speaking directly to them. My hope is that this book will play a role in helping some veterans find a way forward after war and military service.

After war and military service, many veterans are left with challenges so intense that even the most psychologically and emotionally mature monk or psychotherapist would struggle to navigate them. And yet, young warriors, who are in no way trained or prepared to find their way through the challenging terrain of an inner crisis are forced to do so—*often without much support.* After war and military service, life *demands* that we endure a complete and total psychological transformation—that we adapt our psyches from the task of warfighting to the task of finding a new self and new identity, and relating to family members, friends, coworkers, and our civilian peers, so that we can experience and take part in an entirely different side of life most of us have not known since we were children, if then. This is a monumental task that continues to be underestimated and underappreciated by mental health professionals.

Whether we like it or not, we veterans have been initiated into a realm of psychological experience that has changed us permanently. There is no going back to the way things were. We cannot simply wish our way back into an identity we possessed before we put on the uniform. That person is gone—*forever*. Neither can we remain the warrior we became as a result of war and military service—not if we want to experience any depth of connection and contentment in civilian life. Even if you're destined to be a warrior your entire career, one day that career will end, and when it does, you are left to live a life outside of war or the prospect of it. When the warrior's outer role comes to an end, a new version of ourselves has to be born through a process of transformation—a process called *individuation* that has been explored and studied extensively by Carl Gustav Jung and laid out in the awe-inspiring and immense body of his life's work.

After war and military service, we have to undergo yet another initiation, whereby the unconscious transforms our personalities and introduces us to a person who we do not yet know and cannot know until that transformation has run its course. After war, the Greek mythological hero Odysseus undergoes precisely this sort of ordeal. His journey, or odyssey, transforms him from a battle-hardened and rather insensitive warrior into a man who is capable of great emotional depth and sensitivity, who can navigate his inner world with the same quality of expertise he possessed in battle. His story is history's greatest roadmap for life after war, which is why I lean on it so heavily here. This book is my attempt to introduce my fellow veterans, their therapists, and others who support them to the kind of inner work that is necessary if we are to successfully navigate the post-war or post-military transformation process.

This book is not a "how-to" manual offering veterans step-by-step instructions to get rid of symptoms, as I don't think such a thing is really possible, nor that it would actually be helpful. I offer *Odysseus & the Oar* as an education in the *psyche* (Greek and Latin for *soul*) and its patterned functioning, specifically in the lives of veterans. If we better understand the nature and functioning of the psyche, we can attune ourselves to the unconscious and find our unique paths home. In the pages that follow, I hope to help veterans discover the bridge to their inner worlds, so that they might understand their pain and transform through it. The soul—through dreams, images, and symptoms—is trying to take you somewhere. This book is meant to help veterans read their souls' unique maps, and to help those who support them to be better stewards of veterans' souls' journeys.

— — — — —

Carl Jung is one of the great fathers of depth psychology, and he emphasized the importance of *archetypes*, images and motifs that repeat themselves in our dreams, myths, and images. According to Jung, archetypes are "innate and inherited. They function, when the occasion arises, in more or less the same way in all of us."[4] In other words, when individuals find themselves in a specific situation —like leaving the military or coming home from war—it's common for certain archetypal themes to present themselves as the unconscious attempts to help us navigate the challenges we face.

You can think of the unconscious as the totality of the psyche that lies beneath the conscious personality and our awareness—and according to the Jungian point of view, the unconscious is the source of all psychological life. When the conscious personality meets its limits or loses its way, it is the unconscious that presents a solution as we transform and discover new possibilities within ourselves. Ultimately, archetypal images are an important way the ego can begin to see and understand the life that is stirring within the unconscious, as these images depict (*in a symbolic way*) psychological realities.

In my own journey "home" from the Iraq War, and in my work as a psychotherapist with other veterans, I have noted the degree to which archetypal themes permeate the dreams of returning veterans—and I've been amazed to witness uncanny parallels between these dreams and ancient myths about warriors, like the *Odyssey*. From the perspective of depth psychology, myths (as in mythological stories) express deep wisdom and psychological realities that have unconscious roots, and so myths from societies across the globe can be strikingly similar. I've found that exploring myths like the *Odyssey* can offer veterans a new perspective on their challenges and help them navigate the transformation process of returning "home."

This book and a not-yet-published companion volume explain my interpretation of the *Odyssey*. The other volume is longer and more technical, for clinicians and those with a passion for depth psychology, to help them understand the problems veterans face from the perspective of the unconscious. It's important, I believe, to challenge the dominant paradigm that focuses on trauma-based *symptoms*, so we can help therapists better understand veterans' *entire* psyches. I personally suffered when I was pushed to reexperience traumas rather than understand my soul's journey. It was the latter that ultimately set the stage for me to begin examining and processing some of the trauma I experienced in war.

The interpretation of the *Odyssey* presented here is based on my direct experience, personally and professionally. I have lived it. Through more than fifteen years of recovering from war and over six years in Jungian analysis, dozens of dreams have shown me how much Odysseus and I have in common. I do not see Odysseus as a role model, but as a symbol to respect, appreciate, and learn from. In the end, Odysseus reminds us we are only human and we must submit ourselves before the archetypes of the collective unconscious, and for this, I am indebted to Homer's retelling of Odysseus's journey.

Over the past fifteen years, I have carefully studied my dreams and become keenly aware of the archetypal themes of the returning warrior. I have had the privilege of undertaking analysis and formally studying Jungian psychology. And I have had the fortune and experience of working with hundreds of other veterans since 2014 in a professional capacity, and have witnessed the same archetypal themes in their lives and dreams. This rare combination of lived experiences is a blessing that allowed me to see this myth as, I believe, others have not, and so I feel it is my duty to share the *Odyssey* in the way that I have experienced it.

At this point I want to note that there is always some difficulty when a therapist shares psychological material, especially as it relates to one's clients. While I feel a responsibility to share what I have learned, I also feel a responsibility to protect my clients to the greatest extent possible. In writing this book, I have relied as much as possible on my own dreams to provide examples of how these archetypal themes appear in the dreams of modern veterans. And, when suitable, I have used the dreams of other veterans who've shared their dreams publicly, while also leaning on other examples that already exist in published literature. In cases where I do reference my own clients, I have disguised certain details to avoid the possibility that they might be exposed or harmed in some way, and I have restricted myself to only referencing clients who have completed their treatment.

Though I have a unique vantage point other veterans, psychotherapists, and writers may not have had, my viewpoint is still limited. Perhaps one of this book's greatest limitations is the fact that it is based on the experience of a male veteran/psychotherapist, who served in the military primarily with males (six of my eight years in the Army were with all-male units), and whose veteran-patients are mostly males who served in combat arms units—and it is these personal and professional experiences that have shaped my understanding of the *Odyssey*, which, of course, is also a myth that focuses on the experiences of a male combat veteran.

Though I've worked with over one hundred female veterans in a psychotherapeutic context, most of that has been through group programs and clinical interviews that did not provide the same kind of deep learning opportunity that I've gained from conducting long-term, depth-oriented individual psychotherapy with male veterans. Ultimately, it was through my own analysis—which brought an understanding of my own psyche, especially working with dreams—that I was able to understand what my later male veteran-patients were also tasked with working through. My in-depth work with hundreds of male veterans gives me a high degree of confidence that such lessons do apply to the overwhelming majority of veterans, and especially among those who have served in combat. I cannot say with the same degree of confidence that the specifics explored in this book as it relates to *the archetype of the warrior's return* will apply to the majority of female veterans.

But I can say that my conversations with female veterans have repeatedly affirmed my intuition on this matter, that the same general problem faced by most male veterans is also faced by many —though certainly not all—female veterans, namely that military service and the experience of combat causes the warrior— regardless of sex or gender—to adopt a warrior-centric attitude, or adaptation for the sake of survival, which can be disruptive to the individual's   ability to connect with others and themselves. Ultimately, regardless of sex or gender, any person who serves in the military runs the risk of becoming possessed by the warrior complex or archetype, or identifying with the warrior persona, and losing touch with their objective personality or true self. In the end, giving ourselves over to warriorhood can cause us to become entrenched in a narrow part of our personalities, which has psychological and emotional consequences. And, regardless of sex or gender, one's unconscious does not tolerate such deviations from our objective center for very long, except during times when our survival depends on it.

How do such psychological experiences play out in the unconscious of female warriors? To answer this, one would need to study the dreams of dozens of female veterans over a long period of time, especially during the critical stages of their homecoming and recovery process, to make a judgment whether the archetypal imagery and patterns described in this book are applicable to female veterans as well. I have a strong belief that the archetype of the warrior's return is applicable to many female veterans, but since I have not studied women warriors' dreams to the extent I have men's, I lack an adequate vantage point and critical experience to address the matter in depth. Such questions may ultimately fall to another who is better positioned than I am to undertake this work. At this time, I can only relay that my female veteran friends who are attentive to their inner worlds have expressed they share my opinions on this matter. In a recent conversation on this topic, a female veteran friend shared, "I feel like the bulk of my work since leaving the military has been letting go of my inner warrior and reconnecting with my femininity." She shared military service demanded that she become a version of herself that left little room for who she really feels herself to be.

There is another challenge we're confronted with if we explore whether the archetypal experiences of males and female veterans are similar or different. What I call *the archetype of the warrior's return* is not just based on the dreams of modern veterans—it is also based on the same pattern of imagery that we see in several ancient myths about returning warriors. That's what makes it, by definition, archetypal—we have a pattern of psychological experience mirrored with corresponding symbolic imagery that repeats itself in various cultures throughout history. Not only do I not have a good vantage point to understand, precisely, the inner world of female veterans through their return and recovery, but I'm also not acquainted with substantial mythological or archetypal material that focuses on returning female warriors. Without being able to pair the two together, examining how the dreams of modern female warriors compare to the mythological record of the returning female warriors of antiquity, it becomes difficult to make an informed judgment—especially if one lacks lived experience. It may be that the female warriors of this generation are on a new frontier, facing realms of psychological experience rarely known to women of previous generations, while lacking adequate mythological mirrors or maps that portray their psychological journeys.

That leads to a final limitation: the inadequacy and imperfect nature of any theory. Jung's theory of psychology is vital to understanding both mythological and archetypal material, especially dreams. Without Jung's theoretical contributions, I and many others would be lost. Understanding both the *Odyssey* and the dreams of modern veterans would be difficult, if not impossible, if we did not have his concepts or lexicon of terms. Yet, since Jung began to introduce his theories well over 100 years ago, the world as a whole and our culture have transformed significantly, along with our understanding as it relates to our psychological experiences. Even in the last few years, perceptions surrounding gender in our culture have evolved dramatically—with fresh criticism around the gendered terms *anima* and *animus* (which occupy a significant place in Jung's theory of individuation). We can only guess how he might have perceived gender if he were alive today, as there's no doubt a man born nearly 150 years ago would have a different perspective from the average person today. And, we have to confront the reality that those practicing psychology 100 years ago studied individuals whose psyches and psychologies are quite different from those of today. Much has changed, requiring all of us to be thoughtful and open-minded to new ways of seeing and understanding the psyche and the challenges we face.

In my exploration of the archetype of the warrior's return, I stick to the psyche's own imagery and that of the *Odyssey* and comparable myths: where a male warrior creates problems for himself after war which contribute to his progressive undoing, only to be helped along by a female figure—a figure Jung would have referred to as an anima figure, who serves as a bridge to the unconscious and inspires his individuation adventure and transformation process. I have personally experienced this archetypal theme in my own dreams, and have observed it in the male warriors I've worked with. It's impossible to avoid the gendered and heteronormative aspects of this pattern. I do not have answers for differences that may exist among female, non-binary, or transgender warriors or for warriors who identify as lesbian, gay, queer, or homosexual. Ultimately, how the unconscious presents itself to the ego is a highly individual experience, and we have to be aware of the reality that there is no single archetypal pattern or set of images that fits every person. In the end, I ask that readers accept this work for what it is: a limited exploration of the archetype of the warrior's return, whereby we examine how the symbolic images of the myths of antiquity compare to those that appear in the psyches of *many*—or most, though certainly not all—modern veterans. Though the pattern explored here may not be a fit for all veterans, my hope is that it will serve as a template for each individual veteran to begin to explore what archetypal pattern(s) or what myth(s) are living inside them.

A final note before we begin: Readers unfamiliar with the *Odyssey* may wish to visit the appendices, where you will find some details about Homer (the attributed author of the tale) and the *Odyssey's* origins (Appendix I); a chronology of Odysseus's story of going to war and the long journey home (Appendix II); a list of primary figures who appear in or are closely related to the tale (Appendix III); a glossary of Jungian terms (Appendix IV); and general guidelines for therapists (Appendix V). Or you may wish to read one of the many excellent translations of Homer's *Odyssey* that are available today.

Odysseus & the Oar

I

THE WARRIOR'S RETURN

Speak through me, o muse
of that man of many devices
who wandered much
once he'd sacked the sacred citadel of Troy.
He saw the cities of many men
and knew their minds,
suffering many sorrows
in order to win back his life-soul
and the return of his companions.
In the end he failed to save them,
in spite of his longing to do so,
for through their own heedlessness they perished.
Fools—who ate the cows of Helios-Hyperion,
and the day of their return was taken from them.
Of these matters, goddess, daughter of Zeus, speak through us
beginning wherever you will.

— Homer, trans. by Stein

The psychological trouble in neurosis, and the neurosis itself, can be
formulated as an act of adaptation that has failed. ... a neurosis is,
in a sense, an attempt at self-cure ...

— C.G. Jung[5]

This book is for veterans, therapists who work with veterans, and others who may have an interest in the psychological journey that veterans experience after war and military service, though I believe there are lessons here that can benefit just about anyone. My aim is to examine what I call "*the archetype of the warrior's return*," which can be understood as a roadmap to healing and transformation after war or military service. We will follow the ancient Greek warrior Odysseus in his attempt to return *home* to Ithaca after fighting in the Trojan War. As we'll see, the imagery in this myth parallels images found in other stories about returning warriors in various cultures all over the world, and these same themes and images appear in the dreams of modern veterans. Through understanding the archetypal imagery of our dreams and in myths like the *Odyssey*, we can deepen our capacity to transform and heal through the inevitable traumas that come with serving in the military and combat.

I offer this book to help veterans navigate their inner journeys home, which is often a chaotic and painful rebirth. Discovering a meaningful and satisfying life after serving in the military or fighting in battle is not easy. My hope is that these shapes of printer's ink we call words and letters might string together in a way that create a map of the transformation and healing process. The *Odyssey*, like our dreams, is a map, but to read and understand it we need to lean on ancient and largely forgotten symbols and wisdom—which the early psychologist Carl Jung sought to awaken through his psychology. This journey is our own odyssey, so that we too might rediscover who we really are and, in the process, heal ourselves.

After I returned from a tour of hunting roadside bombs in Baghdad in 2007 and 2008, I spent most of my first year back in the States drunk, angry, bitter, and resentful. I wanted revenge. Then, a year after coming home, I had a huge breakdown, and I was flooded with anxiety, panic attacks, and fears that left me wondering if I'd become psychotic. Each time I returned to my apartment, I would look around to ensure there were no bombs or enemies lurking in hidden places. In the middle of the night, as I wrenched in terror from panic attacks, I would call my friends and family for help. No one knew what to say or do. I felt terrified, and largely alone.

I went to the local Department of Veterans Affairs (VA) hospital, where they put me on meds that made me feel worse than I already did. My psychiatrist told me, "This will never go away. Post-Traumatic Stress Disorder (PTSD) has no cure. You're just gonna have to live with it." I asked how I could do that, and if she could connect me to a Vietnam veteran who'd had the experience and could show me the way. She couldn't, but she connected me with a psychotherapist in their clinic. These days, the VA has a wonderful peer support program, and I'm sure that would've helped me a great deal—but it didn't exist yet. During my first therapy session, the therapist told me to tell him about the experiences that affected me most. I think his exact words were, "What was the worst thing that happened? Let's start with that." As a therapist myself now, I cringe at how unwise this was; it can be dangerous to expose patients to traumatic memories before they're emotionally ready—before they feel able to express and hold themselves through their pain. We didn't get very far that day. The therapist fell asleep while I was talking about a terrifying ambush I was lucky to survive during the Battle of Sadr City, where I had to risk my life in the heat of battle to treat a wounded platoonmate. After that, I lost confidence that the VA could help me.

Instead, I sought out psychotherapies in the civilian world and paid out-of-pocket, which I couldn't afford—I accumulated a significant amount of debt just trying to get quality therapy for the trauma I accumulated in service to the US government. Yet I knew it was an investment I had to make if I wanted to survive. During those first five years home, I had many painful episodes where I was inundated with unwanted suicidal thoughts. Still, seeing civilian therapists was far more productive, because I felt I could trust them more, and each six-month stint in therapy did help the symptoms become more manageable. But the benefits had an expiration date. Symptoms came and went like the tides, ebbing and flowing once or twice each year and sweeping me off my feet, and I couldn't understand why. Now I think I do. For those who have had similar experiences, I offer this book and Odysseus's story to help make sense of possible causes of these kinds of symptoms.

Throughout my first two years of therapy, I had huge dreams at night that I knew were important. Some were horrifying, others had a spiritual quality. When I asked one of my therapists if I could share a dream with him, he asked, "Aren't dreams just garbage left over from the day before?" I didn't know what my dreams meant, but I knew they weren't garbage. Several years later I learned that depth psychotherapies, such as Jungian analysis, treat dreams as having central importance to a person's therapeutic process. From this point of view, dreams reflect a *psychic reality*, showing us what is happening from the viewpoint of the unconscious. Often, dreams express the dynamics between different aspects of our psyches. When a person has a "big dream," it's often obvious that it has a meaning and purpose. Take for instance this dream, which came during my final year in the Army. When I had it, something in me changed, and I developed an intense curiosity about what the dream was trying to tell me.

The Refusal of the Call, and the Emergence of the Self

I'm in a foreign, mountainous land. It seems like Israel or maybe Afghanistan. I am the commander of a small military unit, and we are fleeing from the enemy. At night, we hide in caves, and I remind my troops to put out their fires so they don't give our position away. I'm going to have to leave my unit to go into town by myself to meet an informant who has critical information about the enemy.

I put on plain clothes and go into town. I'm waiting for the informant, but I have no idea what he looks like. Suddenly, a blind man approaches me and asks if I'm Adam. I say, "Yes, I am," and he says to follow him. He leads me to the corner of the building and invites me to follow him down a dark stairwell into a basement. I come close to the door, but I feel too afraid. I'm not sure I can trust him, so I back away. All of a sudden, chaos breaks out in the building. The enemy is here! I'm terrified and look for a way to escape. People run in all directions. I head toward the hallway to make my way outside, when I see three converging flights of stairs coming out of the basement, and I see a band of warriors dressed in purple. The leader gives a powerful speech preparing them for battle. At the end of his speech, he says, "Out of the desert, Israel come running!" As I begin to wake from sleep, a voice seems to whisper in my ear, "Adam, this message is from Michael."

It seemed obvious that this dream had meaning and it was my job to try to make sense of it. Other dreams followed, and I began writing them down, pulled by a sense they would be important someday. My intuition proved correct.

Years later when I looked back on this dream I recognized that, *psychologically speaking, I was still at war.* Unwanted memories of combat consumed me, along with painful symptoms. I did not feel I was truly "at home." In the dream I was trying to evade something that was expressed as "the enemy." At that time, I imagined my symptoms and suffering as an enemy—one that I wanted to avoid as much as possible. The work of the psychologist and Jungian analyst, Donald Kalsched (whose work will be reviewed in greater detail later), helps illuminate this imagery and its meaning. I now believe "the enemy" in the dream represents the maladaptive psychological defenses (which arise from trauma) that were causing my suffering.[6]

In this dream I am looking for help and information that will help me to overcome the enemy, and the man who has this information happens to be a blind man—an important archetypal figure. In myths, blind men, like Tiresias in the *Odyssey*, tend to be guides to

6

the underworld, the realm of the unconscious. While such archetypal figures lack outer sight, they tend to have inner sight and familiarity with the inner world, and so these aspects of the self help initiate us into the knowledge of the unconscious. In getting to know our inner worlds, we discover aspects of ourselves we don't know (which are unconscious), and in the process we develop a greater capacity for healing and transformation. In the *Odyssey*, Odysseus cannot "get home" until he undertakes a journey to the underworld. While there he meets Tiresias and receives critical information that will help him to navigate the hardships before him and return to his home on the island, Ithaca. In my dream, the blind man invites me into the underworld of the unconscious, but apparently at this point in time, that task was too daunting for me. I simply wasn't yet able to face the discomfort such an adventure would entail. Despite my refusal to answer the call to adventure, it was forced upon me anyways. The enemy— and my suffering—was impossible to avoid. It was enveloping me. Yet, there is some other mysterious, supportive force which arises from the unconscious to provide me with the critical aid I desperately needed.

While much more could be said about this dream, for now my main objective is to demonstrate there is much more to dreams than just "leftover garbage from the day before," and that they have archetypal roots that are inherently meaningful. They tell us stories—our stories—on a deeper level so that we might transform, heal, and rediscover who we really are. They bring us into relationship with other aspects of ourselves, and the unconscious, which we experience as the spiritual world. Throughout this book, as we explore the *Odyssey*, we'll do so in a way that attempts to deepen our awareness of the realities of the unconscious, so that we might better navigate the challenges we face.

Dreams aren't the only way that the unconscious makes itself known. As I grow in experience as a psychotherapist, I continue to be amazed at the seemingly endless ways in which the unconscious expresses itself, and how our behaviors tend to have a symbolic aspect to them which go much deeper than we tend to appreciate.

One fellow combat veteran I worked with repeatedly found himself having affairs despite a sincere desire to be faithful to his wife and family. Once, when lamenting about his inability to restrain himself, he said, "It's like I can't help myself." Something within him (in his unconscious) would overpower him. As an elite operator who prided himself in being able to overcome anything, he re-marked, "The only thing in the world that can take me down is a woman." What we eventually came to understand was that his uncontrollable longing for actual, flesh-and-blood women was a problem that was symbolic in nature. This hardened, rigid, intensely driven, masculine warrior had adopted an attitude towards life that was suitable for the military, but it was not a fit for his civilian life as a father and husband. It was not a suitable attitude for relating to himself in a healthy way either. What he needed was to learn to relate to himself and those around him in a softer, more flexible, and more receptive manner. Ultimately, the women he sought out embodied what he was missing in his conscious personality. Only when he began to cultivate a relation-ship to this so-called feminine aspect of the psyche—mirrored by the immensely powerful female figures of the *Odyssey*—did the desire to act out through affairs begin to decrease.

Importantly, this veteran shares a great deal in common with Odysseus. His symptoms and psychological experiences had mythic parallels. We could say he was being held captive in the domain of Circe and/or Calypso—in an unconscious state overpowered by the neglected aspect of his psyche—which left his home and family in a state of chaos and peril, not so different from the state of Odysseus's home in his absence. He had to get in touch with the underlying meaning of his experiences to have a real chance of resolving the problems he faced. Whether doing my own inner work, or in my work with clients, I like to ask myself questions like, Where am I? What mythic realm am I in? What myth is being lived? What archetypal pattern is playing itself out? For practitioners of Jungian psychology, the task of discovering what myth or archetype we are living in is a central question that we must ask ourselves again and again.

It's often said that Jung's contributions to understanding our inner worlds is as significant as Einstein's contributions to understanding the outer world. Jung saw that our dreams, the stories we create, and the products of our imagination have an inherently mythic nature. He discovered that if we view our experiences—*and symptoms*—from a symbolic perspective, it enriches our lives as they are guided by a deeper wisdom that resides beneath life's surface. Jungian psychology focuses on the unconscious and all that it produces, from dreams to myths. The power of the unconscious and its inherently spiritual nature are undeniable for those who've stayed true to the root of psychology. As noted, *psyche* is Greek and Latin for soul, the breath of life.

Since 2014, I've spent much of my time working with other combat veterans, and this experience has, over and over, deepened my conviction that looking to the wisdom of mythic narratives of antiquity and of our own dreams can be an extremely valuable part of the therapeutic process. I think this is especially true for warriors and civilians in roles of service that can be especially dangerous and chaotic—those who sacrifice their own well-being by putting themselves in overwhelmingly chaotic and dangerous situations to protect and care for others. These individuals are likely to find themselves in the same archetypal situations as ancient warriors like the Greek Odysseus, the Celtic Cúchulainn, the Norse god Thor, and the Navajo twin brothers. In this book, I intend to illuminate the archetypal patterns of experience that will help warriors and those close to them navigate the process of healing and transformation.

The word *archetype* was introduced by Jung to discuss symbols and patterns of experience that repeat themselves throughout humanity, not limited by space or time. When you find yourself in a certain situation—such as trying to find your way home from war or transitioning out of the military—the psyche *expresses itself* through certain symbolic images, and when these images tend to repeat themselves and form a pattern on the collective level, that's when we are dealing with an archetype.

The pattern-producing nature of the unconscious can be understood better by observing the effects of sound. There are videos of experiments online in which sand or salt is sprinkled across a metal plate, and as different frequencies of sound cause the plate to vibrate, the salt or sand arranges in unique patterns. And as the tone or frequency changes, the patterns change too. These patterns are known as *Chladni figures*, named after the German physicist and musician who made them known in the late 1700s. This is not altogether different from what happens in our psyche from moment to moment, or from one psychological state to another. As we find ourselves moving from one experience to another, such as leaving war or transitioning from the military and seeking to heal from our experiences, the unconscious expresses its view of the situation by presenting certain images, or archetypes, in patterns. And we can discern those patterns through our dreams, by examining our life experiences in analysis, or by studying mythology.

This helps us understand why myths about returning warriors from all around the world contain the same themes and follow certain patterns (what I call *the archetype of the warrior's return*), and why modern veterans' dreams contain these same mythic themes, despite the veterans' lack of awareness that such themes exist in the psyche or in literature. In repeating these patterns, the psyche is attempting to guide us through our own healing process. We can't go to war with the mindset of a civilian, and we can't come home from war and heal with the combative mindset of a warrior. The unconscious possesses remarkable wisdom, and it always tries to provoke change in us when our conscious personality has met its limits, or we've gone off track or lost our way. Our job is to attune ourselves to the unconscious and learn to follow its guidance. This is a critical lesson Odysseus must learn on his journey home—and one we must learn as well.

The images throughout the *Odyssey* and myths like it portray the psychological tasks those returning and recovering from war need to undertake. It's not surprising then that the imagery in such myths parallels the images in the dreams of modern veterans. Context matters. As Jung stated, the archetypes are "innate and inherited. They function, when the occasion arises, in more or less the same way in all of us,"[7] When one returns from war or leaves the military, it is to be expected that an inner drama will unfold according to the archetype of the warrior's return, as one's psyche attempts to redirect the personality in a way that makes healing and transformation possible.

We can see examples of the archetype of the warrior's return in the *Odyssey* from ancient Greece, in an ancient Celtic tale about the warrior Cúchulainn returning from battle, in a Navajo story about twin brothers after heroic adventures, and in an ancient Norse myth about the theft of Thor's hammer. In each of these tales, what we can describe as an imbalanced and emotionally wounded warrior finds himself in a situation where he meets his limits and is unable to overcome his challenges without transforming. Each of these warriors must leave behind his warrior-centric tendencies and learn to relate to himself, his inner world, and others differently. The attitude, way of being, and style of consciousness required for healing is a radically different from the ways needed to survive and withstand the hardships of war. Fittingly, in all of these myths, the warriors finally heal and transform when they come into contact with female figures (or, in Thor's case, when he himself becomes like a woman) who initiate them into a new and different way of being. Such imagery is symbolic, and it depicts inner realities rather than outer ones. Interpreted through the language of Jungian psychology, we might refer to such figures as "anima figures," which Jung believed serve as a bridge to the unconscious and therefore they occupy a key role in his conceptualization of the individuation process.[8] Each of these experiences can be understood as an *initiation*, whereby the individual is transformed. Initiation is itself an archetype, and initiation processes tend to have shared characteristics that consist of an archetypal pattern, with consistent underlying themes repeating themselves within these processes.[9]

Basic Combat Training or "boot camp" is a communal initiation to help civilians become warriors so we can perform our duties as soldiers and withstand the hardships of our roles in battle. In boot camp, the pre-military, civilian personality is supplanted by the warrior identity, which then takes the stage with all of its particular military-style characteristics. I don't think anyone questions why this is so important and necessary. Obviously, it isn't just the skills of a warrior that allow for war's grizzly tasks to be done. We could teach a civilian to shoot rifles and to use military equipment, but that doesn't mean that individual will be mission ready. The warrior's strength and that of his unit comes from the archetypal, psychological center of warriorhood itself—the warrior archetype. Warriors must be in touch with a martial, warrior spirit which has an unsettling intensity and aggressiveness that makes them capable of violent, life-taking action, and yet a profound degree of discipline, professionalism, and pride. Good warriors can be neither weaklings nor unrestrained, violent beasts. Boot camp, as an initiatory process, makes warriors' psyches able to carry the archetypal warrior energy in such a way that it can guide their actions and make otherwise impossible tasks possible. What it *does not* do is psychologically prepare warriors for the reality that it may overtake them, and undo them.

The archetypal warrior energy, all by itself, is a force that can make warriors' lives difficult, potentially causing them to live a one-sided life. But, the real challenge comes with the duality of warriorhood's gifts and consequences: that serving in the role of a warrior comes with meaning, purpose, and the opportunity to engage in history-altering experiences of individual and global consequence; and that many warriors endure horrible, tragic, and traumatic wounds that leave chasms in our souls and devastate our nervous systems. One combat veteran client of mine shared about taking the life of an enemy combatant and remarked, "At the time I didn't fucking care. Killing him felt good. I was even proud that I fucking killed him. Later, it was like I sobered up and was tortured by it... couldn't get it out of my head. It's like I was an animal and now that I'm human again I have to find a way to live with it." This veteran's therapy process wasn't just about tending to the trauma he experienced, but also about tending to his soul and the archetypal dimensions of his experience—unraveling his identity from the warrior complex that had come to possess him.

As individuals and as a nation we fail to recognize that the reverse of boot camp is also critical for warriors. My experience leading intensive therapeutic group programs for veterans has taught me that warriors benefit immensely from communal therapeutic processes (whether post-service initiations, rites, or rituals) that help them a adopt an identity as *veterans* after service, along with a new attitude, skills, and adaptations that can make our transition and recovery to civilian life healthier. Yet, such processes hardly exist. *The Battle Within's* Revenant Journey program is one of few examples.

From time immemorial, initiations around the world have helped individuals through transitional phases. In ancient societies, boys were initiated into manhood, girls into womanhood, men into warriorhood, and warriors back into civilian life. The Navajo "Enemy Way" ceremony is one such example of a post-war initiation experience, meant to help free warriors of the ghosts that might haunt them after battle.[10] Jung understood the importance of such initiation processes, and spoke about how some societies would help warriors to navigate the transition home by forcing them to take a lowly, humble position so that they might disidentify from the "godlike" heroic energies that tend to intoxicate a person who has been inflated by the intense experience of combat.[11]

Each transitional task exists within an archetypal context, and each has unique and specific psychological demands which are not to be confused with one another. One veterans organization, which I shall not name out of respect for its team and its noble aims, has made the critical error of thinking that male warriors suffer because they have not had a proper initiation into manhood. This error is born out of a belief made popular by the mythopoetic men's movement, that a lack of a proper initiation into manhood is at the root of many of society's ills and men's general unhappiness in the modern world. While this general insight remains valuable and worthy of consideration, it should be obvious that the problems of veterans are distinct from civilians, and thus it fails to offer an adequate explanation to the issue at hand, let alone a hint toward a solution. Having not even passed basic logical scrutiny, this theory never should have developed into interventions that were then passed on to veterans who have participated in this organization's programs, where it is suggested that their problems are because they haven't been properly initiated into manhood or adulthood. It is offensive and absurd, to say the least.

This organization fails to grasp the archetypal context warriors exist in, and how it is different than the archetypal context of adolescents transitioning into adulthood. The lessons of the mythopoetic men's movement on the subject of initiation are not universally applicable to all populations for all transitional challenges. Each unique transition requires new (and different) adaptations to meet the demands of the new (and different) developmental stage or societal task. In other words, something which has never been conscious before must become conscious, so the individual can meet challenges it does not yet have the ability to face, and the tasks of returning from war or transitioning out of military service are exceptionally challenging and unique from other developmental or transitional phases faced by the average civilian.

For warriors to successfully return home, to heal and rediscover a satisfying life filled with meaning and purpose, we must be transformed once again from the inside out. When a communal initiation process is absent or when traditional psychotherapies meet their limits, it falls on the warrior to go the way of the shaman and to heal himself or herself. The *Odyssey*, in my assessment, is a myth that can be understood to depict the inner challenges veterans tend to face and illustrates through its story-telling and symbolism how best to navigate them. It's a quintess-ential example of *the archetype of the warrior's return*, probably the most elaborate one. It tells us what kind of post-war or post-service initiation is needed, whether we're talking about an organic, individual process of transformation or organized processes that set the stage for healing in groups of warriors, like the one I designed at *The Battle Within*.

Many years ago, I was leading a group of veterans and first responders, and as members of the cohort became curious about dreams, one shared a dream with me, which in turn led to another, and then another, and so on. All were quite archetypal, and in line with what I'm used to experiencing when working with this population. Two of the veterans in the group shared painful dreams in which they were separated from the women they loved—like Odysseus separated from his wife, Penelope, as we'll read. One of these dreams ended with the veteran wandering around lost, trying to "get home." In his book *What it Is Like to Go to War*, Karl Marlantes, a highly decorated Vietnam Veteran, shared a dream that reflects a similar situation, and he diagnosed his problem well.

Twenty years later I had a dream in which I was going to a wedding. The bride was waiting. A friend asked where the groom was. I had to explain to him that the wedding wouldn't occur until the groom came home from Vietnam. I had been reading a lot of women writers. This time I got it. The hypermasculine warrior energy has to be balanced by the feminine energy, but it must come home to do this.[12]

Dreams and myths are intrinsically symbolic. They rarely speak literally, but instead depict *inner, psychological realities*. If we are disconnected from the women we love in our dreams—just as Odysseus was separated from Penelope as he struggled to "get home"—it implies we are separated from our own inner wife, which is what Jung called the *anima*. This problem is similar to the problem of the combat veteran I shared about earlier, who repeatedly fell into affairs.

In essence, when Jung discussed the anima, he was referring to what he understood as the unconscious half of a man's soul (Jung called the equivalent for females the animus). Jung understood the anima and animus to have a compensatory relationship to that of the *persona*, which is the mask we wear to navigate our way through the outer world. He believed that what was left out of the persona became a defining characteristic of the anima or animus, and that dreams often included opposite-sex figures whose characteristics were the opposite of the individual's outer personality.[13] Importantly, as it relates to what I understand as the *archetype of the warrior's return,* I believe that this is why we see so many mythological examples of ferocious, battle-hardened warriors who are saved, supported, and transformed by female figures—and why we see the same theme in the dreams of modern veterans. While military service and war compel us to become defined by a particular side of our personalities (the hardened and stereotypically "masculine" side), the reality is that the healing and transformation process require fundamentally different psychological qualities (qualities that are stereotypically imagined as being associated with the "feminine" aspect of the psyche). Ultimately, the unconscious will bring forth these unconscious qualities when they are needed most —which is what we observe in the symbolic imagery of myths about returning warriors all around the globe.

Jung believed that opposite-sex figures in dreams or myths were often distinct from same-sex figures in terms of their psychological meaning, so he assigned the terms anima (meaning "soul"—which he associated with eros) and animus (meaning "spirit"—which he associated with logos). In depth psychology, soul and spirit are imagined as being distinct: soul being grounded in the chthonic, earthy realm of the body; and spirit being ethereal, not bound by the body or physical objects. Jung's thinking, based on his obser-vations of people who lived in a world that is quite different from today's, was that men tended to lack connection to the inner, sensual world of soul and eros (being focused in outer pursuits), while women tended to lack connection to the ethereal world of spirit and logos.[14] He wrote:

If, therefore, we speak of the *anima* of a man, we must logically speak of the *animus* of a woman, if we are to give the soul of a woman its right name. Whereas logic and objectivity are usually the predominant features of a man's outer attitude, or are at least regarded as ideals, in the case of a woman it is feeling. But in the soul it is the other way round: inwardly it is the man who feels, and the woman who reflects.[15]

Here we can see that Jung's rather black-and-white generalizations about the differences between men and women do not fit the realities of our time—even if they may have fit his own. Given the differences of how men and women lived in the world in his time (with women being far more constrained by society relative to men), Jung believed that the individuation process asked each to develop the contrasexual aspects of the self which were left out of their lives. So, simply put, according to Jung's theory, life may bring circumstances where men may need to develop the so-called "feminine" aspects of the self, while women may need to develop the so-called "masculine" aspects of the self. We have to appreciate that we live in a different world today, where people have a great deal of freedom to live and express themselves as they like, with less arbitrary judgements about what men or women should or shouldn't do. And, since we are living in a world that is so different, the psychological tasks and problems—and perhaps how they show up through the images of the unconscious—are not the same as they were in Jung's time.

The terms anima and animus, and the way they are understood as symbols, have been challenged and reimagined since Jung's time. It is beyond the scope of this book to explore the debate surrounding these terms, but I want to emphasize a basic psychological fact as it relates to any figure or symbol that is not the storyteller or the dreamer. Such figures or images are sometimes referred to as "non-ego" images, meaning that they are, by definition, something other than the ego—something unconscious. Regardless of the sex or gender of the dreamer or the symbol, the important thing to remember is that these "other" figures represent something in us that we are not identified with—they are something other which we can benefit from getting to know for their own unique qualities.

In the end, whatever the term used and whatever the sex or gender of a figure in my dream or Homer's myth, my goal is to treat the figure or image or person in my dream or in a myth as a living thing—something that has psychological life, which is not me and which is, in some way, inviting me to direct my attention toward it. Whether it's a man or a woman or an animal that approaches me in a dream, I am obliged to welcome them as whatever they are—and not as they are theorized by someone else to be—and certainly not reduced to a theoretical term and the dogmatic assumptions that come with it. It is my job to feel and explore the image and what it evokes in me and tells me about myself.

For the purposes of sharing my insights and experiences working with veterans, I will continue to use Jung's terms as he posited them, along with his theory of individuation, not as gospel, but as rich grounds worthy of exploration with the goal of healing and transformation. In returning to Marlantes' dream, above, note that he had an inner bride (classically an *anima figure*) longing for her betrothed to return from war. This dream paints a heartbreaking picture of the painful separation between differing aspects of his own soul—and this dream specifically depicts this separation as being between a bride and her groom who had not yet returned from Vietnam.

Jung theorized that as the persona helps mediate our relationship to the outer world, the anima or animus help mediate our relationship with the inner world.[16] [17] From his point of view, if you are disconnected from your anima or animus, you will be disconnected from the unconscious, and your life will grow stale and lack meaning. To be disconnected from the anima or animus is to be disconnected from half your soul, so it's no wonder these dreams are disturbing to those who have them. To speak in the language of myths, if the inner queen is lost or endangered, your kingdom will become a wasteland without fertility.

Another veteran at the same program shared a dream where hostile figures were trying to harm his wife and children. He struggled to fight back, but his weapon wouldn't work. There are two motifs in this dream—the loss of functioning defenses (in the weapon that won't work) and the hostile figures threatening the dreamer and his precious loved ones. The loss of functioning defenses echoes a motif seen in a myth about the theft of Thor's hammer, who couldn't fight back against the giants because his weapon (or defense) had been stolen. Psychologist Abraham Maslow is famous for saying, "If all you have is a hammer, everything looks like a nail." When Thor, the Norse hammer-wielding god associated with lightning, thunder, storms, strength, and the protection of humankind, lost his hammer, he had to adopt a new approach so he could get it back—he had to embody and relate through the archetypal feminine, which is a theme we see repeatedly in myths about hardened warriors.[18] This story of Thor is unique relative to other myths that depict the archetype of the warriors return, in that he actually dresses up and pretends to be a woman. When we go too far in one direction, we generally have to go the opposite direction to find balance and overcome the challenges we face. When the weapons of our dreams start to jam, break down, or fail, it's a sign that our old adaptations have met their limits and a new approach is needed. This is a good indicator that it's time for therapy. The same theme is reflected in the research of Harry Wilmer, a Jungian and Freudian analyst who worked with Vietnam vets at the VA and was a veteran himself. Here is a dream from one of his patients:

I am in a goddamn firefight. People are getting hit and firing back. Explosions are going off. Commands are being given. People are crying. We are tangling with the NVA in some small valley. We could see them coming over, and we seemed to be moving toward them. My damn weapon jams. I pull the damn cartridge out, but the automatic gun won't fire. By this time they are all over us. … I am scared shitless.[19]

One question we need to ask is what do the hostile figures in these dreams represent, which cause veterans to feel so threatened? To answer this question, it is helpful to understand a bit more about the nature of the psyche and the numerous underlying causes of suffering. While this will be discussed in much greater detail in later chapters, psychological defenses comprise the foundation of the psyche, and they allow us to feel safe in the world. They also shape our experience of reality, and we have a variety of different defenses for different purposes.[20] When our psychological defenses (the weapons in our dreams) start to become maladaptive or when they break down or fail, we tend to experience a greater degree of anxiety, depression, or other unpleasant symptoms—and that's when these sorts of dreams start to arise. We have to ask ourselves what effect these hostile figures have on the dreamer—in other words, how do they make the dreamer *feel?* The Vietnam veteran above said, "scared shitless," and others say things like they feel tortured, threatened, or on edge. This is exactly how PTSD symptoms make a person feel, and these symptoms result from specific maladaptive psychological defenses that get stuck in the "on" position.

Depth psychologist and Jungian Analyst, Donald Kalsched, spent decades studying the dreams of trauma survivors, and he found that our dreams often contain the same theme as the dreams above, where hostile figures chase, threaten, torture, or kidnap the dreamer and precious others. We see these hostile aspects of the psyche expressed in my first big dream, shared above, as I was running from some enemy. At the time, I was running from my suffering and my symptoms. Kalsched and other analysts believe these threatening figures represent the maladaptive defenses that cause us to suffer, as trauma often causes defenses to turn against the person, leaving them to feel tortured.

Jungians generally recognize that "special children" in dreams tend to represent a vital core of our personalities—even the soul itself—that which makes us feel full of life and leads us to our future potential. This is sometimes referred to as the archetype of the divine child. In contrast, special women (especially in the dreams of men) tend to be associated with the anima, or something precious, deeply valuable and longed for, which is distinct from the ego and its qualities. If our connection to these vital aspects of our personalities is threatened, life loses its flavor, and this happens if we are too one-sided or if we experience severe trauma that causes hostile defenses that cut us off from life.

So, if we consider the dreams above, we can see that the dreamers' adaptations, which were necessary in war, hamper our well-being back home, and threaten our relationship to vital, lifegiving aspects of our own souls. This is by no means uncommon. Several years ago, Jason Kander, a public figure and Afghanistan veteran, shared about his own struggles with PTSD with a reporter.

When night fell and everybody else in the house was asleep, Jason Kander went on patrol. Tormented by nightmares about intruders breaking in and kidnapping his wife and son, the Afghanistan War veteran and one-time rising Democratic Party star would rise from his bed and keep watch over his home. "I went almost 12 years without a good night's sleep," Kander said.[21]

Kander's dream and the dream of the veteran I shared previously appear to be related in terms of their meaning. I have also had dreams like this one, and have worked with at least a dozen other veterans or trauma survivors who've shared dreams with the same kidnapping motif, where the dreamer and loved ones are threatened by hostile figures. We can learn even more if we amplify the imagery of these dreams by looking to mythological examples. In the *Odyssey*, while Odysseus is trying to make his way home from war, hostile suitors threaten to steal Odysseus's wife, Penelope, and kill his child, Telemachus. Odysseus's kingdom is threatened, just as many veterans' inner worlds are imperiled because their experiences in the military and trauma have caused parts of their psyche to turn against them. But the *Odyssey* tells us it is possible to dispatch the suitors and restore justice in the kingdom. Like Odysseus, we can reclaim our lives and find peace once again.

As you'll see throughout this book, if we better understand the inner meaning of dreams and myths by paying attention to the archetypal patterns, it can tell us a great deal about how we might navigate our own post-service or post-war challenges. By adopting a mythic, archetypal perspective of our experiences, we can understand our situation more clearly, seeing where we are and where we need to go.

The world-renowned mythologist Joseph Campbell used the Greek word *nostos* in discussing the journey of Odysseus as he sought to return home from the Trojan War. Contrary to what it may seem, the *nostos* or return is not an easy part of the hero's journey. Transformation is akin to rebirth, and birth is hardly easy. Often for those like Odysseus who are especially heroic, the journey home is a humbling one. It generally requires setting aside one's heroic tendencies and learning to adopt a different approach to life. The journey to healing tends to show us our human limitations and forces us to see, honor, learn from, and listen to our pain. In depth psychology, it's said that *there's a gift—or gold—in the wound.* But to find this gift, we need an authentic transformation. *Who we were* has to be replaced by *who we're meant to be.* Until we learn to listen to our symptoms as a voice of the soul, we won't be able to transform, because our suffering is not an aberration to be overcome or suppressed, but a divine messenger to help us find and follow our unique paths home.

In myths and dreams, *home* is not a literal, physical place. It's a symbolic reference to what we yearn for the most—the place that allows us to be in touch with our *true self,* or objective personality. The true self is who we really are, far beneath the surface. In Jungian psychology, we recognize that a number of things—including complexes and maladaptive psychological defenses—can distort our personalities and cause our true self to be lost. The journey home is a healing adventure, where we work past all the barriers that separate us from the true self. Odysseus's journey home from the Trojan War is symbolic for his healing-and-transformation process. Jung called this process *individuation*—becoming the person you are meant to be, as you make the unconscious conscious and cultivate wholeness in the personality. This doesn't mean becoming a lone wolf, adopting ideals of rugged individualism. It means exploring your inner world to discover parts of your personality that have not yet to be expressed, and freeing yourself of those aspects of the psyche that rob you of life. To return "home," Odysseus's personality must be freed of all that distorts it, and he must be transformed into the person he truly is at his core. Only then does he reconnect with his son, Telemachus, and his wife, Penelope. To get home, he must overcome these obstacles, and today's warriors are no different.

-2-
THE RAID OF ISMARUS:
POSSESSION BY THE WARRIOR
COMPLEX

I entered the realm of Mars [the Roman god of war] for a time in Vietnam. Some of us get swallowed up by these energies or archetypes and some of us reemerge to carry on with other activities. Recognizing that we share these energies, but need not dedicate our lives to them, allows us all to use them, but not be used by them ... How are we to be warriors who essentially perform violent acts yet still maintain our humanity? Our only hope is to see this Mars energy clearly so we can become aware of ourselves as distinct from it yet a part of it. There is no hope for limiting the tragedy of warfare and violence if we don't see it. It will take us over, obliterate our egos, turn us all into people overwhelmed by our dark sides.

— Karl Marlantes[22]

The *Iliad* and the *Odyssey* are Greek epic poems attributed to Homer, dating to somewhere around or between the 7th and 6th centuries BCE. They are the oldest existing pieces of Western literature. The *Iliad* is set during the Trojan War, the ten-year siege of the city of Troy (Ilium) by a coalition of Greek states. It focuses only on a few events that occurred in the final weeks of the war, emphasizing the quarrel between King Agamemnon and the warrior Achilles. The *Odyssey*, a sequel to the *Iliad*, is the classic journey of a warrior returning home after war. It focuses on Odysseus and his ten-year journey home to Ithaca after the fall of Troy.

Those familiar with the *Odyssey* probably noticed how Odysseus is often his own worst enemy, especially early part of his journey home from war. He seems incapable of *not* creating his own undoing. VA psychiatrist Jonathan Shay observed that this is a common theme among modern combat veterans who he says "get stuck in combat mode."[23] Just as one cannot go to war with the attitude of a civilian, one cannot return "home" from war successfully with the attitude of a warrior. The warrior's attitude and way of being is healthy in only one environment: *war.* Beyond that chaotic and hellish realm, it sows only seeds of destruction, disconnection, and suffering. Military training and culture cultivate and sustain this attitude, because the military has a duty to ensure its members are ready to act violently in the heat of battle. Yet, there is a high cost for those who leave the combat zone or military, without ever having experienced a post-war or post-military counter-initiation process that makes possible their recovery and transformation.

Odysseus's first stop after leaving Troy is Ismarus, the city of the Cicones. Unprovoked, Odysseus and his men act as if they're still at war. They sack and loot the town and murder innocent people. Odysseus wanted to head out immediately, but his men behave belligerently, and they pay a significant price as a result. When the townspeople counterattack the next morning, dozens of Odysseus's men lose their lives—an unnecessary tragedy that could have been avoided if Odysseus and his men hadn't been possessed by their warrior-centric way of being. One can't help but think of how this scene mirrors the tragic loss of life that is seen too often in newly returned warriors, whose excessive risk taking often has deadly consequences. However, I do not intend to interpret or understand the Odyssey so literally. Instead I want to focus on how this imagery can be understood symbolically, which tells us more about the psyche's inner workings, with the hope that this insight will drive us deeper into the kind of transformative work that is necessary to transform veterans' souls.

Unless veterans take part in a postwar initiation that rebalances their psyches to prepare them for life in the "civilian world" while teaching them how to heal from their wounds, they can expect to encounter serious challenges. Sadly, Odysseus didn't have such an initiation when he left Troy—just as many veterans don't when they leave war or military service. It seems even leadership at the Department of Defense (DoD) and the Department of Veterans Affairs (VA) fail to appreciate how important the post-military transformation process is, as they continue to neglect the need to provide a counter-initiation experience that might help veterans navigate post-military life.

It's important to understand how veterans end up "stuck in combat mode," and useful to have some psychological theories to help frame our understanding. Let us begin with the psychic law of inertia:

Newton's law of inertia—the fundamental law of bodies —that every body perseveres in its state of rest, or of motion, unless it is compelled to change that state by forces impressed thereon, seemingly affects not only "bodies" but anything which appears in time and space. In the psyche inertia is seen as a tendency toward habit formation and ritualization.[24]

Jungian analyst Anthony Stevens frames the importance of this concept in a way that is helpful to our understanding:

> Every pattern of adaptation, outer or inner, is maintained in essentially the same unaltered form and anxiously defended against change until an equally strong or stronger impulse is able to displace it.[25]

Civilians have a pattern of adaptation (inner and outer) that fits their role in society. When a civilian enters military service and goes through combat training, their patterns of adaptation change, and they become warriors, with new adaptations (both inner and outer) such as a particular way of being, speaking, dressing, and reacting to whatever situation they are in. One's personality is then fundamentally altered as the expression of psychic energy shifts course, finding itself reinvested according to a different psychological pattern. Where before there was a civilian, thereafter there is a warrior—a human being with the potential and responsibility to wage war, wherein they unleash the most extreme force possible, including death, upon their enemies.

War is no place for gentle-hearted common people, and the United States military has an interest in producing the most ferocious and professional fighting force it can possibly assemble. Military leaders —especially non-commissioned officers who've been to war— consider it an immensely personal endeavor to prepare their troops for the worst. So, the preparation for war continues after basic combat training, once soldiers arrive at their units and throughout their careers. If you know you're going into a year-long gun-battle with twelve soldiers that you're personally responsible for—and your own life may be lost or spared depending on their readiness— you're going to make damn sure they're ready for anything, including unleashing an unforgiving hell upon those who threaten you. The average person, in an untrained and uninitiated state, has no place in war. To be adapted for war, one must be in touch with parts of oneself scarcely known to the average civilian.

When we experience our initiation into the military the warrior archetype is constellated in our unconscious, and that particular form of psychic energy is activated. Once the warrior archetype is activated—*brought into motion out of a state of rest via initiation*—it has force. It becomes a *complex* of increased power, and has the power to redirect conscious energy in a certain direction. It even has the power to take over us, or possess us, and we can lose ourselves to it.

At this point, it is important to talk about complexes in greater depth, because they're so important to understanding many of the problems veterans face. Complexes essentially behave as foreign or independent bodies of psychic force, while existing as collections of feeling-toned images that reside in the unconscious. As Jung wrote, when certain associations trigger, activate, or constellate the energy contained by a complex, they are ignited and have the power to redirect our consciousness.[26]

> Everyone knows nowadays that people "have complexes." What is not so well known, though far more important theoretically, is that complexes can *have us.* The existence of complexes throws serious doubt on the naïve assumption of the unity of consciousness, which is equated with "psyche," and on the supremacy of the will. Every constellation of a complex postulates a disturbed state of consciousness. The unity of consciousness is dis-rupted and the intentions of the will are impeded or made impossible. ... The complex must therefore be a psychic factor which, in terms of energy [*or power or force*], possesses a value that sometimes exceeds that of our conscious intentions [our egos], otherwise such disruptions of the conscious order would not be possible at all. And in fact, an active complex puts us momentarily under a state of duress, of compulsive thinking and acting ...

> What then, scientifically speaking, is a "feeling-toned complex"? It is the *image* of a certain psychic situation which is strongly accentuated emotionally ... The image has a powerful inner coherence, it has its own wholeness and, in addition, a relatively high degree of autonomy, so

that it is subject to the control of the conscious mind to only a limited extent, and therefore behaves like an animated foreign body in the sphere of consciousness.[27]

The central point here is that a complex can disrupt how we feel, think, and act. When a complex gets activated, the ego loses its power to direct consciousness. In fact, a complex can just take over the whole show, while the ego goes along for a ride. Our whole experience of the world can be influenced by complexes—especially if we're not aware of it. While Jung's words help us begin to understand complexes, I want to examine complexes from a few additional angles. First, we'll explore complexes as elements of the psyche which arise based on experience. Jungian Analyst June Singer discussed the nature of complexes as sometimes having roots in traumatic experiences, while also discussing why some complexes seem to have a greater amount of energy or intensity behind them.

It is not the superficial psychic jolts and bumps that occur which give rise to the formation of complexes, but only those wounds which lay bare the vital, pattern-forming elements of the psyche, the elements which Jung has called *archetypes*. Those experiences which threaten our deepest beliefs—in our gods and ourselves—those are the ones which give rise to complexes. Jung proposed that the nuclear element of the complex is characterized by its feeling-tone, the emphasis arising from the *intensity* of the emotion involved. This emphasis, this intensity, can be expressed in terms of energy, a value of quantity. In direct relation to the amount of energy, the energic quantity, is the capacity for a nucleus to draw associations to it, thereby forming a complex. The more energic quantity, the more associations, hence the material from everyday life experiences gets drawn into the complex.[28] (emphasis added)

Singer is alluding to trauma-based complexes that arise as a result of significant experiences that reshape our experience of the world. In this instance, a "psychic jolt" or "bump" might be something that wounded us—like a getting hit by a roadside bomb or IED or getting caught in a gnarly firefight. The more intense the experience that injured us, the more powerful the trauma-based complex will be, because it will have more energy. The more energy it has, the more associations from our psyche it can draw to it, and the more power it will have to disrupt our consciousness and send us into *reexperiencing* the past as if it were happening all over again.

Imagine this kind of trauma-based complex as a black hole sucking things into it. The more power or energy it has, the more associations it can suck into it, and when other (later) experiences arise which evoke associations related to the complex, it can "trigger" the complex—the entire web of emotions and sensations that are woven together with these "images" of the past. In Jungian psychology, the term "image" refers to more than just things you see, as it refers to all psychological experiences that register internally. Sounds (like an explosion or a certain song) or a smell (like a burning car or grandma's pie) reflexively evoke *images*. A song might take you back to a particular moment in time—and this memory is experienced as an *image with a certain feeling tone*. We can't separate our psychological experiences from images. They're foundational to the psyche's functioning, and everything we experience ties to an image—hence Jung's emphasis on images.

If we consider the *associations* tied to certain traumas, like the sounds (gunfire, explosions, people yelling), sights (highway, crowd, flash of light, smoke rising), smells (gunpowder, smoke from a fire, dust), and so forth, we see how they all become part of the web of a trauma-based complex. We also have to appreciate other associations we didn't (*consciously*) register in moments of trauma, because we were too disconnected from reality. Because of *dissociation*, a powerful psychological defense that protects us from feeling the overwhelming sensations and feelings that happened during life-threatening events, we might not feel much at all during and for a period of time after some traumatic experiences. In the heat of combat, your body was likely wrenching with tension, and there was probably overwhelming amounts of anxiety, fear, and even sadness that were not able to be consciously experienced, let alone process. Dissociation cuts us off from our bodies and our feelings to protect us, so we can function and survive. But these are not forgotten, and when other reminders of trauma are evoked ("triggered"), they may be brought back to life.

I'll never forget how, when I was still in Iraq, me and my

platoonmates had to warn one another before we took a picture while utilizing a flash at night, or even before somebody tried to spark up a cigarette if it was dark out. Same thing if we were shutting a hatch or door on the vehicle, because the sudden and unexpected "*thud*" or flash of light could scare the shit out of someone. When a bomb goes off, there's an instantaneous flash, and if you're a few vehicles back from the blast, you might see the flash before you hear the *BOOM* of the explosion. Sometimes, we'd forget to warn each other. The unexpected flash of a camera or a cigarette lighter might cause you to jump, and your nervous system automatically kicks into action. You might feel tense, anxious, and agitated for a while afterward, on high alert. In this case, the "image" of the flash or spark, or sound touched on a complex—a psychic content composed of the web of images, sensations, and emotions that have the power to disrupt the normal flow of energy through the psyche. *The complex would then have us in its grip, no matter how much we wanted to ignore its power.*

Jung's theory of complexes explains why so many veterans have a hard time in crowds, driving down the highway, hearing fireworks, or facing other reminders (*associations*) connected to their trauma. Thanks to neuroscience, most of us are now familiar with physiological explanations of how trauma changes the brain and nervous system, causing us to suffer and react to stressors more easily. We now know that chronic stress and trauma lead to increased activity in the brain's limbic system, which is the essentially the alarm system that sends us into fight, flight, or freeze mode. At the same time, other parts of the brain that normally balance and hold the limbic system in check become inhibited.

Over time, chronic stress and trauma cause this system to react to potential threats (*which are experienced as images*) with greater sensitivity, activating the psychological defenses that are intended to help keep us safe, but which often cause us to suffer.[29]

Here I must stress that without complexes, even a dangerously hyperactive limbic system would have nothing to react to. There would be no "trigger" to set it off. We have to appreciate the centrality of complexes and images as it relates to our psychological and emotional experiences. They are pillars in the foundation of our consciousness, and the images we encounter have the power to alter our consciousness for better or worse. If we can learn to appreciate the role of images in how our brains and bodies respond to trauma, then we might also learn to appreciate the role of images in the healing process, understanding the importance of dreams and myths.

We have to appreciate how far-reaching the effects of images and complexes are. Some persons are said to have "negative mother complexes," or "negative father complexes," along with a legion of others. Whatever the central image of the complex is—whether mother, father, or warrior—the related images and associations that tie into the complex can trigger or activate it, causing us to experience all of the psychological, emotional, and physiological reactions that automatically follow. Importantly, not all complexes are problematic. Some are simply foundational elements of the psyche itself.

Consequently, in Jung's view the complexes per se do not

necessarily represent pathology. Everybody has complexes. They are, in Jung's terms, "focal nodal points of psychic life which … must not be lacking, for otherwise psychic activity would come to a fatal standstill." Complexes contain the driving power of psychic life. "Suffering is not an illness; it is the normal counterpole to happiness. A complex becomes pathological only when we think we have not got it." Because then it has us.[30]

This brings us to the next fact we have to face with complexes, which is that not all complexes are based in trauma, nor are they pathological. They're the "focal nodal points of psychic life" that lie beneath our experiences. *Without complexes nothing moves*. As Jung pointed out, the ego itself is a complex, which he referred to as the *ego-complex*—our idea of "I" or "me" as an independent personality.[31] One way of understanding the ego-complex is that it's like a collection of images that, in Jung's words, "has a fluctuating composition," changing according to how we imagine and experience ourselves throughout time.[32]

At this point, we can return to the key task at hand, which is to understand the nature of what I'm calling the *warrior complex* and its impact on the psyches of those who serve in the military. The warrior complex is a collection of images and associations that relate to warriorhood and the quintessential image of the warrior. It evokes certain attitudes and modes of behavior, Standard Operating Procedures (SOPs) that go along with the image of the ideal warrior. Boot camp helps establish this complex so that the individuals who are to serve as warriors will be able to fulfill their duties, and, if necessary, act with the absolute most lethal and violent energy possible to be effective and victorious combatants, which will increase the likelihood of their survival. Boot camp, subsequent military training, and war itself—basically the entirety of military life—amount to powerful initiatory experiences that set the psychic energy associated with the warrior image into motion, progressively increasing its power.

In drawing from Jung's theory on complexes, we can understand that the warrior complex (1) has its own wholeness and can behave like a foreign element of consciousness (it can be imagined almost like a separate personality within us that becomes conflated with the way we imagine our own identity); (2) that it is not the ego, it is separate from it, but that it can overpower the ego or possess it; and (3) the greater the energy behind this complex (based on the nature or power of the experiences that activated it), the greater the ability of this complex to displace the ego and distort the personality and its perception of reality. In short, the warrior complex can and does *possess* the personality of many service members and veterans. If this happens, the complex must be *deactivated*, which requires that it be made conscious and relativized by other forces in the psyche so that equilibrium and balance are restored.

When your warrior complex gets activated, you might start behaving in the ways warriors do—perhaps as if you're in combat again, lashing out aggressively, looking for someone to fight. Or if a trauma complex gets activated (by a "trigger" that reminds your nervous system of combat), you might find yourself inundated with

PTSD symptoms, such as feeling on-guard, anxious, stressed, numb, or having unwanted and painful memories. The reaction is unconscious and automatic, and happens when complexes assert their power over us. Jonathan Shay's books make clear the extent of this problem, though he interprets things differently from the way I do here, as he focuses on behavior more than on underlying, unconscious causes or meaning. Of course, as we explore the *Odyssey*, we'll get a clearer sense that the ancient Greeks saw this problem as well.

After we are initiated into the military through combat training, the warrior archetype or warrior complex become dominant components in the psyche, while other aspects (such as the archetypal feminine or usual civilian dominants) occupy a less powerful position—sometimes becoming totally repressed. The warrior archetype or complex becomes *anxiously defended against change until an equally strong or stronger impulse is able to displace it.*[33] In other words, military training, culture, and war itself set psychic energy in motion that transforms our personalities to prepare us for war, and our psychic energy will continue to express itself along this gradient until a time comes that a new experience (or an accumulation of experiences) causes a redirection of psychic energy that leads to a new adaptation. Leaving the military or coming home from war doesn't automatically change our inner, psychological dynamics. The warrior complex doesn't just "turn off," which is evident if we review the countless examples in literature about combat veterans, especially in Shay's work.[34, 35] It remains a powerful force in the psyche, one that is often problematic outside the realm of war, causing us to lose an authentic connection to ourselves, others, and the world. The warrior complex has to be made conscious, relativized by other psychic forces, and deactivated—and the *Odyssey* helps us understand how this process can unfold.

I have witnessed at *The Battle Within* how an appropriately therapeutic counter-initiation experience that follows the archetype of the warrior's return can bring about dramatic changes, and I have also witnessed the limitations of similar programs that do not follow this archetypal pattern. Even without such a post-war or post-military initiation experience, the psyche will push for change —through dreams and, ultimately, through suffering. We who have served in the military tend to maintain our tough guy or gal military persona long after our time in the service, failing to understand the myriad ways this creates barriers to a healthy and fulfilling life. The first part of Odysseus's journey highlights this problem, at the same time illustrating how the psyche attempts to correct course through its self-healing, wholeness-seeking function.

To recap, after Odysseus and his men left Troy, the wind carried them to Ismarus, the city of the Cicones. There Odysseus and his men "sacked the town and put the people to the sword. [They] took their wives and also much booty…"[36] Odysseus wanted to be on his way quickly, but his men would not obey him, and they sat on the beach drinking wine and killing sheep and oxen. The next morning, the Cicones came back with skilled reinforcements from inland, and a battle raged that lasted most of the day until finally Odysseus and his men were able to escape. Odysseus lost six men from each of his twelve boats—at total of seventy-two men, which represents a significant loss of power as a result of this error.

My interpretation of this myth comes from an application of Jungian theory and its modes of understanding. I approach the story's imagery as I would any other symbolic products of the unconscious, including dreams. From a Jungian perspective, all imagery is inherently symbolic and all the elements in a dream or a myth represent inner aspects of the individual. So we can understand the figures in the raid of Ismarus—and the myth as a whole—to represent aspects of Odysseus's own psyche. For readers who do not want to take my word for it and are academically inclined, I encourage you to explore Jung's writings so you can understand the rationale for this approach.

From a Jungian perspective, one way we can imagine this is to understand Odysseus himself as a symbolic representation of the *ego*—the part of our personality we are aware of, the part we call "I" or "me." All the other figures in this tale represent what Jungians call the *shadow*, which is everything in the personality we're not yet aware of, whether we repressed and hid these parts of ourselves due to shame, or whether life has not yet presented us with an opportunity to get to know these parts. Some shadow aspects are positive and helpful, while others may be negative and challenging to deal with. The same can be said of the ego. Not all the qualities we idealize about ourselves are, in reality, positive, and not all the qualities we devalue about ourselves are actually negative. The difficulty comes in distinguishing between what parts of ourselves are truly healthy and which ones aren't. Determining which is which is an important task, and because dreams present an objective, psychic reality, it's helpful to turn toward them to separate the grain from the chaff.

For example, perhaps you take pride in your drivenness and beat up on yourself when you're too emotional or soft. Our society, and especially military culture, encourage hard work and drivenness and devalue emotional expression, even shaming those who show how they really feel. In actuality, one can be *too* driven. Sometimes we get caught up in *doing* things, even compulsively, and this can be a problem that points to underlying issues which need to be addressed. Maybe our drivenness is a way of distracting ourselves from our pain or feeling of purposelessness. Often, beneath compulsive tendencies there are wounds that could benefit from therapeutic work. Maybe our ego's perspective is wrong—maybe our drivenness is not actually helping us; maybe it's standing in the way of our healing. In the same way, maybe the pain we so desperately wish to avoid—which we judge to be negative—is actually what we need to *feel*, and even express, so we can heal and transform.

Several years after I came home from Baghdad, after completing a couple of years of therapy, I was still wrestling with a lot of anxiety. What I needed to do was surrender to my feelings and let go, and to hold myself through my experiences in a caring and supportive way. But I was fighting them. This is typical for warriors, because fighting is what we do. In my driven, warrior-centric way of being, I thought I might overcome my hardships through the kind of heroic response I learned in the military. I planned a solo backcountry camping trip in Joshua Tree National Park, which was an emotional stretch for someone who didn't even feel safe at home. Being alone in the desert, I was a nervous wreck. I thought this adventure would be an initiation to help me to connect with my power and overcome my anxiety by force, but I was wrong. I was so hypervigilant I could hardly sleep, fearful I would fall victim to some attack. I couldn't have been more paranoid. My first night alone in the desert, I had this dream:

Rejection of the Anima and Feeling

I'm sleeping in my tent when a naked woman comes to me. She is beautiful, but something is wrong. She wants to be with me, but I am concerned because she seems sick and very scared. I ask her if she has a disease, and she says she has shingles. Nervous about embracing, I resist her. Suddenly Hitler comes riding up on a horse with a group of Nazi soldiers and the woman runs for her life. Hitler and his men have been looking for her and it seems they want to kill her.

In this dream, the female figure would represent an aspect of the self that is in need of care and nurturance due to some sort of sickness, and, classically, Jungians would associate this female figure in a man's dream with the anima. Regardless of whether we accept the classical Jungian association of this figure with the anima, the clear and unfortunate reality is that this aspect of the self is seeking a connection with the ego, and yet, some other hostile, non-ego image is violently driving it away. The dream does not depict the part of me needing care as a male figure, but as a female one, and the unconscious's own specificity and the context of my situation at the time leads me to believe this dream is depicting my own hostility toward aspects of myself stereotypically associated with the feminine—especially my emotional life. I feel this part of me was reaching out for connection, asking me to embrace it as I suffered, because I had not really cared for myself in a nurturing or compassionate way. I had tried to deny my feelings and push them away, believing (as many warriors do) that suffering and emotions are signs of weakness. My ego's view was distorted, because I was possessed by a hostile complex. Our emotional experiences possess a wisdom of their own and must be acknowledged and held, not rejected or ignored. In the dream, Hitler represents a prejudiced, hostile, authoritarian attitude or complex which caused me to devalue my feelings and treat them as threats to be eradicated by force. I wanted to kill off my feelings through heroic one-sidedness, and this dream was my unconscious telling me, "*You are possessed by an inner tyrant, and you're causing yourself and precious parts of your soul extreme harm.*"

At the time, I had no idea what the dream meant. I had not yet begun my own analysis or begun to study depth psychology. Yet the dream caught my attention. I couldn't sleep the rest of the night, tormented by fear. I was forced to recognize that denying my feelings would not make them go away; it's impossible to overcome feelings by force. My warrior-centric adaptation to reality had met its limits and no relief could be found without transformation.

If we turn back to the *Odyssey* and the Raid of Ismarus, we might question Odysseus, his men, and their behavior, just as we might question our own attitudes and the unconscious influences that shape them. Odysseus's soldiers are at his side—aligned with the ego—but are they really being helpful? In this part of the story, his men act belligerently and destructively and keep him in a dangerous position. I believe Odysseus's soldiers represent counterproductive, warrior-centric shadow elements whose combative, aggressive, insensitive ways of being imperil his chances of returning home to Ithaca—not to mention cause harm to innocent people. If we understand this part of the myth symbolically, aspects of Odysseus's own personality are endangering him and causing harm, suggesting a need in Odysseus for transformation.

Why would Odysseus and his men attack innocent people? We veterans have a tendency to get "stuck in combat mode," as Shay suggested, and we continue to act as if we're in the military or at war even when we aren't.[37, 38] Because we're unaware of this reality, we can say it's unconscious. That Odysseus's men don't obey him suggests that his ego was overpowered by the unconscious part of his psyche, and these warrior-centric forces (within him) prevent him from doing what is best.

In the language of Jungian psychology, we can say that Odysseus is *possessed* by his warrior persona, the warrior complex, or that he is *identified with* the warrior archetype. The persona is a mask we wear to navigate our relationship with the outer world. Some people's personas make them appear as warriors, while others might present themselves as cowboys, hipsters, intellectuals, or sophisticated folks with lots of class. The persona functions, in essence, as a particular expression of our identity, what we want to show the world. We wear these masks so we can find acceptance in certain environments and live out our roles in society. As we shift from one situation to another, our persona might change a little.

Imagine yourself in a group of cowboys, and think about how you might act, talk, or what you might choose to talk about. If you planned to spend a day with such a group, you might even wear different clothing. And what if you were with a group of businesspeople in an office, or around a bunch of church folks on a Sunday afternoon, or with your family? How would you feel in each of these groups—nervous, excited, at ease? Will you wear the same mask, or persona, in each situation? Will you relate in the same way? Does your image of yourself, how you feel, how you present yourself, change? Imagining these different expressions, we get a sense for the persona as a concept and how our identity and behavior might shift depending on the circumstances.

Many of us wear the mask (persona) of the warrior for so long, we forget we're wearing it. In military service, we don't spend much time interacting with civilians or even with our families, and so we grow accustomed to having *one persona*. Military culture demands that we uphold a military appearance and embody its ideals. We become *possessed by our mask*, and after a while, our true self (which resides in the unconscious) reminds us that we want to live authentically, as our deepest self. Whenever our personality gets distorted or one-sided, the unconscious reminds us to live in alignment with who we really are.

Sometimes these reminders take the form of hardships or suffering, dreams, or other experiences that challenge the way we imagine ourselves. In this part of the *Odyssey*, the Cicones challenge Odysseus and his men. It doesn't mean the Cicones or Odysseus's men are "bad." We can understand the Cicones as shadow elements trying to challenge Odysseus's warrior persona. Though his warrior identity got him through a horrendous war, it no longer serves him. The unconscious, in an attempt to correct course and balance this dangerous imbalance, challenges the ego. Whenever the ego—or conscious personality—is out of touch with our true self, the unconscious will present shadow elements to balance things out. This creates an inner conflict that produces anxiety, as a genuine challenge to the ego. Odysseus loses seventy-two men, a significant reduction in his ego's power. In Jungian terms, we can say the ego is being *relativized* by non-ego elements of the psyche— and in the big picture, this is a necessary and healthy part of the individuation process, even if it is painful.

There are parts of us we like and are happy to identify with and parts our ego rejects. Many veterans have an ego-position that rejects feelings, the emotional side of our nature. But *when we deny something that is true, we do so at our own peril*. The unconscious will find a way to challenge ego's denial to help us acknowledge what we've been ignoring. If you insist you're a hard-ass who doesn't feel sad or never expresses your feelings, there's nothing like a bout of depression or anxiety to shake you free from that limited view of yourself and help you to learn to include emotions in your life. In this part of the *Odyssey*, Odysseus and his men are overly warrior-centric, aggressive, and destructive, and so they need to be challenged by the Cicones, who represent the innocent qualities they have forgotten.

It will be helpful here to look a bit more deeply into the nature of archetypes and complexes. The warrior *archetype* is the collective, stereotypical image of a warrior. Warriors have existed throughout space and time, although in each culture they have a unique form. Archetypes represent an uncontainable power which can only be relativized through relationship with other archetypal powers. If too much of a single archetypal power is activated in your psyche, you run the risk of becoming possessed by it, and so it's important that the warrior archetype be balanced by other, opposite forms of energy.

In myths, the *archetypal feminine* is often the counterbalancing force that helps contain the destructiveness of the archetypal warrior. We see this in mythology. The Greek god of war, Ares, has limits on his warrior energy by his opposites, Aphrodite and Athena. We see the same in the Navajo myth about twin-brother warriors who are transformed by a mother figure after returning from battle and becoming sick, and frightening their tribe with intense energy.[39] Another example exists in an ancient Celtic myth about the rage-filled warrior Cúchulainn, who lashed out at his own charioteer and allies after battle. In this example, women lead the effort to calm and disarm Cúchulainn before he is dunked in three vats of water, which brings him back to a state of balance.[40]

When we live the role of the warrior, the energy or images associated with the archetypal warrior move through us. Without the archetype of the warrior and its associated energy, we would not be able to go to war. Archetypal images course through us, but they are not "us." Once this energy is switched on, it can alter and dominate our personalities, and we run the risk of being consumed by it. Jung recognized this reality, and wrote:

> You see, whenever one is caught in an archetype, one forgets oneself completely, one is in a heightened condition, just inflated; then one lives on and can see later that one has suffered from an inflation. Primitives know that. When a man has a great excitement, an uplifted condition —when a man who has been a successful warrior and killed other men for instance—he must go through a *rite de sortie* in order to disidentify from the archetypal hero, the godlike figure he has become. Otherwise he works havoc, he goes on slaughtering his own tribe perhaps, or becomes so impertinent that he is insupportable. Therefore, in certain tribes the successful warrior is not received in triumph as we would treat him, but is sent to a lonely place where he is fed on raw vegetables for two months in order to thin him down, and then when he is quite meek he is allowed to come back.[41]

When Jung speaks of inflation, he is referring to the tendency to think one has more power and potential than they really have. When you have the power to take life, or to control other people (such as commanding soldiers in combat) it may feel as if you are God, godlike, or all powerful. Obviously, since the psyche will seek to correct the inflation or imbalance, it is to our benefit if we can have an experience that will restore equilibrium without having to experience a complete breakdown or some sort of catastrophe—which is where the sort of counter-initiation in the tribes Jung mentions above comes in. When reading of this kind of corrective experience, it's hard not to think of the terrible treatment received by our Vietnam veterans, and to wonder if perhaps there was some kind of unconscious wisdom at work that escaped our under-standing. I am not suggesting that civilians who shamed and criticized Vietnam veterans were doing them a favor, but rather that the lack of support for warriors of that era could be under-stood as an unconscious, compensatory response by the culture as a whole that might have prevented some returning veterans from feeling as if they were gods to be revered—as some warriors of my own generation seem to think. I do not believe it is a good thing if warriors are abused or treated badly upon returning home, because obviously that just leads to more wounding. But, to worship those who serve or hold them up as a sort of superior citizen is not productive either. This just encourages an endless and unhealthy identification with one's former role as a warrior. We need a communal response that tends to the warrior without inflating him further—that brings him back to his humanity, and helps him to disidentify from the archetypal warrior energy that might have possessed him.

In contrast to the collective nature of the warrior *archetype*, the warrior *complex* is a personal element of the psyche. How we react to an image depends on the nature of our personal complex which is associated with it. If we take the image of a warrior, for example, different people may have very different reactions if they see someone in uniform. An old man who once served as a warrior himself might feel a sense of pride and perhaps even become teary-eyed, as an image of a warrior reminds him of a special time in his life. A young boy might become full of inspiration, imagining the warrior as a hero—or perhaps even as a sort of demi-god in the flesh. But, in every war, there have been stories of warriors who've raped, injured, or killed innocent people. Those who've experienced such horrors, or who've been pained simply by hearing such atrocities (or who may have been victims of something similar) may have feelings about warriors that are intensely negative—and encountering the image of a warrior may evoke sadness, fear, anger, and even hatred. All of us (warriors or civilian) have a unique warrior complex—an internal collection of images and associations that have a particular feeling-tone—and all of us need to explore how that affects our perceptions of actual warriors, and what it means for how we relate to that part of ourselves.

A *complex* has an archetypal (and collective) core, and a personal shell, which is a collection of feeling-toned associations based on personal experiences or other influences, including cultural ones.[42, 43] So, the core of a warrior complex is the universal warrior archetype. For each of us, our feeling-toned associations with various images or complexes will be different. My association with what a warrior is differs from yours, at least to a degree, because our experiences are unique. Some people imagine a warrior as violent, angry, aggressive, defensive, and dangerous. But others may see warriors as honorable, strong, courageous, just, valorous, heroic protectors of society.

At the cultural level, we see examples different warrior complexes throughout history. We can assume the average citizen's warrior complex in ancient Greece around the time of the Trojan War differed greatly from that during the US Revolutionary War, or from today. The warrior complex in each time and culture is colored by different influences. The British of the eighteenth century imagined a professional warrior as a gentleman who marched into battle with propriety. The American revolutionaries imagined warriors as skillful woodsmen who could defeat their enemy in ambushes, using hit-and-run guerilla tactics.

Differing warrior complexes color our styles of fighting and our overall behavior, while also influencing our behavior after our service is complete. After reading Joseph Plumb Martin's firsthand account of serving in the Revolution, I had the impression that the warriors of the Revolution were nowhere near as psychologically imbalanced as the warriors of today, and that they did not hold themselves to the same degree of toxic masculinity that we experience. Being more balanced, I suspect our ancestors were better prepared to manage postwar challenges of healing and transformation.

Our American ideas of warriorhood have evolved since the Revolution, through the Civil War, two World Wars, Korea, Vietnam, Desert Storm, and every other conflict we've been in all the way up to today. The heroic ideal of warriorhood after World War II crashed hard in the 1960s and '70s. Events like the My Lai Massacre in Vietnam have colored our associations and changed our image of warriors. After World War II, the US soldier was seen as a hero; after Vietnam he was seen by many people in our society as a savage baby-killer. The American imagination shifted in a way that warriorhood became seen as calloused and imbalanced, all the more so after two decades of war in Afghanistan and Iraq. It's gotten to a point where some veterans proudly claim the title of "dysfunctional veteran" and wear shirts labeling themselves as such. It's hard to imagine the veterans of WWI or WWII doing the same —how we imagine ourselves as warriors has changed.

The way we imagine warriors and the way warriors imagine themselves has become increasingly inhuman. Today's warrior, covered in high-tech tactical gear, appears more robotic than human. The way we're trained has been perfected in its aim to take humanity out of the picture. Repeated drills train us to see *targets* rather than human beings on the other side of our rifles. We train to adapt to hardship through dissociation, becoming numb to our pain and the world around us. We learn to shut off our humanity —our sensations and feelings and all that brings us a sense of connection to life. What remains when we complete our training, combat, and our time in the service is not a common human being. For those who've been immersed in battle for extended periods, there is often a hardened warrior who often feels unsure of who he has become when the job is done. The human who once related to the world in a satisfying way is permanently changed.

I think back to a night on the front line, Route Gold, during the Battle of Sadr City. My platoonmates were taking care of an explosively formed projectile (EFP) we'd spotted, and we got ambushed, our second ambush that night. Earlier another truck (a

Huskey) was completely immobilized after being hit by another EFP. We sat blacked out in the midst of a sandstorm without air support. Visibility was zero. There were so many explosions it was impossible to tell what was going on and whether everyone was okay. Sometimes when a truck takes a bad hit, they lose radio communications, and in this environment, it seemed like one of our trucks could get hit at any point and we might not even know there was a problem. We had some M-1 tanks and a few Bradleys with us to provide support, and there were moments when the fighting was so thick and overwhelming we couldn't tell the difference between the tanks returning fire, or bombs, mortars, and rocket-propelled grenades (RPGs) exploding. It was a fucking nightmare.

I was in the backseat of an RG-31, which doesn't give me the option to fight or return fire, so I sat there, essentially blind, as the horror of the experience tore through me. When you're in a fight or flight situation, and you don't have the option to fight, it's torture —it's traumatic. My body told me to run, but where? There was no safe space. My body felt like a powerful, wild animal, begging to do *something, anything*, to fight back against the enemy and the horrible sense of powerlessness I was experiencing. I was tempted to get out of the truck and throw lead in the general direction of the enemy, but given that we had machine guns, tanks, and Bradley's already doing some serious shooting, it seemed like an unnecessary and stupid risk for me, as the medic and lifeline for my platoonmates, to expose myself to danger for the sake of hurling small arms fire towards an enemy I couldn't even see. Dissociation kicked in, numbing me to the terror around me, and the warrior complex shifted into overdrive to ensure I maintained the hardened discipline necessary to do my job. I remember feeling at war with myself, trying not to be overcome by fear, and digging as deep as I could to locate that ferocious and unforgiving spirit that any warrior needs if he is to survive in combat. I found it, and adopted the mindset I needed to survive and be an effective member of my platoon.

On a number of other occasions, the same kind of challenges presented themselves. Around the same time, a platoonmate was wounded in an ambush where we took back-to-back hits from EFPs in Sadr City. We were escorting a group of US Army and Iraqi Army infantry to a location that had to retreat from hours earlier, near the intersection of routes Charlie and Gold. On our way up Charlie, it was eerily quiet, and we knew we were going to get hit—we just didn't know what the cost would be. The anticipation was worse than most people can imagine. Our company had just had two soldiers killed about two months before this, including a soldier from our platoon. That attack also resulted in the severe wounding of one our platoon's most courageous and capable soldiers, who (at the time) was still fighting for his life. We knew the risks of this moment were extreme.

When the ambush began with dual, deafening explosions, someone accidentally triggered the key on their radio, and all we could hear was screaming—we didn't know what vehicle the screams were coming from, who was hit, or how bad it was. I just started putting on my gloves and getting ready for action. I felt that familiar spirit of rage and aggression rise up inside me as I prepared for the worst. I was called on to expose myself, all alone, sprinting for my life to get to my friend so I could take care of him. I'm not sure I've ever run as fast or felt as strong or as focused as I did in that moment. When I got to the truck, the several hundred-pound armor door wouldn't open when I pushed the button that typically opens the door with a pneumatic hydraulic. But the air tank on the truck had been penetrated by shrapnel rendering the hydraulic opener useless. So, it had to be opened by force, which isn't an easy task. While another comrade had been trying to push it open from the inside, I pulled from the outside—and somehow we threw the door open with ease. I remember the intensity and sense of power I felt in that moment, as I took charge and moved my wounded platoonmate back to the MRAP where my aid bag was waiting.

I had no idea what my friend's wounds were until I got him back to my truck. I soon I discovered that shrapnel had torn through the underside of his upper arm, near his brachial artery, and that he'd been hit again near his kidney area on the right side. A large piece of shrapnel tore through most of the twelve inch width of his back armor plate, from one side to the other, steadily progressing deeper through most the plate—before it finally, and barely, penetrated. Had the angle of his body been just a bit different, the shrapnel would have torn through his core and caused such horrific damage there would have been no chance of saving him. This close call, like so many others we experienced, was haunting. Death never seemed very far away from us, at times coming so close it felt like it was taunting us. In the moment, I remember almost laughing, thinking of how lucky he was. Years later, when I was reflecting on the experience, I wept. I became acquainted with the spirit that possessed me in combat, and came to see how different it was than "me," at most other times.

Adrenaline aside, some factor in the psyche made possible a spirit of ferocity that allowed me to be the kind of warrior I needed to be in those moments. While there are neurochemical explanations for what I experienced that night, I believe those explanations alone are insufficient—because they don't account for the corresponding psychological experience of warriorhood itself. If not for the underlying foundation of the archetypal warrior inside of me, which had developed into a well-formed personal warrior complex through my training and experiences, we cannot assume my reaction would have been possible at all. I believe it was my *fantasy of myself—my imagination of myself as a battle-tested, experienced warrior—* that made possible my response to a serious test of my courage and abilities. I could be wrong, but I sincerely doubt an uninitiated individual, or most civilians, would be capable of having the same psychological experience in that moment.

Obviously, under normal circumstances, most human beings would not put themselves in harm's way like this. But war requires that we allow the archetypal warrior energy to make a home in us. If you're a former grunt, think about the sort of energy and violence of action required to kick down doors and clear rooms, or to square up against the enemy in a firefight. If you've never been in these kinds of situations, simply imagine what it must be like, and what it would require. *It takes more than adrenaline, and more than good training. It requires a psychological capacity that comes from one's identification with the archetypal warrior image.*

Ordinary consciousness doesn't allow for human beings to do these kinds of things unless another factor in the psyche is present to support us—and that's where the warrior complex comes in. It has a definite function. Military training activates and hones this element of the psyche, causing it to become increasingly powerful and refined, so that in moments of absolute and dire need we can allow ourselves to be propelled by it. It is only because the warrior complex exerts such a powerful force in our consciousness that we are able to do these extraordinary things. Our warrior complexes keep us alive in battle. For those of us who have been in combat, without allowing that force in our psyches to dominate our personalities, how else could we have managed?

The archetypal warrior energy that pulses through us can save your ass, but it has a dark side that can't be neglected. If you had the misfortune, as I did, of seeing other soldiers act out in unnecessarily violent ways— harming or even killing innocent people, or destroying their property for no reason except to express their rage and hatred—the warrior archetype loses its façade of nobility. Certain associations once tied to it—like honor, justice, and selflessness—go straight out the window, replaced by new associations like shame, darkness, and anger.

Two other combat veterans I was acquainted with were consumed by their darkness when they murdered their wives and other family members after coming home. Another veteran and close friend asked me to help him when he was in a rough spot, then, in his drunkenness, he savagely attacked me and landed me in the hospital. I can no longer look at other veterans and ignore reality, pretending that all service members and veterans are good people. Not everyone who wears a cape is a hero. Those who are severely imbalanced and possessed by the warrior complex are a real danger to themselves and others.

A warrior must be capable of doing much more than just fighting in battle. He or she must also be able to navigate the harsh emotional and spiritual challenges that come with the job. Warriors must be able to regulate their emotions, hold themselves through the pain they will inevitably suffer, restrain their impulses, and display a high degree of spiritual and emotional maturity. Warriors ought to be helped to develop these capacities through their training. Authentic warriorhood requires flexibility and balance: to fight *only* when absolutely necessary and to maintain a highly developed capacity for restraint, emotional expression, relatedness, compassion, self-care, and navigating their inner worlds. If you have not cultivated these qualities, you will very likely find yourself —like Odysseus and his men—acting in a destructive, counterproductive manner that tears the fabric of society rather than protecting it.

When we are possessed by the warrior complex, we are not thinking clearly. We can't see ourselves, others, or the world accurately. Everything looks like a battle to be fought and won; every obstacle looks like something we need to blow through or climb over. It's a huge problem, because our suffering, anxiety, depression, and relational challenges are not things that can be worked through by following warrior-centric tendencies. After military service and war, we have to develop new ways of imagining ourselves and our problems. This way of being in the world leads inevitably to trouble, and this is one of the primary lessons of the Odyssey.

We cannot heal or transform using the way of being and thinking that defined us in the military. If we act like a Drill Instructor or Platoon Sergeant and treat ourselves (or others) like a private who needs to be whipped into shape, we won't find our way *home* to our true self. If we approach the wounded parts of ourselves, or our depression, anxiety, and other symptoms as if they're enemies to be eradicated, we aren't going to get very far. We have to learn to relate to ourselves differently, with compassion, connection, and nurturance.

After we leave the military or the combat zone, our chief aim needs to be to heal and transform so we can discover and live out our life's purpose. Many veterans come to feel that their time in the service was their whole purpose, and everything that follows is meaningless. Generally, such thinking points to a warrior complex and the need for transformation. As long as the warrior complex maintains its hold over us, we long to return to the military and war. If we can free ourselves from the grip of this complex and the mindset that goes with it, we will see a broad horizon full of possibilities.

We have to realize the consequences of living in a nation that (1) worships the warrior image and (2) *that does not do its part to ensure warriors are deactivated and discharged as civilians who hold veteran status.* These two problems lead to another one that is just as significant, which is that we veterans find ourselves unable to transform and discover who we really are. In idealizing the warrior image, we create a situation where veterans feel a sense of meaning only as long as they remain identified with it. Rewarding us for identifying with an image from the past dampens the motivation for transformation and evolution. We need to focus on going forward—on developing a new sense of self and a broader sense of identity. Being identified with the archetypal warrior, we're prone to fall into its outdated modes, with a propensity to be stoic, unfeeling, unrelatable, overly driven, and with an unhealthy dose of heroism that causes us to see everything as a challenge to be conquered or a battle to be won.

We can't *defeat* anxiety and aren't well-served if we *battle* PTSD. They are not our enemies. The challenges we face call for a different approach than we're used to. Anxiety, depression, and PTSD symptoms are overcome by learning to surrender and make space for our suffering, by nurturing and holding ourselves with compassion and nonjudgmental acceptance of all our experiences. It isn't easy to learn these essential elements of the art of healing. War doesn't teach us the art of healing, nor are we provided other venues where we can let healing in. Perhaps our nation's greatest failure as it relates to veterans is the failure to initiate and prepare warriors for *the journey home*.

Without a communal experience that honors and acknowledges veterans for their service, we tend to seek out the recognition we never received. Without powerful, heartfelt ceremonies and rituals to honor our inner warriors and help them step aside and relinquish their place at the center of our psyches, we are likely to go on possessed by the archetypal warrior. Until honored and dismissed, the warrior awaits the change of command, maintaining a life-robbing grip over the psyche that stalls all potential for transformation.

Consider the psychic law of inertia. Since military training, culture, and war itself set the archetypal warrior energy in motion, we need a counter-initiation (whether an organic individual experience, or an organized communal experience) to help to relativize this energy and activate other potentials in the psyche. An object in motion stays in motion, and an object at rest stays at rest unless other forces intervene. Because our military experiences set such powerful warrior-centric energies in motion, we need to undergo powerful experiences that can slow them down, stop, and redirect them, inviting into motion other energies that are necessary for our healing and transformation process. The remainder of the *Odyssey* helps us understand some of the other archetypal elements of the psyche that are helpful in transforming veterans, because through-out Odysseus's journey home, he continuously encounters figures who challenge him and by doing so, initiate him into new phases of development along the path of transformation.

-3-

THE LAND OF THE LOTUS EATERS: THE FEAR OF FEELING

The aggressive, warrior-centric actions of Odysseus and his men during the raid of Ismarus anger Zeus, the god of the sky, lightning, and thunder in ancient Greek mythology, and ruler of the gods on Mount Olympus. Zeus generates a storm that lasts for nine days, and Odysseus and his men are tossed about on the angry sea. Eventually they arrive in the land of the Lotus Eaters, where the lotus flowers they eat are "so delicious that those who ate of it left off caring about home, and did not even want to go back and say what had happened to them, but were for staying and munching lotus with the Lotus-eaters without thinking further of their return." Fortunately, Odysseus is wise enough to recognize the danger, and he drives his men back to his boat right away, and they sail on "in much distress."[44]

From this point forward until he arrives at the land of the

Phaeacians, Odysseus lives in a dreamland, where ordinary reality takes a back seat to the fantasy world. One way we can understand this symbolic imagery is to consider its parallel with intrapsychic dynamics, or in other words, to imagine how Odysseus's experiences reflect inner, psychological events that are common at certain stages of the individuation process. In that case, we could say the conflict on Ismarus provoked an eruption of unconscious energy within Odysseus, which led to Odysseus's immersion in his inner world. The land of the Lotus Eaters is the first of Odysseus's deeply symbolic encounters, beginning the journey into his own unconscious.

In *Odysseus in America: Combat Trauma and the Trials of Homecoming*, Jonathan Shay offers this interpretation of the encounter with the Lotus Eaters:

> Homer suggests that if you forget your pain, you forget your homeland—you "lose your hope of home." To really *be home* means to be emotionally present and engaged. Even without alcohol, stimulants, opiates, or sedatives, some entirely clean and sober combat veterans endure civilian life with all their emotions shut down, except for anger, the one emotion that promoted survival in combat. Homer seems to be saying that if you are too successful in forgetting pain, forgetting grief, fear, and disgust, you may dry up the springs of sweetness, enjoyment, and pleasure in another person's company. This fits our clinical experience. … Selective suppression of emotion is an

essential adaptation to survive in lethal settings such as battle, where numbing grief and suppressing fear and physical pain are lifesaving. Whatever the psychological and physiological machinery that produces this emotional shutdown, it appears to get jammed in the "on" position for some veterans. Do not imagine that this is a comfortable or pleasant state of being. Veterans in this state say they feel "dead" and that they watch life through a very dirty window. They are never *in* life.[45]

I applaud Shay's interpretation here with a few small caveats. To me, this episode doesn't just refer to a flight from pain or emotions, but a flight from consciousness itself. Yet Shay is right. We can only return home by staying in touch with our emotions. If we hide from or avoid our pain, we'll miss out on transformation and recovery. Many psychotherapists repeat the phrase, "To heal it you must feel it." Much of our suffering is rooted in defenses that try to protect us from pain, but actually cause us to suffer more. To repair or transform these maladaptive defenses we have to confront and express the pain they're trying to guard against. But we can't attempt to confront our pain until we have enough inner resources to feel safe doing so. We have to develop the capacity to "hold ourselves" so we can enter the realm of emotion.

While I disagree with much of Jonathan Shay's interpretation of the *Odyssey*—I understand it as an inner journey having to do with the unconscious and archetypal realities of the individuation process—I do appreciate his reading of Odysseus's experiences among the Lotus Eaters. There is no doubt that addiction, alcohol, and substance use among veterans is a real problem, and that this portion of the *Odyssey* seems to highlight the risks of substance use in a potent way. A flight from consciousness via addiction, alcohol use, or substance use is a key way that veterans lose touch with themselves after they come home from war or leave the service.

I understand this problem on a deeply personal level. My first year home from Iraq was mostly a drunken blur, as were several years leading up to that deployment. I was absolutely plastered four or five days most weeks when I came home from Baghdad. A few times, I went on ten-day-long binges, blacking out and making a huge mess of my life. It pains me to think of how much I missed out on because I was a captive to alcohol. Because I could not control my drinking, I lost educational opportunities, hurt myself financially, lost a job, and I ruined precious relationships. I failed to take care of myself, and I didn't dedicate precious time and energy to exploring my life's aims, and instead I pursued goals that didn't fit who I really was. I was lost. Later, I had to go back and correct course, but the damage was done. Although alcohol may have led to some fun nights, and helped me to keep my pain at bay, it robbed me of years of my life. I paid a price. To be honest, I only quit drinking because every time I drank I experienced severe anxiety, and the negative consequences of drinking compelled me to stop. Continuing was not an option. For me, it felt like getting sober was a matter of survival. After over fourteen years of sobriety, I feel grateful. To be honest, I feel like I'm lucky to be alive, and fortunate that a breakdown redirected my life and saved me from what might have been a real tragedy.

At the time, I didn't know I was running from the pain I was carrying from my experiences in combat. But despite my best efforts to keep the pain at bay, there were plenty of moments when the pain would burst through the surface, erupting chaotically. I would think about my friends or civilians who were killed and maimed, and I would break into tears. It would last a few seconds, until I choked it off and made myself think of something else. I couldn't allow the descent into the underworld and face the horrors of the past, at least not yet. I didn't have the inner resources to hold myself through all that pain, so all I could do was run from it.

My own experiences helped me to better understand one of my grandfathers, who was a combat medic in both Korea and Vietnam. After he retired from the Army, he essentially spent the rest of his life sitting in a recliner, sipping down whiskey and smoking cigarettes. He rarely left his house, and almost never talked about the war. In fact, according to my uncles and stepmother, I was one of the only people he ever talked to about Vietnam. Yet, he told me very little—only what type of units he was with, where he was stationed, a bit about their mission. The rest was silence, but the silence was, in itself, a powerful statement. There were horrors in his history too terrible to mention, name, face, or feel. So he gave himself over to whiskey (*we could call it Lotus*), and lived a dim, isolated, and depressing life, practically glued to his recliner and television. His journey "home" stopped there.

In my psychotherapy practice, nearly every veteran I have worked with has (at some point post-service) struggled with alcohol or substance use. More than once I've heard a client's story, and felt reminded of my own. Sometimes, when a veteran tells me about their drinking or substance use problem, I think of Odysseus and his men in the land of the Lotus Eaters. After several months of sobriety, one of my clients remarked, " When I was drinking, I had no idea how many problems I had that I was avoiding. It was honestly like I was in a fantasy world where nothing else mattered." Another veteran who afterwards became a law enforcement officer shared about feeling overwhelmed by two back-to-back tragedies, one of which resulted in the death of a child and the other in the death of a co-worker. When the first anniversary of these events rolled around she told me, "I've been drinking way more than I should. But I can't help it. I don't know what else to do. It's just so overwhelming and drinking is the only thing that seems to help."

We have to appreciate that a lot of people drink or use substances because they're trying to alleviate significant discomfort. In many cases, this is because individuals don't yet possess the capacity to otherwise hold themselves through their pain—to regulate their emotions and tolerate emotional and psychological discomfort without the assistance alcohol or drugs provide. When I'm meeting a new veteran and discussing alcohol or drug use with them, some will attempt to explain that they do not have a problem. I can't count the number of times I've heard someone say, "Well, I just have a couple beers at the end of the day to take the edge off." So, I usually ask, "What edge? Take the edge off of what?" That usually leads to an important discussion about all of the troubles that are overwhelming the person, and it also tends to reveal a lack of other strategies and skills that could "take the edge off" their pain.

Our ability to regulate our emotions is influenced by a number of factors, including how well our parents supported us through emotionally challenging events during our development, because we tend to internalize the way that others have related to us. If our parents were extremely caring, patient, and supportive towards us in difficult times, then we tend to be more caring, patient, and supportive towards ourselves than we might otherwise be if they'd treated us in the opposite fashion. At the same time, how well we regulate our emotions when we're feeling stressed, upset, angry, or down is dependent on whether we're intentional and put in the work when challenging moments arise. It takes dedication and practice.

Emotional regulation skills and capacity are not only linked to how much we suffer, but deficits have also been linked alcohol or drug use, and deeper psychopathology, such as personality disorders. Research has shown that emotional regulation deficits are a strong predictor of alcohol use and dependence.[46] So, we can't overlook the importance of this factor is in the temptation to fall into the what we might call the *lotus trap*. If we don't make space for our emotions and tend to them in a healthy way, we'll be prone not only to suffering, but to addiction and other unhealthy behaviors.

When we're not accustomed to feeling or expressing emotions, we often need help finding our way. Therapy can help us build these skills and practices so that we can improve our emotional regulation and distress tolerance capacity. Our program evaluations at *The Battle Within* have shown significant disparities in emotional regulation capacity between those who attended therapy and those who didn't. Graduates of our five-day *Revenant Journey* program who attended more than twenty therapy sessions had an average score nearly twenty points higher on the Emotional Regulation Skills Questionnaire (ERSQ) than those who attended no therapy at all (which means those who attended therapy had much better emotional regulation skills), and those who attended more therapy sessions also experienced significantly less suffering from symptoms associated with PTSD and depression.[47]

Similarly, we found that those who practiced some form of mindfulness (such as meditation or yoga) on a frequent basis (most days or every day) had far better ERSQ scores (nearly twenty points higher) than those who meditated only occasionally, rarely, or never. Like those who attended therapy, those who practiced mindfulness experienced fewer symptoms of depression or those associated with trauma.[48] One of the gifts of mindfulness is that it helps us to become acutely aware of what we're feeling or experiencing, while at the same time helping us to better understand what lies beneath it. Practicing a mindful awareness of the present moment isn't just about awareness though—scientific studies have shown it actually changes the way our nervous systems function and how we respond to stress or discomfort. One study showed that simply practicing mindful attention to one's breath can improve connectivity between our amygdala (which triggers our fight or flight response) and the pre-frontal cortex (which helps us to stay calm, rational, and emotionally balanced), which is critical for emotional regulation.[49] Simply put, a regular mindfulness practice is a great way to improve our emotional regulation capacity.

Until we can learn to regulate our emotions, the way we express them will likely remain primitive, which means that when an upsetting or challenging situation arises, we can feel overwhelmed and we're prone to act out. A veteran client once told me, "When I feel sad, I get angry. When I feel depressed, I get angry. When I feel anxious, I get angry. Basically, I have an anger problem." I didn't agree with him. I don't think he has an anger problem, but an emotional regulation problem, probably stemming from the fact that no one helped him learn *to hold himself* in moments of difficulty. I also believe anger was a convenient way of expressing pain in a way that felt acceptable to him. Men (and boys) in our society are sometimes shamed by others if they feel sadness, pain, or fear—but men are given the space to feel anger. In fact, anger can be used to set boundaries and create space (which can be healthy or unhealthy, depending on the circumstances), and sometimes people use their anger to drive others away if they're afraid others will see their vulnerability.

Because it's *so* difficult to withstand the stress and discomfort of challenging emotional situations, we come up with all kinds of other ways to run from our pain other than alcohol or substance use, including addictions to video games, porn, TV, or even work. It is one thing to temporarily distract yourself to cope with stressors or hardships (that can be healthy) but it is another thing to lose yourself by being consumed by distractions, while never truly caring for yourself by meeting your emotional and psychological needs.

We need to reckon with why such problems are so prevalent in the veteran and military community. It makes sense. First, we have to admit we aren't the most emotionally developed cohort of individuals on the planet, and second, many of us carry a severe degree of pain. The amount of trauma we endure paired with the lack of practice, skills, and *permission* (from self and others) to tend to our pain creates a situation that is ripe for addiction.

My sense is that if veterans were not so ashamed of their pain, they would not be so prone to turn to drugs or alcohol. We must acknowledge that the shame and stigma associated with suffering is largely rooted in how suffering is pathologized, and imagined to be a sign of weakness. Our culture (as a whole, and within the veteran and military community in particular) is a part of the problem. Even elements within field of psychology play a part in sustaining this negative view of suffering. As long as we imagine suffering to be pathological, an indication of something wrong, people (veterans especially) will be hesitant to accept or express how much they hurt. As it stands now, substance use is more acceptable in the veteran community than authentically feeling one's suffering, and that tells me that our culture and the field of psychology as a whole have missed the mark when it comes to conceptualizing and imagining military-related wounds. Dr. Ed Tick, a depth psychologist who dedicated his career to working with veterans, wrote:

Interpretations of human phenomena are not necessarily correct or true but are rather concepts and practices arising from the cultural matrix of which they are a part. … The modern interpretation of military service and its invisible wounding is culturally derived and determined and in accord with modern dominant values and beliefs. It is not necessarily correct, true, or consistent with the experiences of survivors or of history – and certainly not the only interpretation of war wounding and restoration. James Hillman suspects that PTSD is an American rather than universal response to war trauma. Sri Lankan trauma psychiatrist Ruwan Jayatunge worries about "the Americanization of mental illness." … Roger Brooke agrees, especially regarding veterans: "It is our own culture that has socially constructed this universal as a psychiatric condition, burdening the individual veteran with all the negative consequences that implies."[50]

If we turn to Roger Brooke, a veteran and depth psychotherapist, we get more insight into the reality that there are many ways of imagining and conceptualizing *what exactly* is going on beneath the surface, and *why* veterans suffer.

Tick (personal communication, 2009) has counted over eighty names in different languages for what we have socially constructed as a psychiatric condition called PTSD. The Xhosa of South Africa call this psychological wound of war the *kanene*, which refers to the warrior's insight in the burden he carries. "It follows you like a shadow never letting you forget what you have done" (Sipho KaMbuqe, personal communication, 2009). The

Zulus call it the *Ukuhlanya*, which derives from the world *ukunhlanhlatha*, which means to wander around without direction and to lose one's bearings. It has both geographical and moral or spiritual meaning (Siphiwe Mthethwa, personal communication, 2013). The Lakota Sioux call it *nagi napayape*, which means, "The spirits have left him" (Tick, personal communication, 2009)—reminding us of the many veterans who say that they are numb and have lost their souls. The Hopi call it the *tsawana*, which means "a mind in terror"—reminding us of the hyper-arousal, hyper-vigilance, and flashbacks described as PTSD. In the American Civil War (1861-1865), the wound was called "soldier's heart", which names correctly the traumatized centre of our emotional lives, morality, aesthetics, and capacity for intimacy, or what we call the soul. In sum, the psycho-logical wounds of war are essentially moral and spiritual, and have been addressed as such in all warrior cultures. This is the evidence base indicating that our own therapeutic treatments for traumatized veterans will be successful only to the extent that these issues are addressed on their own terms and not primarily as symptoms of a psychiatric condition.[51]

As we sift through the various ways suffering among veterans is imagined in other cultures, we see some have a different focus than others. The names given do not focus upon the same aspect of suffering. For example, the Lakota Sioux's term seems to focus on the spiritual aspect of suffering, which depth psychologists sometimes call soul loss. In contrast, the Hopi term seems to focus more on the experience of terror, anxiety, and panic arising from hyperarousal, which is closer to our conceptualization of PTSD. The Zulu's imagining of suffering seems to place its emphasis upon the feeling of being lost—not knowing who one is anymore, or where one is going—a disorientation deep within the self as one's understanding of oneself and the world has been altered. One characterization is not more accurate than any other. All are valid and important, and veterans cannot be said to be a monolithic population where one of these problems is *the* prominent problem in every individual.

We have to acknowledge that culture influences how suffering manifests to some degree, and how we respond to suffering when it arises. In the field of psychology, it is understood that there are indeed "culture-bound syndromes," as cultural idiosyncrasies combine with unique factors that give rise to an illness in a particular context. Tick asserted that many Vietnamese soldiers did not have the same problems as American soldiers after the war, as both cultures have unique views of suffering, different ideas about how to hold suffering, and what suffering means.[52] Our imagination of things shapes our experience to a degree, and so our view of suffering among veterans can be either helpful or problematic. Right now, it seems the way we conceptualize veterans' problems is, on the whole, toxic, because it burdens veterans with the shame of being "disordered" when their psyches and brains are doing exactly what they *need* to do to cope with the traumatic circumstances they've endured. And, the fact that we have more or less normalized drug and alcohol use within our society and the veteran community, though we have not normalized suffering, should tell us a great deal about how backwards we've got things.

It is puzzling that the military community is accepting of the avoidance inherent in drug and alcohol abuse, while at the same time it belittles those who honestly and bravely express the painful realities they contend with—which are inherent to warriorhood itself. What could be more courageous than sitting with the terrifying and overwhelming emotions that arise from trauma, and letting them transmit their truths and transform us? In the midst of a panic attack, when fear is at its most powerful, it takes profound courage to consciously surrender to the experience. When the horror of battle returns and the soul demands it be faced, the courageous warrior turns toward it as best he or she can, reaching out for help when it becomes too much. We should be proud to do our inner work, to take a hard look at ourselves and our suffering, and to understand what it asks of us.

The tale of Odysseus helps us see how suffering is an inherent part of the work of transforming into a mature, fully-initiated *veteran*, whereas alcohol or substance abuse or a lack of consciousness is a way of avoiding reality and postponing, perhaps indefinitely, the difficult journey ahead. Turning toward this myth helps us reimagine what mature warriorhood really is. While the parallel between this episode of the tale and substance use among modern veterans is obvious, we can also understand Odysseus's encounter with the Lotus Eaters as symbolizing unconsciousness in general.

In 2016, after I had been completely sober for over seven years, I had this dream:

> I seem to be in New York City trying to navigate busses and subways, and I'm having trouble connecting with other people. I hang out with some guy and we smoke some weed and I get high. I'm anxious at first, but then I'm laughing and having a lot of fun. Next I'm with classmates and I'm really drunk. I can't control myself as I'm laughing, and I seem to be in and out of consciousness. I'm forgetting things and not sober, and my classmates seem a little annoyed. At one point, we enter a swamp-like forest within the city. There are snakes and dangerous creatures around. I'm trying to avoid them.

As Jung said, dreams present the *psychic reality* to reflect one's situation from the symbolic perspective of the unconscious. In this dream, I'm high and/or drunk, suggesting my view of reality is distorted and there's an overall lack of conscious awareness. It probably reflects that I was out of touch with myself and others during some period around the time I had the dream. I wasn't impaired by drugs or alcohol, since as I've said, I'd been completely sober for over seven years by then. But despite my literal sobriety, the dream suggests my consciousness was still impaired to the point that my capacity to connect with others was affected. In terms of who the *others* are, this might refer to actual other people, but it probably reflects an inability to connect with *inner* others, in other words with myself. The two are linked: He who (like Odysseus) is not in connection to his inner others will not be able to connect with outer others either.

This dream reflects a type of disruptive unconsciousness, and one doesn't need to be drunk or high to be impaired in this way. Perfectly sober people can suffer from unconsciousness (lack of awareness) by falling in with their inner version of the Lotus Eaters. A person who doesn't care who he or she really is or where they're going might decide to stay with the Lotus Eaters. Forgetting the true self and not caring about the journey to discover it is the same as forgetting your home, and anyone who abandons the journey back to this sacred place of being with oneself truly has been eating too much lotus. Such a person is unconscious, because they've lost touch with consciousness. To regain conscious awareness sometimes requires an inner journey into the seas, forests, and even the swamps of the unconscious.

This dream, like its corresponding episode of the *Odyssey*, ends with a recognition of the dangers of my circumstances and the frightening realities I wish I could avoid. I begin the dream in New York City, which for me at the time probably represented an overdeveloped, one-sided, overly civilized aspect of the psyche that lacks a balanced connection to nature. I had become intoxicated and disconnected from reality. When ego consciousness becomes one-sided, when our conscious position is not balanced by insights from the unconscious, it can lead to disease. Increasing our awareness of the unconscious by immersing ourselves in it can produce greater awareness and consciousness. We can regain our bearings and get back on the path homeward.

At the end of the dream, I enter a swamp-like forest. The forest is often a symbol of the unconscious in that both are unfamiliar realms where the unknown awaits us, and in the dream it helps me come into contact with the things I wish I could avoid (snakes and other dangerous creatures). These anxiety-producing creatures likely represent the anxiety-producing things I was trying to avoid, like my emotions. Though I saw these creatures as dangerous, in truth they probably were not—just as many trauma survivors tend to fear their overwhelming emotions which, when they stop and allow themselves to feel them, are not as threatening as they'd seemed.

It's widely noted that when people start sobering up, they begin to become conscious of their underlying suffering and other issues their addiction distracted from, and this can be frightening and challenging. The same is true when we begin to intentionally cultivate consciousness within ourselves. As we deepen our relationship to our bodies, emotions, and other inner experiences, the dark creatures that have been haunting our inner worlds (like anxiety or psychosomatic symptoms) can turn out to be guides that help us navigate the difficulties we need to face.

This mirrors Odysseus's recognition that he and his men will be in danger if they don't return to *sea*—continuing their journey to explore *the unconscious*. While some might wish to avoid discomfort by remaining in Lotus Land, the task of continuing onward to face the inherent difficulties of the journey home is necessary for those who wish for a life of substance. Those who continue their inner journey will soon meet the shadow, the unconscious aspects of the personality, as the *individuation process* leads them homeward, toward the true self.

-4-

MEETING THE CYCLOPS, MEETING THE SHADOW

In the journey home from war, there must come a time when we are able to adopt a sober, open, and honest relationship with the unconscious, all our internal experiences, and the remainder of our personality. If we have pain, we acknowledge the pain, find the means to express it, and seek to understand what it is calling for. If there are parts of us that long for expression—perhaps creative desires or longings for lifegiving passions—this means finding a way to bring these things into being. If we find parts of ourselves that we're ashamed or afraid of, such as troubling thoughts or emotions, we try to understand what these parts of us need and might teach us. For those courageous enough to examine their inner worlds, it's inevitable they'll encounter parts of themselves they've never known before, and this in itself will leave them transformed.

These unconscious (unknown, unrecognized and/or undeveloped) parts of ourselves are what Jung called *shadow*, and they sometimes appear in dreams and myths as primitive or untrustworthy figures. The ego tends to devalue or be suspicious of what it doesn't understand. If we can learn to relate to the shadow and integrate its elements, we are transformed. If we don't, our potential for growth and transformation remains limited, because these aspects of ourselves remain left out of our development. When we encounter our limits and find ourselves at a standstill, growth comes when we endeavor to cultivate a relationship with these unrealized potentials that reside in our unconscious.

If we imagine a rigid, masculine warrior who has almost no relationship with his emotional life, we can say that this part of his shadow is likely undeveloped in terms of feeling. One combat veteran I worked with years ago shared a dream in which a gorilla was hiding in his room. He felt this big, hairy, powerful animal threatening him, and had a lot of anxiety about it. He described the gorilla as primitive and unhinged—like it could blow up or attack at any moment. It's possible this image could represent an aspect of his shadow, and that it may have had something to do with the fact that he was so disconnected from his emotions.

If we can develop our capacity for feeling, our relationships with these neglected aspects of ourselves can change and become healthier. But this takes work and conscious effort, and if we stay stuck in the habit of fighting against challenges, we won't be able to change much. We can't transform and mature by avoiding, resisting, or fighting the obstacles we face. We cannot integrate shadow by trying to kill it. Because warriors are often prone to heroic tendencies, we often fail to approach our inner worlds or shadows in any other way. This was Odysseus's next major mistake.

After leaving the Lotus Eaters behind, Odysseus and his men arrive in "the land of the lawless and inhuman Cyclopes … [who] neither plant nor plow, but trust in providence, and live on such wheat, barley, and grapes as grow wild without any kind of tillage".[53] After their arrival in the land of the one-eyed Cyclopes, Odysseus notices spring water coming out of a cave and they enter it, but can't see a thing due to the darkness. This can be understood to represent that Odysseus could not yet see or navigate in the cave of his unconscious and thus cannot receive the lifegiving benefits of the spring.

Odysseus's men begin killing the goats on the island to feed themselves, then enter the cave of Polyphemus the Cyclops, who appears to be quite well-off despite his primitive nature. Polyphemus is a shepherd with "more lambs and kids than his pens could hold."[54] He makes his own cheeses and dairy products, and appears to be doing fairly well for himself making his living off nature alone. Despite his earthy, simple, seemingly primitive nature, he has a certain kind of wealth and power.

Uninvited, Odysseus and his men enter the abode of Polyphemus and take pretty much whatever they want, acting as if they own the place. When Polyphemus returns, and notices his unwelcome guests, a conversation sours when Odysseus lies to Polyphemus. Odysseus says his name is "No Man," or *Outis* in Greek. The play on words has meaning. While the word *outis* means "no man," *me tis* means "someone" − and *me tis* also alludes to a primary quality in Odysseus's personality − his *metis*, or his cunning intelligence, wit, wisdom, or craftiness.[55] While the author of the tale seems to have inserted this symbolic reference intentionally, it appears important that Odysseus identifies as the opposite of what he is known for, while at the same time failing to own his true identity.

Polyphemus gets the sense Odysseus is lying and, offended, gobbles up a couple of Odysseus's men. Odysseus and the rest of his men are trapped as Polyphemus stands near the entry to his cave. He's stuck in an anxiety producing situation, like many folks tend to be when they are in a conflict with the shadow. Here Odysseus, the combative warrior, makes an unwise decision. Instead of learning to relate to Polyphemus, he gets the him drunk (relying on his *metis*), then stabs him in his only eye and blinds him. When Polyphemus calls for help, he says, "No Man" has hurt him. Hearing this, the other Cyclopes ignore his calls and Odysseus and his men escape Polyphemus's cave.

Odysseus then foolishly and repeatedly taunts Polyphemus with immense arrogance and pride, imperiling himself and his crew even further. As he flees, Odysseus, apparently seeking bragging rights, pridefully discloses his true name to his gigantic adversary. He wants others to know that it was he, the cunning Odysseus, who blinded Polyphemus. Later, Odysseus will pay for this error.

At this point, they learn that Polyphemus is the son of Poseidon— the god of the sea—the very god no sailor can offend if he wishes to travel on the water safely. As Odysseus and his men try to sail away, Polyphemus hurls rocks at them, nearly destroying their ships. Six of Odysseus's men die in this misadventure, while the rest barely escape with their lives. The conflict leaves Odysseus in a weaker state than when he entered the cave of Polyphemus.

If we look with an archetypal lens, there's so much we can learn from the symbolism in Odysseus's encounter with the Cyclopes. Polyphemus is a quintessential shadow figure. If we *amplify* the image of Polyphemus as a wild man, given his primitive nature and closeness to the earth, we see similarities with the figures of Enkidu in the *Epic of Gilgamesh* and Iron John in the tale named after him. If shadow figures like these are related to appropriately, they can be sources of a new life, aiding us in our transformation process. The Cyclopes did not need to plant or plow because their land provided all that was needed. This suggests that what's natural in us provides exactly what we need to flourish. Our shadows—often symbolized in myths and dreams as these kinds of wild figures who are close to nature—can help us get in touch with what is precious, natural, and lifegiving in our own souls.

Gilgamesh was a rotten king who, like Odysseus early in his journey, behaved quite unjustly. Ultimately, Gilgamesh matured through his relationship with Enkidu, the wild man who begins the tale more animal than human. Covered in hair at first, Enkidu quickly takes on more human qualities after a transformative encounter with a priestess, who initiates him into the realm of sensuousness and feeling. While the relationship between Gilgamesh and Enkidu became a positive, life altering one for Gilgamesh and his kingdom, it began with an epic wrestling match—*a conflict.* At first, Gilgamesh experienced Enkidu as a threat to be overcome by force, but as the story goes on, Gilgamesh realizes their relationship is empowering.

In the language of Jungian psychology, Gilgamesh can be

understood to represent the inflated ego, Enkidu a counter-balancing shadow figure, and Shamhat (the priestess) an anima figure who helps these figures to relate to the unconscious. Without Shamhat, Gilgamesh would not have been able to relate to his shadow (symbolized by Enkidu), and we'll see this same motif later in the *Odyssey* when Odysseus meets Circe. Gilgamesh and Enkidu are both rather primitive at first, but by the end of the *Epic of Gilgamesh*, Gilgamesh is a mature, just, and balanced king. To achieve this transformation, he needs Enkidu, who ultimately leads him into the realm of adventure, emotion, and suffering.[56]

In the tale *Iron John*, Iron John appears first as a primitive figure covered in hair who lives in the depths of a pond (water is another popular symbol for the unconscious). Iron John repeatedly offers support to the tale's developing youth-prince-hero, helping him develop and transform through a series of challenges. At the end of the story, we learn that Iron John, the central shadow figure, is actually a prosperous and handsome baron who was put under a witch's spell, and the spell isn't broken until the prince undergoes his own transformation, culminating in marriage to a princess (an anima figure). Only after the prince learns to relate appropriately to the archetypal feminine does he learn Iron John's identity, see his true nature, and gain access to his own wealth of riches.

We see a similar motif in the Old Testament. Isaac has twin sons who are opposites, Jacob and Esau, the latter is covered in hair. The tension between these opposite brothers is palpable, and it hits a height when Jacob steals his brother's birthright. Years later, while Jacob is on the run from his brother (trying to avoid the conflict), he wrestles with God in a dream and he is renamed Israel, "He who wrestles with God." In the course of our development, inner conflict is unavoidable, and it is within the course of inner conflict that we tend to be transformed. The day after his dream, the long separated brothers peacefully reunite. Thus, encountering and integrating what is not conscious is a spiritual affair that affects one's very identity.

Our own shadows (which have innumerable aspects) have the same capacity to enrich us, but according to classical Jungian theory, we need the help of the anima (or animus, for females) to relate appropriately to the unconscious and to receive the gifts of this relationship. Since Odysseus lacks a connection to his anima (up to this point in the story, there are no female figures), he lacks the know-how to relate properly to Polyphemus.

Odysseus has lost touch with the breadth of his personality by becoming identified with only a portion of it, his warrior persona, and Polyphemus shows up as a shadow element meant to redirect Odysseus's psyche toward a more balanced position. What stands out about Polyphemus (despite his name, hinting toward "many," *poly*) is that he has just one eye, lives in a cave, and seems primitive. Odysseus sees the Cyclopes, in his own words, as lawless and inhuman. But, Polyphemus is the son of Poseidon, close to nature, and well-off despite his seemingly uncivilized nature. He is large and powerful, with the capacity to reduce the power of Odysseus, just as the shadow has the power to challenge and relativize the ego.

Polyphemus's name hints at the fact that there is more than one aspect of the psyche which requires relating to. Our shadows are not just a single undeveloped or unknown aspect of the self. The shadow has many faces. Polyphemus's name beckons us to appreciate complexity and the polytheistic reality of our own inner worlds. We have many parts that all yearn for expression. One-sidedness starves us of life. A healthy psyche is a flexible one with a diversity of qualities and resources. In fact, we might say that's what resilience really is: having enough inner diversity to allow us to be flexible and adaptive in the face of hardship. The more diverse our inner world is, the greater we can adapt to situations and enjoy life's many aspects. The ideal warrior is not just one who can fight, but one who can tend his wounds after battle, too—one who can lean into his sadness and grief, anxiety and fear.

Polyphemus having just one eye can have several possible meanings, symbolically, especially if we understand Polyphemus as a symbolic aspect of Odysseus's own psyche. First of all, having just one eye reduces our capacity for depth perception, reflecting Odysseus's own lack of capacity to see with depth at this point or appreciate that his aggressive, warrior-centric ego is not the full extent of who he is. When we become one-sided, we lose sight of the breadth and depth of our own interiority.

Odysseus's encounter with the Cyclopes arises *after* he and his men have raided the city of the Cicones, murdering and robbing the innocents of Ismarus, and after they've stopped among the Lotus Eaters. So, the Cyclopes enters the scene following Odysseus's own aggressive, devouring, primitive, *narrow-sighted* behavior. We don't see much evidence of Polyphemus being "lawless," as Odysseus accused him of being; but Odysseus's behavior at Ismarus is damning. Odysseus fails to recognize his own one-sided tendency toward aggression, lawlessness, and primitive behavior. We might say that Polyphemus shows up to help Odysseus see just how ugly and off-centered he has become. Polyphemus is an exaggerated version of Odysseus himself—Odysseus on steroids—but Odysseus doesn't see it. He remains in a rather unconscious state. His perception of the Cyclopes is clouded by projection. Jung said, "Everything unconscious is projected."[57] Because of projection, Odysseus accuses the Cyclopes of being the very things he himself has become.

Another way to understand having just one eye is spiritual seeing. The widely revered Norse god Odin had one eye, having relinquished his second eye in exchange for wisdom. In the East, there's the sense of a spiritual eye in the center of one's forehead. And in the Greek tradition, figures who are blinded (like Tiresias or Oedipus) gain spiritual sight, even the capacity to see into the future. Downing calls this "soul sight," noting that it was Athena, goddess of wisdom, who bestowed this upon Tiresias.[58] Odysseus will meet Tiresias later in his journey, and he will play a critical role helping Odysseus to navigate crucial challenges.

Polyphemus's spiritual power is symbolically reinforced because he lives in a cave, one of many symbols of the unconscious.[59] Because Odysseus botches this first descent into a cave, he'll have to repeat it in a different form later. Polyphemus's spiritual nature is further strengthened by the fact that he's the son of Poseidon, god of the sea. Sea and water are also symbols of the unconscious, which is timeless, with enormous depth, always stirring, beyond our capacity to tame, and full of both life and terror.[60] Importantly, it is meaningful that Odysseus has entered Polyphemus's cave, because it suggests that Odysseus is beginning to encounter his own unconscious material so he can understand what's there.

Polyphemus the Cyclops is one who sees and experiences the world differently from Odysseus. His closeness to nature and contentedness with simplicity suggests a spiritual maturity that the compulsive, overly-heroic Odysseus lacks. If Odysseus can learn to relate to his shadow—these potentials within himself—it could have spiritual benefits and the capacity for a new kind of sight. But he misses the opportunity and (metaphorically) shoots himself in the foot. By blinding the Cyclops, he angers Poseidon, and this will haunt him later. One who learns to recognize, value, and relate with his shadow will have an easier time of finding his way home. One who treats his shadow as an enemy to exploit or battle will have difficulty discovering his true nature and navigating the road of transformation and recovery.

Unless we learn to be more receptive and adaptable *internally*, opening ourselves to non-ego images from the unconscious (such as Polyphemus), we won't be able to change. Non-ego images (things that are *not* part of the "ego" we identify with) represent aspects of ourselves we need to build a relationship with, so our sense of self can transform, leading to healthier adaptations. Learning to relate to these images inevitably alters the ego itself if we're receptive enough to let ourselves be changed. As long as the ego mows down all challengers, nothing new can happen. The overly heroic individual prolongs the journey home, tearing up a peaceful future as if it's still his violent past. And so our hero Odysseus vanquishes Polyphemus, and moves onward as the (delusional) warrior-centric trickster he has become.

We've all made mistakes like this at times, and it's okay. It becomes a problem when we become too rigid to change. One of the ways this manifests in the veteran population is the tendency to devalue civilians and anything feeling-oriented, feminine, or soft. These are symbols of our own shadow side—the parts of us that remain unconscious and undeveloped which can, if related to, lead us to healing. As mentioned, Jung noted that everything that is unconscious tends to be *projected*, as we displace our inner realities onto others. When we project something, we imagine others have qualities or feelings that we actually have, but we're not yet ready to realize or "own" it. We can project our so-called negative or positive traits or experiences onto others.

Once, I was working with a client who told me he was concerned that a mentor of his was annoyed with him. He needed to rely on his mentor's assistance, and so he repeatedly reached out to persuade him to help with his situation. When he felt he had annoyed his mentor, he checked it out with him (*a wise move on his part!*). They had a conversation, and the mentor denied feeling annoyed at all, and shared he was happy to help. Yet, my client continued to feel he was a burden, was convinced that he really had annoyed his mentor. He felt terrible about himself, and for having needs that required attention. As I explored this with my client, I asked him to name what he was feeling. The primary thing he noticed, at first, was guilt. He even referenced a feeling wheel (a pie chart that lists a multitude of feelings to help us find words for our feelings) and nothing else stood out—he wasn't aware of any other feelings.

This client's upbringing was far from ideal—he was often asked to meet the needs of others, including his mother, and so there was always pressure for him to ignore his feelings and needs and to focus on the needs of others instead. Moreover, anger really didn't have a place in his household. It worked out much better for him to be a good boy, and he had to repress his anger. As he and I continued to explore his experience with his mentor, it became clear that these old patterns were still alive and his perceptions were clouded by projection—and he realized it wasn't the mentor who was annoyed and frustrated, but he himself. He soon realized he was angry because his mentor hadn't upheld his end of the bargain, and he resented being put in a position where he had to repeatedly remind the mentor of his responsibilities, per their agreement. Projection is a powerful, and deceptive force that can distort our understanding of ourselves, and others.

We also do this with our best qualities when we aren't ready to "own" them. Our self-image may be too damaged to let in that we are good at something, or enjoy something. I had a therapy client who was a talented artist, but she was shy and afraid to share her work with the world. One day she showed me a piece of artwork she created of a powerful, exotic looking woman with golden skin —an obvious shadow figure, given the figure's otherness and rich nature. I asked her to describe the woman in the drawing to me, to explain what she was like. This young artist told me the golden woman in her drawing was powerful, confident, and creative—all the things she herself was but could not yet own. In helping her recognize that she was projecting these qualities onto this figure which was born out of her own unconscious, over time, we were able to do some therapeutic work that made it possible for her to reclaim these aspects of her true self.

Jung noted that when aspects of our personality remain unconscious, those aspects are sometimes *perceived* in a negative light and devalued.[61] Sometimes we make negative judgments about disliked personality features or qualities, and we intentionally drive them underground or push them away. This helps explain why some hard-ass, emotionally avoidant warriors tend to have such negative opinions of anyone who's in touch with their emotions. I can't count the times I've heard veterans talk shit about "snowflakes," knowing they bury their own emotional pain far beneath the surface. Healthy human beings experience and express pain—so if we carry negative judgement about that, it's a red flag that says we need to examine ourselves closer. Myths and fairy tales teach us the value of turning toward what we devalue. We see one example of this in a Grimm brothers' fairy tale called *The Frog Prince*. In this story, a princess drops her precious golden ball (symbolizing psychic energy) into a well, and only a slimy frog (who is actually a handsome prince whose identity is distorted due to a spell) can retrieve it.

The frog in this story can be understood as a symbol of the shadow, who appears primitive because he represents unconscious, undeveloped contents. Something wicked distorted this figure's true nature and appearance, causing him to dwell in the well of the unconscious. The stuck-up princess (the inflated ego) wants nothing to do with this detestable frog. She devalues him because she can't see his true nature (or her own). Only by learning to relate to her own shadow, represented by the frog, can she transform what is "underground" back into its true nature, in this case as a wealthy prince. Doing so, she ultimately enriches herself and finds true love.

We accuse other people of being sensitive or overly emotional when, in fact, we're just as sensitive. We just hide our sensitivity through a thick façade, a persona. Warriors who mock "snowflakes" ought to ask themselves, "Who's more sensitive: the man who has the courage to openly express his pain and cry, or the man too afraid to be honest about how he feels?" So-called snowflakes let emotions flow through them naturally, and they don't injure others in the process. Only when you stop up your emotions do they become destructive, causing us to lash out at others and cause harm. Expressing emotion doesn't make you weak. It makes you strong and resilient. The minute you accuse someone else of being a snowflake, you are probably projecting your own shadow— your sensitivity and fear of emotions—onto the other. Don't be afraid to melt. Have courage and remember that the qualities that we tend to depreciate most are often the qualities that have the greatest potential to enrich our lives and transform us.

When Odysseus assaults Polyphemus, he assaults himself. By failing to relate to his own shadow, he prolongs his painful journey and makes returning home much more difficult. In the same way, modern veterans do themselves a disservice by failing to integrate their own shadows. Ultimately, our ability to transform and relate depends on the extent to which we remain open to our inner worlds and aspects of ourselves that are *not yet known* to the ego. This requires humility—we must be "No Man" to discover our true identity. Joseph Campbell's commentary on Odysseus's temporary adoption of a humble position is quite helpful:

> … the symbolic name Noman [suggests] self-divestiture at the passage to the yonder world: because he did not assert his secular character, his personal name and fame, Odysseus passed a cosmic threshold guardian [Polyphemus], to enter a sphere of transpersonal forces, over which ego has no control.[62]

An ego-position of receptivity and humility is essential in the presence of the shadow. If we want to enter the world of the unconscious and reap the benefits of a transformational inner journey, we have to have the correct attitude. Egocentricity needs to be replaced by receptivity to our own complexity and multi-faceted-ness. All that is *other* can teach us something about ourselves.

While this encounter between Odysseus and his shadow marks an important development in his transformation process, it's just the beginning. Odysseus's experimental adoption of humility serves him a little, but he continues to rely on his cunning and aggression, so we see that he hasn't really changed. What did happen was an unforgettable encounter with a challenging force that reduced his power to some degree, and no doubt, it was an experience that shook him. To return home to Ithaca, he will have to change more, and that will require facing additional challenges. While a brief encounter with our shadow material might result in a modest degree of increased awareness, the likelihood of integration and lasting change requires more intention in our relationship with the non-ego aspects of the psyche.

-5-

THE BAG OF WINDS
& THE BREAKDOWN

After Odysseus and his men escape the land of the Cyclopes and sail on, they arrive at the island of Aeolia (north of Sicily), where King Aeolus greets them kindly, sharing luxuries and feasts. Aeolus was the mythical keeper of the winds. They stay for a month, then Aeolus grants Odysseus a bag of winds to assist them on their journey home. For nine days and nights they sail smoothly. Odysseus commands the rudder without sleep in hopes they'll get back to Ithaca faster, and his men begin to feel jealous and start to wonder what's inside the bag. Among themselves, they say:

'how this man gets honored ... See what fine prizes he is taking home from Troy, while we, who have traveled just as far as he has, come back with hands empty as we set out with—and now Aeolus has given him ever so much more. Quick, let us see what it all is, and how much gold and silver there is in the sack he gave him.'[63]

On the tenth day, they see Ithaca on the horizon; their home is in sight. But Odysseus, completely exhausted, cannot stay awake. When he falls asleep, his men open the bag of winds, and it blows them all the way back to Aeolia. Arriving there again, Odysseus begs Aeolus for help getting back home, but the king replies, "Vilest of mankind, get you gone at once out of the island; him whom heaven hates will I in no wise help. Be off, for you come here as one abhorred of heaven."[64]

I imagine many veterans, like myself, will feel some connection to Odysseus's men, who saw their superiors walk away from war with far greater benefits although they had the same or in many cases far worse experiences than those with higher ranks. In many units, those ranking E-7 and above come home from their tours with Bronze Stars, even if all they did was manage the chow line on a large base, far from any real danger. Meanwhile, many low-ranking soldiers in combat units who are subjected to the life-threatening, soul-torturing heat of battle day after day, walk away with no awards at all, or perhaps a small achievement medal. Even many soldiers entitled to combat awards for meeting specific criteria while engaged with the enemy were never given them because of administrative failures by others serving in the rear. Sadly, those of us who legitimately fought receive a disproportionate share of suffering and sometimes far less acknowledgment. In that sort of situation, warriors of today (like Odysseus's men) feel ripped-off, because they haven't been properly honored for their sacrifices, while others reap benefits merely because of rank. While not to be overlooked, this parallel is not the only that has meaning.

Let's consider the symbolic, psychological nature of this ordeal. Odysseus controls the ship and thus represents the ego. His control is total and complete, to the extent that it's self-defeating—he has all the resources, while no one else has anything. This is a picture of psychological imbalance. It's an ego that doesn't know its limits, and because of this one-sidedness, it *undoes itself*. Odysseus does not embody a balanced position as he attempts to steer his way back to Ithaca all by himself, without sleep. Not once does he look to any *other* for help. In trying to rely solely on himself—his ego and the power at his disposal—he brings about his demise. He falls asleep, into unconsciousness, which provokes a compensatory response from the neglected aspects of the psyche (his crewmembers, who we can understand to represent various aspects of shadow).

It's impossible to truly return home to the true self without diversity in the psyche. When all of our inner resources and psychic energy are focused in a single area, the parts of ourselves that are not invested in remain primitive, and will appear like a jack-in-the-box when their opportunity arises. Getting back to Ithaca, returning home, requires that all parts of the psyche receive their due.

We can understand Odysseus's men to symbolize the aspects of his shadow that have not received the resources and attention they require, and they yearn for recognition. As Jungian analyst Marion Woodman declared, "Since the natural gradient of the psyche is toward wholeness, the Self will attempt to push the neglected part forward for recognition."[65] Along the same lines, Edward Whitmont explained:

> The law of the preservation of energy applies also to the psyche. Whatever is repressed, while then lost to consciousness, still does not disappear. It becomes an unconscious compulsive force which then has primitive and potentially destructive characteristics.[66]

> But that which supports life also crucifies us; salvation and the fullness of life may also come through loss or renunciation of what had appeared to be the only life— the life under the ego's conscious will, devoted to the satisfaction of its demands.[67]

Odysseus's men—representing the unrecognized parts of his personality that are longing for expression—open the bag of winds simply because they must. The psychic energy hoarded by the ego has to be released before transformation can happen. Had Odysseus gotten back to Ithaca without undergoing a real transformation, he might have destroyed his relationship with Penelope and Telemachus and even been driven to suicide. There are too many tragic stories of returning veterans like this. I can think of several well-known veterans who appeared to be shining examples of resilience and success—who seemed to have made it to Ithaca— but ultimately took their own lives. We have to think about homecoming differently—that helping veterans "succeed" after war and military services needs to be more about inner adaptations (focused on the richness of one's emotional and psychological life), and less about outer ones (degrees, jobs, income, social media followers, etc.).

We can imagine that Odysseus's men, representing aspects of the hero's shadow, saved Odysseus through this *seemingly* counter-productive act. A regressive experience is generally necessary for change to happen. When only Odysseus steers the ship, when the ego ignores the other aspects of the psyche, it's inevitable that a (self-engendered) crisis will erupt. If other non-ego (non-Odysseus) figures had been allowed to direct the wheel, perhaps Ithaca could have been reached, but since they are not allowed to, they must undo what *seemed* like progress so that *real progress* can happen. When recurring problems present themselves and this sort of undoing takes place, it's a sure sign we need to direct our attention toward our inner world so we can learn and grow in new directions. The unleashing of the bag of winds may be painful and frustrating, yet a blessing in disguise.

In *Odysseus in America*, Shay shares examples of Vietnam veterans who've made their whole lives into a "mission," which ends up straining or wrecking relationships and creating a host of other problems. He illustrates how many hardworking veterans find themselves in crisis situations because their compulsive work tendencies ultimately distract them from deeper challenges requiring their attention.[68] Driven by heroic and warrior-centered consciousness, such individuals cannot help but see everything as a mission to be accomplished, an obstacle to be vanquished, a battle to be won. Such a person *continues to be a warrior* even when wearing different clothes and taking part in a different mission. Shay explains this strategy as inevitably doomed, giving examples of how it affected some of the veterans he worked with.

> Now the typical Vietnam veteran newly admitted to the program [at the VA] worked the same job for ten to thirty years making good money, and then "broke down," incapacitated by combat-related symptoms and emotions. … The event triggering a "breakdown" from a long successful job history has usually been some external event that prevented the veteran from keeping the workaholic schedule he had followed. … But most of all, he lost the setting in which he could perform his "mission." He became depressed, suicidal, and flooded with intrusive symptoms related to the ambush of his assault support patrol boat in the Mekong Delta the night before Thanksgiving 1968.[69]

This veteran's work habits—his tendency towards *doing*—were a defensive adaptation for the purpose of keeping traumatic symptoms at bay. When he lost his job he lost his purposive distraction and a crisis ensued, as the psyche demanded that the needs of his inner world be tended to. In other words, his conscious adaptation failed when his outer situation changed. This brought about a regressive experience *so that the inner problems that led to his mission-focused way of being could be dealt with*. We might say his own shadow unleashed a bag of winds, as an abundance of psychic energy spilled forth, taking him all the way back to his days in Vietnam— just as Odysseus was carried back to Aeolia.

Psychoanalyst Joseph Bobrow, who has done a great deal of work with veterans, also discussed the reality that a compulsive tendency toward *doing* can be problematic.

> … we each have an *inner* world. Not all anguish can be successfully addressed by "doing something." This includes altruistic public service, and using one's experience to help others. Undeniably noble and often useful to others, we sometimes end up ignoring and bypassing our own inner ghosts and postpone addressing them, sometimes tragically. Some dedicated and well-meaning people and organizations in veteran services today don't fully appreciate this. We underestimate the inner world at our peril.[70]

It would be far better if we tend to our inner work before we seek to apply ourselves in the outer world. Woodman reminds us that if we open the chrysalis for the butterfly or disrupt its natural transformative process by pushing it into the world too quickly, it won't fly.

> The chrysalis is essential if we are to find ourselves. Yet very little in our extroverted society supports introverted

withdrawal. We are supposed to be doers, taking care of others, supporting good causes, unselfish, energetic, doing our social duty. If we choose to simply *be*, our loved ones may automatically assume we are doing nothing, and at first we may feel that way ourselves. … We argue with ourselves, "I should be out there doing something useful." But the truth is I can't do anything useful if there's no *I* to do it. … That is what going into the chrysalis is all about —undergoing a metamorphosis in order one day to be able to stand up and say *I am.*[71]

We need to value the regressive process and appreciate the need for isolation—more aptly referred to as solitude. Our society and the field of psychology have damned veterans' isolating tendencies as they seek time alone and away from the world—time and space that is vital for deep changes in the psyche to happen. Of course, solitude has its shadow, and it's important to recognize that not all time spent in isolation is healthy, but neither is it the beast it's often portrayed to be. Our extraverted society fails to appreciate how important it is to encourage veterans to turn inward as they seek to transform after war.

Instead of rushing veterans to find jobs or pour themselves into serving society, I encourage other veterans to *first* turn inward. It is important for returning or transitioning veterans to spend some time getting in touch with themselves on a deep level—to find a way to connect with their pains, passions, and longings. Spend some time in the woods, immerse yourself in painting, writing, drawing, music, movement, or dancing. The point is to get enough space so that we can discover those quieter voices inside of us, and to find a way to let them express themselves so that we can be transformed by them. We're looking for an *experience* of being touched or moved by parts of ourselves that we typically don't listen to or notice. That tension in your shoulders and gnawing sensation in your gut is saying something, but what are these symptoms saying? Is there sadness or fear you've been running from? As you sit with your discomfort, what images come to mind? What other voices inside of you are crying out, unnoticed by the heroic ego which is always too busy with day-to-day tasks to listen? We must create space and time to hear what various aspects of our souls are saying, and we must establish some way for these sacred messages to pour out of us—to express what cannot be said with words. For each of us, this is different. You must find *your own way* to cultivate a relationship with the most lifegiving parts of yourself, and let them unfold. This is an essential part of learning to relate to the unconscious. Let the non-warrior aspects of your personality steer for a while, and be careful of hurling yourself into another heroic adventure, where only one aspect of your personality finds expression.

Breakdowns are both meaningful and necessary, as are the symptoms that come with them. In these situations, our symptoms and dreams can lead us to the transformation we require. Without the breakdown, no change happens. James Hillman, a prominent Jungian analyst and Navy Corpsman who served the severely wounded during World War II, stated that working with dreams and images, as we're doing here, is important because it functions to "*save the diversity and autonomy of the psyche from domination of any single power.*"[72] Since Odysseus is the *single power that dominates* the attempted journey home to Ithaca, he creates a situation that leads to a breakdown, and to the following events that transform him further.

Without any help from the wind—wind can be understood to represent psychic energy—Odysseus and his men row for seven days until they reach Telephylus, the city of the giant Laestrygonians. When they arrive, exhausted, Odysseus sends three of his men ahead to scout out the place. They soon meet Artakia, the daughter of King Antiphates. Artakia points Odysseus's men to her father's house, and as they approach they find a giantess, the Queen of the Laestrygonians, who immediately calls her husband. King Antiphates arrives and immediately snatches up Odysseus's men and eats them, at the same time alerting the other giants. Soon a whole city of giants swarms down on Odysseus and his men, spearing some of them like fish and throwing huge boulders on others, destroying eleven of Odysseus's twelve ships and killing most of his men. Only Odysseus and the men on his ship escape, his power reduced to a fraction of what it had been. This is an image of nearly complete devastation.

One way of understanding this aspect of the story is by considering it as a continuation of Odysseus's regressive experience, where his ego loses its power as psychic energy retreats away from the conscious personality and falls into the unconscious. The giants, in this case, are powerful agents of the unconscious which confront the ego and relativize its power—hence the meaning in the loss of Odysseus's men. As symbols, the giants represent a power in the psyche that brings an experience which Odysseus cannot beat by force—and whether these are elements of his own shadow, or symptoms (as Shay believed) arising from the unconscious, the important thing is Odysseus is powerless to resist them. All he can do (at least at this point) is run from it. Such a defeat for the ego is painful, but critical for our transformation process. Most, if not all, warriors eventually endure this on their journeys home. When our former survival strategies no longer help us navigate new challenges, we need to adapt, and sometimes that requires a complete transformation. Our psychic energy (the wind), once in alignment with ego's goals, suddenly and violently withdraws, leading us deep into the unconscious where we tend to feel overwhelmed and powerless (as Odysseus does here), but often such an experience can lead us to discover other ways of being, and unrealized parts of ourselves.

I think Odysseus's choice to run from the giants has important meaning in terms of how we relate to ourselves in times of distress. Peter Levine, widely considered a leading expert in treating trauma and somatic approaches to therapy, argued that above all, we must allow traumatized persons to use their instincts to navigate uncomfortable situations. Levine shared the case of his former patient, Nancy, who was referred by a psychiatrist who suggested that Levine provide relaxation training because she was having intense panic attacks. However, Levine found the relaxation training only made her situation worse, because it put her in a position where she was forced to face her discomfort head-on, which only increased her discomfort and exacerbated her condition.[73] At this point in time, she did not yet possess the inner resources to withstand traumatic discomfort without being further retraumatized. Through Nancy's experience, Levine learned that we must help trauma survivors to follow the body's innate wisdom and its impulses to free itself from the threat of harm, and in her case, that meant allowing her to run away from the potential threat versus being forced to lay there helpless while being tormented by it.[74]

Keep in mind, this kind of running away isn't a means of pathological avoidance (such as through alcoholism or drug use), but a running away that took place in a therapeutic context that mobilized her body's instincts in the service of healing. This activated a necessary defense she didn't have access to when she was experiencing the original trauma—and activating it in a therapeutic way empowered her to have a sense of control over her situation. Also, its important to remember this was only one stage of Nancy's recovery. As a trauma survivor's development moves forward and one makes progress in tolerating discomfort, one might be able to sit with it, and safely surrender to the discomfort in a way that is cathartic and helpful. So, we must appreciate that in Odysseus' experience with the threatening Laestrygonians, at this stage, he needed to run away. He could not yet face the threats they presented. They were too big, too powerful.

We experience such a moment as a full-blown crisis, filled with anxiety. It feels like the world is coming apart, as it did for Odysseus in the city of the Laestrygonians. These giants—larger and more powerful than Odysseus and his men—can also be understood to symbolize a shadow that is growing in its ability to overthrow the ego. The more we neglect our shadows, the more power they have over us. If we neglect our feeling side, for example, when a situation arises that provokes emotion, we might be toppled over by it.

Up to this portion of his journey, he has experienced a continual depletion of his energy and power, but the encounter with the Laestrygonians was decisive. His old way of being in the world—as a combative, aggressive warrior—was not serving his efforts to return home and heal, and so his unconscious drew his psychic energy into his inner world so that something new could emerge from within him.

Many veterans know this experience. They find themselves in situations where they're easily overwhelmed and unable to accomplish goals or meet challenges. They might feel exhausted, anxious, terrified, sad, or lost, or feel like there's no way out of some problem they face. Daily tasks can seem like unclimbable mountains or we might feel like we're falling apart. When a crisis hits, we have to appreciate the psyche's power. At that point, avoiding our unconscious is no longer an option.

About a year after my return from Iraq, my own strategies of avoiding my pain collapsed, and I had a sudden and complete breakdown—as if giants had come and decimated me and my entire life. I felt I had lost all of my power and the ability to continue living as I had. One day after a night of heavy drinking, I began vomiting blood, and it was in that moment everything unraveled. I panicked, convinced I would die. It felt like I couldn't breathe, my hands went numb, my left arm started hurting, and I thought I was having a heart attack. A good friend rushed me to the hospital, and in the emergency room they told me I was having a panic attack. I was in denial. At first I thought it was an isolated event, but after that, every single time I drank I had another one. I went to the VA and was diagnosed with post-traumatic stress disorder (PTSD) and began having panic attacks two or three times a day. I could barely get into the car without feeling overwhelmed, developed agoraphobia, and soon I was unable to leave my house.

The strategies (adaptations) that had helped me feel safe—alcohol, repression, and denial—were suddenly useless, and the pain could no longer be kept at bay. The crisis forced me to encounter the overwhelming emotions I'd been carrying around in secret. My body, which I was largely dissociated from at that time, demanded (like a terrifying beast) that I listen to and attune to its needs, and all of the psychosomatic, emotional suffering that was stored in its tissue. For six months, I felt like I was being tortured and I seriously considered ending my life. I feared I might lose control and kill myself in the midst of one of my panic attacks. They seemed unending, and unbearable.

What I didn't know then—but wish I had—was that the crisis I was enduring was part of a transformative and necessary initiation process meant to correct my dangerous psychological imbalance and begin the long process of healing from war. My true self was buried, hidden behind a toxic and destructive warrior complex, layers and layers of maladaptive psychological defenses, and emotional pain that needed to be tended to. I was avoidant of my feelings because they terrified me, and given the stigma of PTSD, I didn't want anyone to think I was disordered or dysfunctional.

At this point, I was in the Army National Guard and had just been promoted to Sergeant. As a non-commissioned officer (NCO) who hoped to deploy to Afghanistan the following year, I wanted to make the pain disappear so I could go on with my life as it had been. I immediately took action to clean myself up in hopes that I might quickly get through the crisis and move forward. I stopped drinking completely (and never went back), quit smoking, began therapy, and started a variety of self-care practices. I thought if I did the right things, the crisis would be put behind me and life could go on as it had before. But my psyche had other plans.

The unconscious is not interested in whether you're checking the boxes to do the right things. While surface-level changes might improve your situation to some degree, the unconscious is concerned with deeper matters—the underlying, toxic elements preventing the true self from finding opportunities for expression. I was living a false life; I was not on *my own path*. The unconscious simply wouldn't allow me to continue living as I had been—just as Odysseus had no choice but to find a new way forward after his power was robbed in the devastating encounter with the Laestrygonian giants.

In my work with veterans, this is where therapy often begins. Only when we're desperate do we tend to reach out for help, and consider finding a new way forward. It is a painful place to be. After Odysseus lost eleven of his twelve ships to the giants, there's no doubt he was overwhelmed with grief, anxiety, and terror. Many veterans can relate to the experience of going through a transitional or existential crisis, and finding that it's impossible to continue living as before. The encounter with the giants put Odysseus in a position where *he had to change, just as our painful emotional and psychological experiences do the same for us. Symptoms are a voice of the soul—not indicators of illness to be ashamed of.* This crisis ultimately sets the stage for Odysseus to be re-forged into the person he is destined to be, as we'll see as we continue to follow him on his journey home.

-6-

CIRCE'S ISLAND: MEETING THE ANIMA

Anima means soul … the soul is the magic breath of life …
— C.G. Jung[75]

Being that has soul is a living being. Soul is the living thing in man, that which lives of itself and causes life. … With her cunning play of illusions the soul lures into life the inertness of matter that does not want to live. She makes us believe incredible things, that life may be lived. She is full of snakes and traps, in order that man should fall, should reach the earth, entangle himself there, and stay caught.
— C.G. Jung[76]

As they left the land of the giant Laestrygonians, Odysseus and his men were at an all-time low. Most of their comrades were dead, and the survivors on Odysseus's last remaining ship barely managed to escape. Gripped by grief, anxiety, and other symptoms of trauma, they were increasingly powerless to overcome all that they were up against and were discovering that the journey home can be as difficult as war itself.

When veterans find themselves at this stage of the journey, overcome by pain and torn between a past they can't return to and a future they cannot fathom how to reach, some humbly submit to their circumstances and do whatever they must to heal and transform, while others become apathetic or nihilistic, and sadly, some resort to suicide. Hillman argued that suicide can be understood as a desire for instant transformation—to end our current state and enter a different one.[77] The antidote is to recognize and appreciate the call for transformation, and to learn how to attain it. Transformation is an imperative, but if the path of development is blocked because a person is too rigid or because they don't have the inner or outer support to hold or make sense of their suffering, things can take a dark turn.

There's a saying, "If nothing changes, nothing changes." In my work as a therapist, I've observed that *some* veterans are stubborn and resistant to change. This was certainly true of me—and maybe still is in certain respects. Unfortunately, some psychologists write research papers accusing veterans of being "treatment resistant" or "non-compliant" whenever treatments don't perform well. I find this frustrating, because while it's true that our community can be resistant to change, I also think that mental health professionals have a tendency to scapegoat their patients even when it's because the approach is not well-suited to the problem. Obviously, if patients are "resisting treatments" (*whatever that means*), we need a new approach to address what underlies the resistance (i.e., the warrior complex or lack of emotional regulation skills which pushes one toward avoidance). Maybe if psychotherapists recognized the reality of the warrior complex and developed therapies that help it to transform and relinquish its control over the psyche (as we have at *The Battle Within*), instead of applying one-size-fits-all "trauma-focused" treatments, they'd be more successful. But, they're stuck in a narrow approach to their problems, just like veterans are at times. So, veterans aren't the only stubborn people out there who are resistant to change—therapists can be that way too.

When the warrior complex won't let go of a person's ego, it can cut off the desire and the capacity to transform. The hardships at this stage of the path help explain why many veterans return to the service, the combat zone, or to similarly challenging roles as first responders. There, the tried-and-true adaptation strategies work, and you can go on without having to endure the trials that come transforming the personality. It's also true that many warrior-types were born for these roles. For some, it's a calling we need to appreciate. Those who are marked by Ares or Mars, meant to live this live in service to the warrior archetype, need to be especially adaptive if they hope to maintain their emotional and psychological wellbeing, and keep healthy, intimate relationships with others. Importantly, one can let this archetypal energy be the guiding force of one's life without being possessed by a warrior complex—but one must be especially conscious and reflective to do so. Such warriors must become experts at emotional regulation and learn to hold the tension between powerful opposites, so they can act fiercely in some moments while being able to be extremely compassionate and nurturing with oneself and others in times of difficulty.

Odysseus and his men are, by now, physically and emotionally exhausted. We might guess they went to engage in battle in Troy with about 720 men, left the war with somewhere between 500 and 550, and now they're down to about forty-six. The psychic energy that powered them in the past is slipping from their grip, and they're falling deeper and deeper into the unconscious, *requiring new adaptations* to make the return home possible. This is a potent image of what life after war can feel like. No matter how much you want to "return home" or heal or feel like yourself again, you just can't force your will into existence; and instead you feel tortured, threatened, and with zero energy to go on.

Odysseus is at a new low point, although before the journey is done, he'll sink even lower. Even more troubling than his debilitating encounters with fierce shadow figures is the absence of female figures, or the anima, which Jung describes as "the bridge to the unconscious" and a representative of the soul.[78] Until now, there have been no gods or goddesses in the story. Odysseus is *all ego, all hero, all warrior*. To this point, the *Odyssey* has described Odysseus's limitations and the trouble he gets into without well-applied direction and support.

As discussed earlier, the loss of Odysseus's men represents the loss of psychic energy and support to help the ego direct the flow of life. When the ego finally recognizes a need for change and adopts a position of receptivity, the dynamics necessary for transformation appear. It's in the painful experience of defeat that change can finally occur. Odysseus and his remaining men arrive at the mythical Aeaean island where the goddess Circe lives. Disoriented and terrified, they want to avoid *experiencing* more traumatic situations. For two days and nights, they lay on the beach in "sorrow and weariness eating [their] hearts out."[79]

On the third day, Odysseus goes hunting and kills an especially large stag to feed his men. On one level, the stag can be understood to represent masculine power, and slaying this creature may indicate that Odysseus is finally undertaking a necessary psychological task that can provide nourishment for him and his men:

> When the child of morning, rosey-fingered Dawn, appeared, I called council and said, 'My friends, we are in very great difficulties; listen therefore to me. We have no idea where the sun either sets or rises, so that we do not even know east from west. I see no way out of it; nevertheless, we must try and find one. We are certainly on an island, for I went as high as I could this morning, and saw the sea reaching all round it to the horizon; it lies low, but towards the middle I saw smoke rising from out of a thick forest of trees.'

> "Their hearts sank as they heard me, for they remembered how they had been treated by the Laestrygonian Antiphates and by the savage ogre Polyphemus. They wept bitterly in dismay ..."[80]

The sense of disorientation and the fact that there is "no way out of it" for Odysseus brings to mind something Jung wrote:

In the majority of my cases the resources of the conscious mind are exhausted (or, in ordinary English, they are "stuck"). It is chiefly this fact that forces me to look for hidden possibilities… I know only one thing: when my conscious mind no longer sees any possible road ahead and consequently gets stuck, my unconscious psyche will react to the unbearable standstill.[81]

Soon after arriving on the Aeaean island, half of Odysseus's men, led by Eurylochus, hesitantly venture forth to recon the island. On patrol, they hear the goddess Circe singing and are invited into her home, where she feeds them a potion which turns them all into pigs, and she takes them captive. Circe—representing the anima and the archetypal feminine—has a transformative effect on Odysseus's men that appears to be negative, but further examination suggests otherwise. From a Jungian viewpoint on dream interpretation, all the figures tend to represent aspects of the dreamer. If we interpret this myth as if it were a dream, Odysseus's men (and Circe) are all aspects of Odysseus. By transforming his scouts into pigs, the anima figure initiates a transformative dynamic in which Odysseus might get a different sense of his true nature.

Hillman describes consciousness of anima as turning toward our inner world. She is the *source of consciousness* that makes reflection possible. Without her, we cannot be aware of inner realities:

… consciousness of anima means first of all awareness of

one's unconsciousness. She brings the possibility of reflection in terms of the unconscious; i.e., in which way does this image, event, person, idea, feeling that is now the content of my reflection produce unconsciousness? … For, before we can become conscious we must be able to know where we are unconscious, and where, when, and to what extent.[82]

Circe makes Odysseus's shadow figures appear as pigs, which is useful because Odysseus can now see what he himself is often like. Was he not acting like a pig when he raided and robbed the innocent people of Ismarus and put them to the sword? Was it not pig-like to rummage through Polyphemus's belongings and barge into the territory of the shadow? Wasn't it pig-like to hoard all of the resources (e.g., the bag of winds), rather than sharing them with his men, by maintaining a singular control of his ship (his psyche)? His warrior-centric ego has been pig-like, allowing no other aspect of his psyche to find expression, *and this has been the main source of his problems*. If we see this story symbolically and reflect on its archetypal implications, Odysseus is finally coming to see his own pig-like—shadow—nature, and this will pave the way for change.

While the pigs might be understood as a potentially negative aspect of Odysseus's personality, I want to make space for their potentially positive aspect as well. They're earthy creatures, who often find their nourishment and sustain their lives by eating what they find in the earth. In ancient Greece, they were associated with feminine goddesses, including Demeter and Persephone, but pigs are also associated with goddesses elsewhere in the world, including in Egypt where the goddess Isis was portrayed riding a pig. In ancient India, the Buddhist goddess of dawn, Marichi, was portrayed as a sow with seven piglets.[83] Thus, pigs in other times and places have not been devalued or seen as negative, but as something holy. Of course, the earth and the mother goddess have a close relationship, as is well-known in our reference to "Mother Earth." This considered, we can also understand Circe turning Odysseus's men into pigs as the anima staking her claim in the psyche, by marking or adopting what once belonged to the ego, and bringing these aspects of the self into her domain. This is an act of transformation, and whether we adopt my first, second, or both interpretations, the effect is a necessary and (ultimately) positive one.

Jung and those who have followed him have observed repeatedly that the anima functions in a complementary manner to the persona.[84, 85] The anima is shaped by the totality of dynamics in the psyche, and so her appearance will be affected by the individual's attitude. Circe, Odysseus's opposite, tells us about Odysseus. Her action can be understood to be the result of Odysseus's one-sidedness, and we should be careful to judge Circe as negative (as Shay seemed to) without appreciating the unpleasant state of Odysseus's character.

Jung wrote:

> … the character of the anima can be deduced from that of the persona. Everything that should normally be in the outer attitude, but which is conspicuously absent, will

invariably be found in the inner attitude. This is a funda-mental rule.[86]

Therefore, all that's left out of the conscious personality—which in veterans is often feeling, nurturance, relatedness, empathy, and compassion—will be reflected by the anima. And when these qual-ities are undeveloped in us, they may sometimes appear dark and chaotic, as Circe seems here. While our introduction to Circe may cause us to judge her negatively and devalue her, soon we'll see that she has invaluable gifts to share with Odysseus and his fellow returning veterans.

When the feminine half of the soul (or any aspect of the psyche) has been repressed, we can come to see and know it by "projecting" it onto others, much like a film is projected onto a blank screen. Sometimes it's a positive projection, and we may idealize and even worship the person who is holding our "inner gold," as Robert A. Johnson put it.[87] Johnson, like all Jungians, argues that learning to recollect our projections—by becoming aware of and reclaiming what we displace onto others—is a critical practice for doing deep, inner work. It isn't easy, and often it takes the help of a therapist who is trained in working with the uncon-scious. This is especially true when the projections are negative. Negative projections related to the anima are readily seen in the veteran population in its widespread distaste for anything remotely considered to be feminine. When veterans express their hatred for hippies, snowflakes, women, effeminate men, or anyone who is different from their macho persona, they are "projecting" their own shadows. In his memoir, Jung wrote, "Everything that irritates us about others can lead us to an understanding of ourselves."[88] And elsewhere he stated, "So long as the anima is unconscious she is always projected, for everything unconscious is projected."[89]

When Circe turned half of Odysseus's men into pigs, this can be understood to represent anima possession. When we have repressed the anima and our inner feminine qualities so terribly, as Odysseus did and many veterans often do, it's not uncommon for a reversal of energy to take place, which Jung called *enantiodromia*. The person who once lived an ironclad emotionless life suddenly finds himself overwhelmed and even ruled by his emotions. I can't count the number of times I've heard veterans say something like this to me, "It seems like everything makes me cry these days. The slightest little thing will just set me off and I can't stop crying." In nearly every case, the veteran judges it as a negative experience and wants me to help them stop feeling the sadness that has overtaken them. And yet, in time, it becomes clear the sadness is a voice of the soul, speaking about wounds that have been ignored for too long. The seemingly ugly, messy thing ends up being a blessing in disguise that plays a role in the process of transformation.

Eurylochus stayed back, and he did not enter Circe's circle with the other scouts or take the potion. Instead, he watched from afar and saw the rest of the men turn into pigs. He returned to the ship to warn Odysseus and tried to convince him they should board the ship and sail away, which would have amounted to more avoidance, more repression, and more denial. Odysseus was wise enough to know he could run no more, and he sought Circe out.

On his way to Circe's dwelling place, Odysseus meets Hermes, the messenger of the gods, who warns Odysseus that he will be in grave danger unless he approaches the goddess in the right way. In the language of Jungian psychology, Hermes is a *Self* figure. Jung used the term *Self* (with a capital *S*) to refer to the objective center of the personality which transcends the boundaries of ordinary consciousness, whereas the *"little-s self"* (or ego) is the subjective center of the personality. Odysseus's subjective sense of self—his idea of who he is—is as a warrior, but this is a narrow and partial view of reality. As Jung proved, there is far more to the personality than is apparent on the surface, and the part of the personality that resides in the unconscious is vastly greater. The goddess Circe is about to initiate Odysseus into the unrealized and unknown parts of his psyche, but in order to navigate the challenge successfully, Odysseus must heed the advice of Hermes—a representative of the *Self*.

In dreams and myths, the Self presents itself as something transcendent and divine that guides the ego personality through the path of individuation. It is an ineffable aspect of the unconscious that possesses wisdom we could not access without its assistance. In dreams, figures like Hermes serve as messengers to this sacred part of our souls. We get into trouble when the little-*s* self thinks it's the totality of the psyche. It isn't. All the gods and goddesses of the *Odyssey* (as in other religious and spiritual myths and stories) are Self symbols, representing the holy, sacred, powerful elements of the unconscious that are transcendent and collective. They represent archetypes, in and of themselves.

Odysseus's larger task is to find himself in proper relationship to Circe, Athena, Zeus, and all the transcendent figures (gods and goddesses) of the unconscious. Hermes is the mediating figure who guides Odysseus on this part of his journey. When we dream, we might say (symbolically) that Hermes has visited us, bringing us a critical message to help us connect with the sacred elements of our souls. In heeding the advice sent us by the Self, our inflated egos are relativized, and we discover deeper, more sacred aspects of ourselves. Coming into contact with the archetypes of the collective unconscious can be overwhelming, even debilitating, which is why our relationship with the unconscious must be mediated.

Hermes gives Odysseus a protective herb to ensure that Circe won't harm him, at the same time advising him how to navigate the situation. Hermes warns Odysseus that Circe will "unman" him if he doesn't approach her in the right way. When our personality is severely imbalanced, we can be at great risk when we begin to face our shadows and integrate long-repressed material. Sometimes, the neglected sides of our personality can strip our egos of their power, leaving us in a vulnerable state.

Around seven years after coming home from Iraq, I began studying depth psychology and this initiated a new phase in my recovery process. Early in my studies, I learned about the anima, the archetypal feminine, and the benefits of turning toward one's emotional life, and at the same time, I became aware of the terrible degree to which I had been cut off from my inner life and feeling in general. During that time, I was in a crisis provoked by the suicide of a warrior I had worked with and the breakdown of important relationships at work. I had just begun Jungian analysis, was completely overwhelmed by traumatic symptoms, and spent most of my time writhing with anxiety and feeling quite depressed. This was the first time I'd ever allowed myself to feel my pain to this extent, rather than just try to escape from it. In the midst of this immersive experience, I had the following dream:

The Horned Woman

I'm with some of my veteran friends, and we're fighting against some evil. I am fighting with a dark woman who has long horns that curl and twist their way down her back. Another woman is helping me. The dark woman draws our figures on a tree to hurt us, as with a voodoo doll. We attack her before she can finish the drawings, but with her magic she easily overcomes us. She inserts a pin into the drawing, corresponding to the right side of my mid-back. I'm almost paralyzed and have to lay down. We need to be rescued from her as soon as possible. Then there is a rescue effort where we try to escape, but a firefight begins and things get confusing. My friends and I are captivated by her powers, and I start to wonder whether she is really bad. Nevertheless, I keep trying to get away from her grip and manage to do so, but I'm injured in the process. Everyone gets away by climbing these massive walls, but I'm not able to because of a horrible leg injury—in other dreams this leg injury happens in Iraq.

In this dream, we see what appears to be the dark side of the archetypal feminine. Like Circe, the dark woman with long horns that curl and twist down her back is no mere mortal.

During this time in my life, I was paralyzed by anxiety and depression and completely overwhelmed by the emotions that were coming up. Never before had I spent so much effort trying to process, express, and understand my emotions, which helps explain why in the dream I am paralyzed by them. This inner figure and the sort of suffering I was having at the time was *experienced as* dark, hostile, and threatening, yet my ego's perception was not the entire reality. Even while my ego was resisting this terrifying experience, another anima figure ("another woman" in the dream) helped me stay steady and safe in a situation I'd spent my whole life running from.

This dark woman, my own Circe, does not "unman" me, but she renders me "almost paralyzed," stripping me of my masculine potential for action. Note that there are two women in the dream. Another side of the archetypal feminine assists me in my battle against the dark woman. Our inner worlds are complex, and the dynamics among these many aspects of us give rise to inner conflicts.

As Hermes tells Odysseus, entering the anima's realm comes with risks we need to prepare for. It's unwise to leap blindly into the inner world without preparation and support. We need to develop our capacity for emotional regulation and affect tolerance to be able to stand in the presence of trauma, whether it is from combat, sexual assault, abandonment, or neglect. Even if we haven't suff-ered such horrific experiences, an encounter with the unconscious is never easy. The greater our capacity to care for ourselves through nurturance, compassion, and good self-care, the better we'll be able to navigate these difficult experiences when they arise. It's also helpful to have reliable outer support, people we can turn to like friends, family members, and a trusted therapist. Having a reliable psychotherapist who can help to navigate our relationship with the unconscious is invaluable, just as Hermes's advice to Odysseus was invaluable in this scene of the Odyssey.

Not long after Odysseus and Circe meet, they have sex, and then Circe's four housemaids prepare a bath for Odysseus. In Jungian psychology, sex is a symbolic reference to integration, as the opp-osites come together to create new life. Odysseus's active, masculine hardness is received by Circe's soothing, receptive softness, changing Odysseus and decreasing his rigidity. Finally he is coming into contact with the feminine aspects of his psyche that will allow him to transform.

Additionally, the number four (in this case, the four housemaids) is significant. Four is associated with wholeness, for example the four seasons, four directions, and four elements. The number four presents itself worldwide in creation myths, such as the Navajo origination story.[90] Once a patient of mine dreamed that he traveled over a sea on a magic boat, passed through a cave, and entered an atrium (an architectural term, but also a chamber of the heart, symbolizing entry into a sacred part of his own soul). Once there, he met four prostitutes who stood as threshold guardians before a room where he needed to change clothes, a reference to an evolution of his persona that he was experiencing. The number four is archetypal, and has spiritual and psychological significance.

Odysseus receives his transformative bath, and the symbols described all suggest that something alchemical, royal, and sacred is underway: the coming together of opposites, the mixing of hot and cold waters until they reach a state of perfection, purple cloth, silver and gold cups and bowls, and anointing Odysseus with oil. This sacred and luxurious experience takes away "the heart-wasting weariness from [his] limbs."[91] Afterwards, Odysseus asks Circe to restore his men, and she does. "They became men again, younger than they were before, and much taller and better looking."[92] What has been transformed and adopted (or held captive) by the feminine is ultimately made better. Again, this is not a negative experience that should be pathologized. Odysseus's encounter with Circe is restorative and healing.

The theme of the archetypal bath appears also in *The Cattle Raid of Cooley*, a Celtic myth. One day after battle, the hero Cúchulainn goes berserk. He's confused and doesn't know where he is. In a fit of misplaced rage, he attempts to fight his allies at Emain Macha (Odysseus's comrade Ajax did the same in his own psychotic rage). Cúchulainn threatens to kill everyone in the court, and when his own charioteer tries to calm him, Cúchulainn attacks him as well. Fortunately, Cúchulainn's allies are wise, realizing that fighting him is not the solution, so instead they send naked women to calm him. The naked women exit the fortified city and approach him. Their behavior is symbolic of the need to allow our defenses to fall away and to embrace receptivity, vulnerability, and compassion. Cúchulainn allows himself to be taken and dunked into a vat of cold water, which boils from his rage and then bursts. They then dunk him in a second vat of water, and the water is said to have boiled as big as fists, so they dunk him in a third. After entering the third vat of cold water, "the water rose to his temperature, but no higher, and the blood-lust left him and he saw where he was and that he was naked."[93]

In both situations, we see an imbalanced male warrior restored through an encounter with the archetypal feminine—the inner opposite who can counterbalance the unrestrained masculine energy. Additionally, in both situations we have the experience of "the bath," along with what can be understood as symbolic sexual imagery. Nakedness implies stripping away one's persona so that what is natural can emerge. It also suggests letting down your guard and becoming receptive so you can be transformed. Nakedness and touch invoke the sacredness of sensuality. Nothing is more precious than being able to *feel*, and to find yourself vividly in touch with others in a way that is lifegiving and restorative. This is the capacity many veterans are cut off from, as the harsh demands of war lead to dissociation, which leaves us disconnected from our sensations and capacity for feeling. Adhering to a hero-centered ego leaves us disconnected from the anima, the one who makes inner reflection possible.

Immersion in water is a common symbol for entering the unconscious, and bathing is a common symbol within the process of alchemical transformation.[94] Jung dedicates an entire chapter to

"Immersion in the Bath" in one of his alchemically focused writings on psychotherapy, and as we explore the nature of this symbolism as part of the transformation process, we can recognize the baths of both Cúchulainn and Odysseus as being profoundly meaningful.[95] During the alchemical process, alchemists sought to create gold, a precious emerald, or the philosopher's stone while starting with the *prima materia*, an original or base material generally considered to be of little value. As he observed alchemical "themes" in the lives of his patients, Jung saw the alchemical process and its imagery was ultimately a projection of the archetypal symbolism inherent to the individuation process.[96] Psychologically speaking, the *prima materia* can be understood as the raw, undigested material of our lives—our childhood memories, traumas, and painful symptoms. Though we're sometimes quick to reject this material, if we turn toward it and work with it, as an alchemist would work with the *prima materia*, we have a chance to discover its gold-like value as we transform. And, "the bath" as an alchemical process is a critical experience in which things really start to change—the old stuff begins to dissolve and new potentials emerge. Obviously, Odysseus's encounter with Circe represents a pivotal moment in his transformation process, and it comes just when he's in the depths of despair.

When men are out of touch with their own inner-feminine aspects, they often seek what is missing through relationships with actual women or anima figures. We may expect the females in our lives to provide what is missing from our inner worlds. The literature on combat veterans is full of examples and discussion about how common it is for warriors to seek out sexual experiences in an effort to sooth their souls. When discussing the sexual addictions of combat veterans, Shay writes about how Vietnam veterans sought out a "steam and cream" in the bathhouses of Vietnam as part of their refuge from battle.[97] In my own work conducting individual therapy with combat veterans, several of my veteran clients have focused upon their relationships with women as a central part of their therapy process. Whether it be sex addictions, serial cheating, or a longing for more emotional support from their wives, many of the combat veterans I have worked with have found themselves in the depths of longing for the archetypal feminine—often projected onto actual women. While there may be biological aspects satisfied by any emotional or sexual connection, we must be cognizant of the *symbolic and psychological* nature of these longings. When we can recognize how we *project* our own our unconscious anima qualities onto others, we can learn to *feel* what is missing from our inner worlds and begin to cultivate it there.

Many veterans are plagued with a high degree of dissociation because of their traumatic experiences. They just want *to feel*—to feel good and to feel safe. Sensual experiences can evoke much needed intimacy and help ground us in our bodies. While sex or sexual activities are one way of breaking through dissociation—when you feel tense or on-edge, few experiences will bring a greater sense of freedom than an orgasm, a powerful way of releasing tension from an overwhelmed system—other kinds of somatic experiences can also feel pleasurable and comforting, like yoga, stretching, self-massage, baths, footbaths, heating pads, dancing, and other kinds of movement. These are all things you can do by yourself to increase your capacity for connection and embodiment, critical to overcoming the dissociative effects of trauma. Odysseus's bath with Circe reminds us that one effective and enjoyable way of entering the anima's inner realm is a sensual, embodied experience.

Circe helps Odysseus back onto the path of transformation. She makes him aware of the fruitfulness of turning toward that which is *other*, and in so doing she restores his sense of well-being. She provides him and his men with food and drink, and it takes a year on her island until they're restored to the level of health and strength they had when they left Ithaca for Troy in the first place. Circe and her servants bathe the warriors and initiate them into the sensual, embodied awareness that is necessary in recovering from war.

> … Circe with loving care bathed the rest of my companions, and anointed them well with olive oil, and put about them mantles of fleece and tunics. We found them all together, feasting well in the halls. When my men looked each other in the face and knew one another, they burst into an outcry of tears, and the whole house echoed[98]

Odysseus and his men are moved when they see one another and recognize who they *really are*, not the men they were forced to become in battle nor the men they've been since leaving Troy. Seeing into the depths of who they really are affects them powerfully.

After a year, Odysseus feels ready to continue his journey, and he requests to go onward. Circe agrees that he can leave, but in order to be successful in his return, he must first go to the house of Hades and Persephone in the underworld to consult with the ghost of the blind prophet Tiresias. Hearing this causes Odysseus to weep. Circe gives Odysseus the guidance he needs to navigate his way into the underworld, instructing him what he is to do when he arrives. Becoming acquainted with the archetypal feminine has paved the way for the descent into the underworld, where the next stage in his healing and transformation can take place.

-7-
THE DESCENT

The night sea journey is a kind of descensus ad in-feros— a descent into Hades and a journey to the land of ghosts somewhere beyond this world, beyond consciousness, hence an immersion in the unconscious.

— C.G. Jung[99]

In the hero's journey, the descent or *nekyia* takes us into the abyss. For Odysseus, the descent begins with his visit to the house of Hades and Persephone; continues with his encounter with the Sirens, Scylla, and Charybdis; and lasts for seven more years, as he stays with Calypso in her island cave. This phase of his painful initiation does not end until Athena implores Zeus to see Odysseus released from Calypso's domain. This lengthy process reflects the experience of psychological and spiritual transformation— regression into the depths of our emotions and pain, immersion in our inner world, and the journey home.

As Circe tells Odysseus, the return home *requires* that he first go into the underworld, then venture through the trials of the Sirens, Scylla, and Charybdis. This initiatory succession is inherently difficult, and anyone who has experienced their own "*dark night of the soul*" knows we are never the same afterward. This is the fire through which we are forged. Its importance is reflected in the *Epic of Gilgamesh*, and elsewhere in the *Odyssey* as it relates to the homeward journey of Menelaus. When Menelaus becomes stranded, the goddess Idothea comes to assist him. Menelaus states:

> I was trying to come on here [to my home], but the gods detained me in Egypt. … We should have run clean out of provisions and my men would have starved, if a goddess had not taken pity upon me and saved me in the person of Idothea, daughter to Proteus, the old man of the sea, for she had taken a great fancy to me. … 'Stranger,' replied she, 'I will make it all quite clear to you. There is an old immortal who lives under the sea hereabouts and whose name is Proteus. … he will tell you about your voyage, what courses you are to take, and how you are to sail the sea so as to reach your home.'[100]

Just as Menelaus has to go under the sea, Odysseus has to go to the underworld. To get there he traverses the waters of Oceanus, then reaches the fertile shores of Persephone's country where he finds the house of Hades. Prior to his departure from her island, Circe told Odysseus that to relate to the other figures in the underworld, the ghosts there will have to consume blood from an animal sacrifice. If they don't receive this blood, relating to them will be impossible, and they'll go away. Odysseus accepts his task, and follows the directions given to him.

I [Odysseus] made a drink offering to all the dead, first with honey and milk, then with wine, and thirdly with water, and I sprinkled white barley meal over the whole, praying earnestly to the poor feckless ghosts ... When I had prayed sufficiently to the dead, I cut the throats of two sheep and let the blood run into the trench, whereon the ghosts came trooping up from Erebus—brides, young bachelors, old mean worn out with toil, maids who had been crossed in love, and brave men who had been killed in battle, with their armor still smirched with blood; they came from every quarter and flitted round the trench with a strange kind of screaming sound that made me turn pale with fear.[101]

Jung discussed the symbolism of sacrifice, specifically as it relates to the *Odyssey*, in one of just a handful of his references to this myth.

By sacrificing these valued objects of desire and possession, the instinctive desire, or libido, is given up in order that it may be regained in new form. Through sacrifice man ransoms himself from the fear of death and is reconciled to the demands of Hades. ... it is a sacrificial offering to the powers of the underworld, like the blood drunk by the shades in the nekyia of Odysseus.[102]

Like Odysseus's sacrifice, our investment of psychic energy (our lifeblood) into the unconscious is a way of paying homage to the gods and goddesses we will discover in the underworld of our own unconscious. Exploring the unconscious and relating to the inner figures that populate it requires real work. Without the sacrifice of our energy and attention, our descent's transformative potential is considerably lessened. Since the descent or therapeutic regression is such a daunting and significant task, where precious energy is invested in this rather than to our day-to-day functioning, we are making a sacrifice to the gods and goddesses, the archetypes of the collective unconscious.

Tiresias gives Odysseus advice on how to return and offers a prophecy for his future. Odysseus is advised *not* to harvest any of the sheep or cattle belonging to the Sun God on the island of Thrinacia when they continue their journey. He tells Odysseus that his return will be hard and full of suffering, and that Poseidon will have his revenge, since Odysseus blinded Poseidon's son Polyphemus.

During this exchange, Odysseus learns for the first time about the suitors who are relentlessly pursuing his wife Penelope and his estate, and the tyranny his wife and son are being forced to endure. These suitors—more than a hundred of them—have been trying to kill his son, and steal his wife and property during his absence. This news must be devastating for Odysseus, while at the same time fueling his desire to return home and restore justice to his kingdom. Tiresias also shares that after Odysseus overcomes the suitors and completes his tasks at home, he must "*take a well-made oar and carry it on and on, till you come to a country where the people have never heard of the sea and do not even mix salt with their food*" [emphasis added].[103] He is beckoning Odysseus to a life of meaning and purpose—to share the boon and lessons of his adventure with those who need it. Those he is to meet are those whose lives lack flavor, who do not know the sea, the source of life—the unconscious. A realm he is (at this point) just getting to know. In discussing Odysseus's interaction with Tiresias, Joseph Campbell writes:

> Not all in the dwelling of Hades are mere shadows. Those who, like Tiresias, have seen and come into touch with the mystery of the two serpents [a reference to Hermes] and, in some sense at least, have been themselves both male and female, know the reality from both sides that each sex experiences shadowlike from its own side; and to the extent they have assimilated what is substantial of life and are, so, eternal. There is a line of Sophocles, referring to the mysteries of Eleusis: "Thrice blessed are those among men, who, after beholding these rites, go down to Hades. Only for them is there life, all the rest will suffer an evil lot." This idea is basic to mature Classical thought and, in fact, is what distinguishes it from its echo in academic neo-Classicism. It is the expression of an organic synthesis of the two worlds of the Greek dual heritage …[104]

When Odysseus sees Elpenor (a young soldier of his who foolishly died while drunk, falling off a roof) he tells Odysseus he must return to Circe's island so Elpenor's body can be buried properly. We can understand this in (at least) two ways. First, most veterans literally lose friends in combat and from suicides and accidents afterward, and it is important to grieve these losses appropriately. Second, this also suggests that a reckless part of Odysseus's psyche must be buried so he can transform. We must mourn actual persons who pass on, and also the parts of ourselves that no longer serve us. We must honor both, paying respect to what was.

We can understand the encounter with Odysseus's mother in the same way, having outer and inner parallels and symbolic meaning. During our absence while in the military, we miss out on important life events at home, including hardships, illnesses, and the deaths of those we love. When we are displaced and in emotionally unsafe environments, we are unlikely to process these losses, and so at some point we need to consciously face what we couldn't in real time.

Symbolically, Odysseus's encounter with his mother can be seen as his "inner mother" and all she represents. We are told she hung herself in grief in Odysseus's absence, which symbolically might be the death of the nurturing, inner mother who cannot bear the ego's participation in war—the hell of battle, the madness, rage, violence, and hatred, flesh being torn open by metal, explosions, gunfire, betrayal, and all the other terrible experiences that are difficult to name or speak of. For an inner mother to be present in this situation would be unbearable. There would be too much feeling, too much consciousness. So, we become like Achilles or Odysseus, possessed by the spirit of Ares, forgetting all that once gave depth and flavor to our lives. If our capacity for self-mothering is nonexistent or becomes unconscious, it belongs to the underworld.

While in the underworld, Odysseus also encounters a variety of other female figures, wives, daughters, and mothers of famous men and heroes, each of whom represents an aspect of the archetypal feminine—those inner "others" who give life and substance to the lives of men. If we take these figures as representing aspects of Odysseus's own psyche, it suggests that military service and combat trauma result in the loss of various aspects of the archetypal feminine in us, and a descent to the house of Hades and Persephone is a way of reconnecting with what was lost, so that it might aid in our ascent and rebirth. Jung observed that:

> Everything young grows old, all beauty fades, all heat cools, all brightness dims, and every truth becomes stale and trite. For all these things have taken on shape, and all shapes are worn thin by the working of time; they age, sicken, crumble to dust—unless they change. But change they can, for the invisible spark that generated them is potent enough for infinite generation. No one should deny the danger of the descent, but it can be risked. No one need risk it, but it is certain that some one will. And let those who go down the sunset way do so with open eyes, for it is a sacrifice which daunts even the gods. Yet every descent is followed by an ascent; the vanishing shapes are shaped anew, and a truth is valid in the end only if it

suffers change and bears new witness in new images, in new tongues, like a new wine that is put into new bottles.[105]

As the women depart at Persephone's command, the males begin to approach. The first is Agamemnon—the one most violent toward the feminine principle. Agamemnon tells Odysseus that his friend Aegisthus and Agamemnon's wife, Clytemnestra, plotted against him and murdered him and his men. Clytemnestra, as Agamemnon's dangerously repressed anima, is an explosive force who takes him by surprise and ultimately subverts him, sending him into the underworld. Agamemnon is remembered as a stubborn, ill-tempered, impulsive, and selfish leader, who sacrificed his own daughter. Jean Houston writes, "Agamemnon's litany is one of unmitigated misogyny," which seems a fair assessment based on the record.[106] We can see Clytemnestra's ascent and Agamemnon's descent as an enantiodromia, the tendency of things to change into their opposites when we go too far in one direction. While Clytemnestra rules the above, grumpy old Agamemnon is subjected to an inescapable immersion in the unconscious.

The tenuous or unhealthy dynamics between Agamemnon and Clytemnestra—male and female—fit a pattern we see elsewhere in Odysseus's descent into the underworld. In addition to the important lesson given to Odysseus on imbalance, we also see the need to respect the gods, along with warnings about compulsive drivenness and being possessed by an overly heroic ego. Achilles, a hero of the Trojan War, considered the greatest of all Greek warriors, tells

Odysseus:

> … what deed of daring will you undertake next … I
> would rather be a paid servant in a poor man's house and
> be above ground than king of kings among the dead. But
> give me news about my son … Tell me also if you have
> heard anything about my father … Could I but stand by
> his side, in the light of day, with the same strength that I
> had when I killed the bravest of our foes upon the plain of
> Troy …[107]

Achilles' accomplishments and fame mean little now that he is
dead—all he cares about is his family, but it's too late. His power to
taste life is gone. This should be a wakeup call for Odysseus *not* to
undertake any more "deeds of daring."

In discussing Achilles in the underworld, Houston wisely speaks to
the symbolic aspect of this encounter, pointing to the limitations of
a heroic approach to living. "[T]he heroic mind can only assert
itself in the world of space and time and cannot look inward into
the timeless, spaceless realm [of the unconscious]."[108] Having a
driven warrior-centric or egocentric way of being does little or no
good in cultivating a relationship to your inner world. The one-
sidedness that brought Achilles fame for his actions in battle does
not serve him in the underworld.

While other dead men in the underworld speak to Odysseus, the
jealous Ajax turns away, still angry because it was Odysseus and

not he who received Achilles's armor. Elsewhere (and much later) in Greek literature, in Sophocles' *Ajax*, Ajax is depicted as severely imbalanced—as an arrogant, vengeful, delusional, and psychotic warrior—*as an example veterans should not follow*. Athena tries to help him, embodying the anima and the archetypal feminine, as she encourages him adopt a healthier and more balanced position. But, he completely rejects her, and does so at his peril. Ultimately, he commits suicide. At the end of the play, Odysseus (who allows Athena to guide him) is presented as a level-headed, wise warrior who acts with compassion, even towards those who wished him ill and treated him with the upmost contempt.

Odysseus also witnesses Tityus, son of Gaia, being tortured for violating Zeus's mistress Leto; Tantalus suffering of thirst and hunger because he disrespected and stole from the gods; and cunning Sisyphus doing his best to complete the impossible task of rolling a boulder up a hill, which was his punishment for tricking the gods and believing that his cleverness was greater than that of Zeus. In all these figures, and especially in Tantalus and Sisyphus, we see qualities of Odysseus—his penchant for cunning and his propensity to live heroically, without respect for the gods. Such encounters provide lessons that equate to warnings. As Odysseus's time in the underworld comes to a close, he meets Heracles, who tells him:

My poor Odysseus … are you too leading the same sorry kind of life that I did when I was above ground? I was son of Zeus, but I went through an infinity of suffering, for I became bondsman to one who was far beneath me—a low fellow who set me all manner of labors."[109]

Here, one of the most famous heroes of all time warns Odysseus about the futility of continuing a heroic way of being. Heracles calls it a "sorry kind of life," that even though he was the son of Zeus, ruler of all the gods on Mt. Olympus, Heracles's habitual heroism caused him and others a great deal of suffering. When Heracles says he "became bondsman to one who was far beneath" himself, it fits Jung's observation that whatever is left out of the conscious personality will, sooner or later, subvert the ego by force.

To the degree that the world invites the individual to identify with the mask [the persona], he is delivered over to influences from within. "High rests on low," says Lao-tzu. An opposite forces its way up from inside; it is exactly as though the unconscious suppressed the ego with the very same power which drew the ego into the persona.[110]

There is a common thread that weaves through Odysseus's encounters in the underworld. We meet a number of sad, aching heroes who now suffer because they lived as Odysseus has. These shades, or shadows (ghosts), are mirrors of Odysseus, and he is forced to see what he might become and what his fate might be *unless he changes*.

As we immerse ourselves in the underworld of the unconscious, we learn from Tiresias and others what is necessary so we can enjoy a successful return and free ourselves from the seemingly endless cycle of challenges that plague us. This advice is critical; without it we'd be left only with the daytime perspective of ego concerning what to do and where to go.

The descent into the therapeutic process can serve us in the same way as Odysseus is served by his descent into the underworld. It is well-known that the variable that most predicts a successful outcome in therapy is the relationship between therapist and client, as this sets the stage for other therapeutic endeavors to be pursued. Catharsis is important to the therapeutic process, but to express yourself, you have to feel safe enough in the relationship to do so. Sometimes we need someone we trust to challenge our maladaptive defenses or patterns, but this is impossible until a solid therapeutic relationship exists.

Trauma survivors need a safe place and an experienced guide to begin the long process of getting in touch with their emotions and bodies. When traumatic symptoms dominate, I tend to favor mindfulness- or somatic-focused approaches to therapy, as well as those that help survivors develop emotional regulation and self-soothing skills. We often need to be intentional and develop the ability to hold ourselves through our suffering, especially if we did not have people to nurture and support us when we were children. When these skills are well-developed and you feel ready to process some of the hardships of the past, some trauma-focused therapies, like Eye Movement Desensitization and Reprocessing (EMDR) or somatic-focused therapies can be especially helpful. However, in my opinion, therapies of depth—and Jungian analysis, in particular—are especially helpful when the time comes to orient oneself toward the inner world so that the personality can be transformed. When the task shifts from developing one's capacity for emotional regulation to "getting home"—rediscovering the true self —an authentic descent and encounter with the inner world and the figures who populate it is irreplaceable. However, one size does not fit all, and a variety of personal factors must be considered to determine what the best course of treatment should be. If you have questions about what type of treatment is best for you, it is always helpful to consult with a licensed mental health professional who is acquainted with a wide variety of psychological theories and therapies.

When Odysseus's journey to the underworld has come to an end, his ascent begins. He boards his ship, and sets sail. At first, he and his men have to row, but soon a "fair wind sprang up" to carry them onward.[111] Here we see evidence of a shift in the flow of psychic energy, and while at first a bit of effort is required to get things moving, soon the psyche helps move him along. Jung called this the progression of the libido, which corresponds with the archetypal ascent—a movement that goes upward and outward, instead of down and in. As Jung noted, a progression of psychic energy and outward movement becomes possible once a suitable adaptation or attitude is attained through a successful regressive immersion in one's unconscious.

In other words, regression leads to the necessity of

adapting to the inner world of the psyche... Thus a complete orientation towards the inner world becomes necessary until such a time as inner adaptation is attained. Once the adaptation is achieved, progression can begin again.[112]

As he promised Elpenor, Odysseus first returns to the island of Aeaea to bury his dead comrade's body. While Odysseus is there, Circe tells him, "You have done a bold thing in going down alive to the house of Hades, and you will have died twice, to other people's once."[113] Homer makes it clear that he viewed the descent-and-ascent as an initiatory rite that resulted in Odysseus's death, rebirth, and transformation. Circe then echoes Tiresias and tells Odysseus of the troubles that lie ahead and how to overcome them. And so he proceeds on his journey to navigate "the road of trials."

First he encounters the Sirens, dangerous creatures who lure sailors with their beauty and their enchanting voices to shipwreck on the rocky coast of their island. To survive this temptation, Odysseus asks to be bound to the mast of his ship while his men stuff their ears with wax. Next he finds himself between the six-headed monster Scylla, who lives high up on a cliff devouring any who come near, and the all-consuming whirlpool Charybdis, who sucks victims down into watery depths. Odysseus is told to rush *between* these two threatening figures—a pair of anxiety-producing opposites—*not even bothering to put on his armor.* He is to remain defenseless, *holding* the tension he feels when between them. Odysseus makes one mistake in this scenario. He puts on his armor, and as a result Scylla eats six of his men. Odysseus once again provides an example of what *not* to do. Still, he manages to navigate the situation well enough to avoid getting too close to either obstacle.

When Circe was coaching Odysseus through this ordeal, Odysseus wondered if he might be able to fight Scylla, to which she replied, "You daredevil, … you are always wanting to fight somebody or something; you will not let yourself be beaten even by the immortals."[114] Again we hear the rebuke of a divine figure who tells Odysseus to surrender to the process of transforming his heroic way of being. This road of trials is, ultimately, meant to help Odysseus accept his smallness, seeing that he is a mere human who must face the terrors and vicissitudes of life. The horrifying monsters on the road home from war cannot be avoided if we wish to know the peace of home again.

Odysseus was told not to put on his armor because it would endanger him and his crew. Armor, which can be understood as a symbol for psychological defensiveness, is not helpful in moments like these. Only by courageously facing what we fear without armor can we successfully navigate these kinds of challenges. Those who find themselves tormented by devouring anxiety, panic attacks, or other terrifying symptoms know that trying to defend yourself or *fight against* your symptoms only makes the situation worse. It's best to have the courage to surrender, even though it can be incredibly difficult to do so.

I understand the Sirens, Scylla, and Charybdis as symbols for the trials we go through that can't be overcome in the way warriors tend to approach problems. Instead of confronting the terrors that lie ahead defensively and aggressively, the way a heroic warrior would, Odysseus follows the guidance of the goddess and faces these fearful experiences with courageous receptivity and vulnerability. Paradoxically, we often find ourselves stronger and more resilient when we give ourselves over to whatever it is that terrifies us. And the things that terrify us generally lose power as we learn to face them. Still, we shouldn't force ourselves to confront these kinds of terrors head-on until we're ready (although often they force themselves upon us whether we feel ready or not). When we endure symptoms of trauma, we often feel pulled between the horror of suffering, and the fear of surrendering, even though it's impossible to fight back. Paradoxically, the way through the road of trials is to surrender, which is why Circe told Odysseus not to put on his armor.

Kalsched wrote about the importance of "suffering into reality."[115] Much of our suffering is caused by maladaptive psychological defenses, and the way to heal and transform these defenses into healthier functioning occurs as we face the pain that the defenses have been guarding against. When a trauma occurs, psychological defenses arise to protect us from the unbearable suffering of the event. These defenses are necessary because they prevent us from having a breakdown in moments of great need, and they also preserve the vital core of the personality—the true self.

In acute, life-threatening traumas or in situations where we face the possibility of bodily harm like combat or abuse, hyperarousal and dissociation are the key defenses that help us through. Hyperarousal helps us become more aware and vigilant so that we can defend ourselves against threats, while dissociation helps reduce the felt impact of the event by numbing our capacity for feeling and sensation. These defenses are what causes PTSD symptoms, leaving us to feel on-guard, threatened, stressed-out, and/or numb and disconnected. These defenses are a normal and healthy response to protect ourselves against harm, and are vital in helping us survive. But when they continue to applied by the psyche long after a traumatic event, when there is little to no likelihood of something bad happening, they end up causing rather than preventing suffering, thus becoming maladaptive. This automatic, unconscious response is generally beyond our control.

What we can do, however, is turn toward the suffering that these defenses attempt to protect us from and the suffering that they cause, holding ourselves in a compassionate, nurturing way. By developing the capacity to face the pain in a gentle, mindful way, we can experience the pain that these defenses guard against, and then let the defenses transform into healthier functioning. We can only do this when we feel safe enough to do so.

Of course, many warriors want to rush into this process and get it over with—that's the typical warrior way—but healing doesn't happen according to the ego's timeline. There are a lot of factors that influence how quickly we recover, like the type and extent of our trauma, what defenses lie under our suffering, how well we learned (or didn't learn) to hold ourselves through our suffering when we were children, our emotional regulation capacity, our attitude, our self-care practices, and how much support we have from friends, family members, or our therapist. No matter what, it takes time—sometimes months, sometimes years. Little by little, though, we do heal. Cultivating a mindful, patient, nonjudgmental approach of acceptance is critical, recognizing, as the Buddhists do, that suffering is an inherent part of life and can actually be an important "teacher."

Bessel van der Kolk, another psychologist specializing in the treatment of trauma, says that mindfulness is the cornerstone of healing from trauma, and he presents a wealth of evidence to argue why this is so.[116] Without mindful awareness, we remain subject to the chaos in our bodies and feel out of control. With mindfulness, we develop the capacity to observe our experiences without judgment and ground ourselves in our bodies in a way that allows our defenses to loosen their control over our psyches. If we can muster the courage to sit with ourselves and notice what's happening in our bodies, holding ourselves as a loving and nurturing parent might, we can create a foundation for emotional regulation that allows maladaptive defenses to fall away.

Additionally, through mindful belly breathing (also called diaphragmatic breathing), we can mobilize the relaxation response of our parasympathetic ("rest and digest") nervous system. This sends soothing signals throughout the body and mind that leave us feeling calmer, helping turn off our flight, fight, or freeze response. These days, you can find classes on mindfulness just about anywhere (including the internet), or attend yoga classes where mindfulness is a central part of the practice. Yoga has the added benefit of increasing a sense of embodiment, which is helpful in overcoming dissociation.

When we practice mindfulness, we try to maintain awareness of the present moment and focus on our breathing. Thoughts, feelings, and sensations are like waves or clouds that come and go. We just notice them without judgment, hold ourselves with compassion, and bring our awareness back to the here and now. Everyone's mind is always bouncing around and our attention is fleeting, drifting off again and again. Everyone feels like they're terrible at meditating. This is normal, don't give up. The important thing is not to try and be perfect in your concentration, but just keep showing up. Trauma survivors should meditate or practice some form of mindfulness every day for at least ten minutes. Having a regular practice is essential, no matter how much your awareness drifts.

Picture Odysseus sailing past the Sirens, Scylla, and Charybdis, and consider the mindfulness meditation instructions above. The Sirens, Scylla and Charybdis are "distractions," like clouds on a windy day, and Odysseus chooses to be immobilized so he will pass by the Sirens, listening to their beautiful and compelling song without pursuing or engaging them in any way. Practicing mindfulness, we notice our inner experiences without engaging them. When a traumatic memory arises and overwhelms you, like passing between Scylla and Charybdis, bring your awareness back to your in-breath and your out-breath, and redirect your attention, perhaps to a soothing sensation or a gentle stretch.

In my second year of Jungian analysis, I made some big discoveries about my past that caused me to see how trauma distorted my personality, causing me to lose touch with my true self. In becoming aware of who I *wasn't*, it brought about the terrifying question of who I really am. I wasn't sure of anything at that time, and I began questioning what psychological forces had pushed me into some of my life's biggest decisions. I was in the midst of the worst part of my therapeutic regression—I was in the abyss of the hero's journey, or the dark night of the soul.

Memories of the war and traumatic events from childhood came flooding back, and I was unable to contain them. I was tormented with relentless anxiety most of each day, and felt terribly depressed. My body ached with severe psychosomatic symptoms. Sometimes, I would wake up dry heaving or even vomiting because my gut was so tight from all the stress.

During this time, I decided to increase my mindfulness practice to about an hour a day, using a combination of meditation and yoga. I also increased my visits to therapy from once to twice a week, as often as I could afford the expense. In the midst of this crisis, a particular few weeks were especially awful. I would have horrifying panic attacks every evening. I was experiencing what I recognized as irrational fears, and worried I would have a psychotic break. I wanted to run away from these experiences and go on with my life. But I knew this suffering was part of my initiation and transformation process and that I needed to use this crisis as what a professor of mine called an AFOG (Another Fuckin' Opportunity for Growth).

When the anxiety would get really bad, I would shut myself in a dark room to meditate. Waves of terror washed over me, and it felt like I'd be torn apart, like I was passing between two monsters. I did my best to breathe mindfully, using gentle stretches to distract and soothe myself. I felt waves of relief pass by, then the waves of panic would return—sometimes big ones, sometimes small ones. Somewhere in the wash of it all, sadness would pour out of me and I would weep. Then, slowly but surely, as I sat with my experiences and nurtured myself through them, I would feel the anxiety lift, as though I had passed through some kind of trial. Around this time, I had the following dream.

Monster on the Cliff

I am leaving a war zone via airplane, and the plane keeps crashing and we have to keep starting over. At first, the plane was overloaded, so over time we take less with us. Each time we take off, the plane crashes and we have to start over. There is an angry general and tanks firing into the air for protective purposes. We finally get out of the ordeal as we begin descending. I am in the cockpit with the pilots, and it's nerve-wracking. Later, I'm on a cliff, and far below is a body of water I need to cross to get to a different airport so I can get home. I'm being chased, and I decide I must jump from the cliff to have a chance of getting home. I plunge into the water below and try swimming across, but the current is strong. The current pulls me toward a dark cave that is sucking all the water in. Fortunately, there's a rock in my path, and I'm able to save myself by moving from rock to rock until I get to the other side. It's still very difficult. A small boy is following me and he is afraid of a monster on the opposite cliffs. He keeps drawing attention to it, and I tell him not to fuss about it because it might hear us and attack. I ask him to keep quiet. Next we ascend a steep hill to the airport to see if we can make our way home.

In the dream, like Odysseus, I'm trying to make my way home from war. And like Odysseus, I run into the same sort of troubles repeatedly. In my case, the plane home keeps crashing, just as Odysseus's ship ends up in one disaster after another. The motif of crashing down out of the sky is a common symbol of inflation and deflation (or as Jung says, positive and negative inflation)—like Icarus who tried to fly with waxen wings, got too close to the sun, and crashed into the sea. This is a central problem for Odysseus and for many veterans. The return "home" to the true self, the objective personality, is impossible so long as we are inflated. We have to come down to earth and face the pain we're ignoring. We can see Odysseus's hardships and breakdowns as attempts to avoid the pain of facing his own shadow and war-related trauma. Finally, it's Odysseus's courage to face this difficult path of trials that brings him down from his one-sided, inflated perspective so he can experience change. Facing our pain in a humble, receptive manner allows us to be transformed.

In my dream, or we could say in my "personal myth," something similar happens. The "airplane" is overloaded—perhaps I was taking too much, like Odysseus trying to steer his ship home by himself—while at the same lacking the ability to fly away from the war zone. The warrior-centric ego must be relativized by other aspects of the unconscious, and one way for that to happen is by facing our inner terrors. The repeated breakdowns in the dream (and my life) ended with a descent, where I was brought down from my inflated perspective.

The next trial in the dream was to cross over a certain body of water, and the imagery here is eerily similar to the *Odyssey*. There's a swift current that would draw me into a dangerous cave that is sucking in the water, so much like Charybdis, while at the same time there's a monster high up on a cliff, like Scylla in the *Odyssey* (I was not familiar with the story at this time). I manage to escape both these risks by facing the horrors and anxieties I feared. Only by taking a leap of faith and facing our pain can we take the next step on our way home to ourselves.

In my dream, I see the presence of the divine child, which is the equivalent of Telemachus, the son of Odysseus, symbolizing the innocent core of the personality, the true self, and the hope of our future potential. Often in the midst of our most desperate challenges, this sacred element of the soul makes an appearance, asking us to protect, nurture, and help him find new life.

By the end of my dream, the trial was complete, and I was in a better position to return home from the war zone. At the time I had that dream, I didn't understand this so I didn't realize something positive had occurred. I was facing horrible challenges every day that I thought would be the death of me, and I was half-right. These challenges would be the death of my outdated, unhealthy sense of self, while at the same time they were birthing something new. Had I known about the *Odyssey* at the time, it might have provided some context and meaning for what I was going through. To see life through the lens of myths and dreams can help us understand our experiences in a new and meaningful light.

As we continue to follow Odysseus's journey home from war, let us remember that the painful, terrifying descent is nothing less than the veteran's initiation into a new stage in his or her development. In the underworld, Odysseus was helped to see the dark side of his heroic nature as he came into contact with those, like him, who suffered because of their one-sidedness. On his road of trials, he had to face anxiety-inducing monsters to learn to accept his smallness and adopt a humbler, more receptive, and vulnerable ego position. Only by allowing himself to face his anxiety and pain could he learn to accept his limitations and be transformed.

-8-

FINDING BALANCE

Both Tiresias and Circe stressed to Odysseus that after his encounters with the Sirens, Scylla, and Charybdis, he would be tempted to harvest the cattle belonging to the Sun-God Hyperion on the island of Thrinacia—and he was explicitly told not to. Throughout the ancient world, the Sun was closely associated with the fiery, active male principle, while the Moon was associated with the feminine principle, especially given its monthly cycle (like the menstrual cycle) from death into new life and its relationship to the lifegiving waters and their tides. Since the Sun represents the masculine principle, Tiresias and Circe's warnings amount to a clear message: *Do not harvest more masculine energy, Odysseus! This is what gets you into trouble! This is a big test—a big moment in your postwar initiation! When you're under pressure, will you return to your old warrior-centric ways, or will you remember the lessons you learned from Circe and the underworld?* Circe's words of caution are abundantly clear:

If you leave these flocks unharmed, and think of nothing but getting home, you may yet after much hardship reach Ithaca. But if you harm them, then I forewarn you of the destruction both of your ship and of your comrades; and even though you may yourself escape, you will return late, in bad plight, after losing all your men.[117]

When Odysseus and his remaining men (about 40 now) reach the island of the Sun God, Odysseus tells them of the warnings from both Tiresias and Circe. He begs his men to return to the ship and be on their way, but Eurylochus responds insolently. Eurylochus's name means "tyrant." In the earlier episode, he was the individual who ran from Circe and missed the transformative encounter the others had there.

Eurylochus makes the case that the men are tired and over-whelmed, and so they should stay. The rest of the men agree, and Odysseus allows it, but he makes it clear that no one must harvest the cattle belonging to the Sun God. Before they have dinner, he makes them swear a solemn oath. That night, the distressed men weep over all those they have lost, and while they are sleeping a storm blows in. What had started as a short rest becomes a long one, and on account of the weather they are forced to stay a full month.

Odysseus repeatedly reminds them of their oath, which initially the men uphold. Before long though, they eat through the stores Circe provided them and they turn to catching birds and fish to avoid starvation. Finally, the temptation to kill the cattle becomes overwhelming—especially to the avoidant tyrant, Eurylochus. While Odysseus is sleeping, Eurylochus misleads the men, violates his oath to Odysseus, and disrespects the gods by killing the Sun God's sacred cattle. Eurylochus (who we might interpret as an element of Odysseus's shadow) seems to want to avoid discomfort, and does so in the same spirit of recklessness that defined Odysseus and his comrades when they first left Troy. Instead of accepting his hunger or adopting a more meek and meager position, he violates his oath and greedily consumes that which is forbidden. Eurylochus remains in an inflated position that lacks respect for the laws of nature while rejecting the authority of the gods and goddesses, or the unconscious, and in doing so, he invites his own destruction.

This is reminiscent of when, earlier in their journey, Odysseus fell asleep at the wheel and his men unleashed the bag of winds gifted by Aeolus. On that occasion, Odysseus was acting foolishly, while his men were ignorant of their actions. This time, Odysseus is doing the right thing, while his men knew their actions were forbidden and yet they acted anyway, without fear of consequence.

The symbolism of "sleeping" is important, and can be understood as falling into unconsciousness. Some unconsciousness can actually be a good thing, if our ego is properly related to the unconscious, and if things in our psyche are in good order. In such a case, the flow of energy can move between the conscious and unconscious aspects of the psyche in a healthy, life-giving manner. Yet, if we're in a place of unconsciousness and things in our psyche are out of order, we can expect things to go awry. That's what seems to be happening here, as it did earlier when Odysseus fell asleep during the bag of winds episode. Despite the evidence of imbalance, it is obvious things are different now, and that Odysseus has changed profoundly. Odysseus (the ego) is not guilty of foolish behavior as he was when he tried to single-handedly drive the ship back to Ithaca. He's trying to honor the gods, and to do what's right. Yet despite the reality that his ego-position is now well adapted, other elements of his personality (symbolized by Eurylochus and other men) continue to be self-defeating. If we take Eurylochus as an inner tyrant—a dark and self-defeating aspect of Odysseus's shadow—then we can surmise that there are still aspects of Odysseus's personality that must be transformed or perish, and that is what happens.

As soon as the weather clears and Odysseus and his men set sail, Zeus strikes their ship with lightning. (In addition to being the leader of the gods on Mt. Olympus, Zeus is god of the sky, thunder, and lightning.) The boat breaks into pieces, and *all of Odysseus's men die*. Odysseus, alone and terrified, is carried by the rough waters back to the whirlpool, Charybdis, and he barely manages to escape by clinging to a fig tree. This tree, like the mast that saved him from the Sirens, is the archetypal symbol of the cosmic tree or *axis mundi*, the connection between heaven and earth.

We see examples of sacred trees in the myths of many religions and cultures. In Christianity, we have the cross where Christ undergoes his initiation into death so that he might be resurrected. In Buddhism, Siddhartha Gautama sits at the base of the Bodhi tree (*ficus religiosa*, or sacred fig) and withstands the torment of

Mara (death, deception, and suffering). He puts his hand on the earth (grounding, humility), attains enlightenment, and becomes a Buddha. In the Norse tradition, the god Odin underwent a similar transformation when he hangs himself on an immense mythical tree named Yggdrasil as part of his initiation so he could drink from the wisdom-giving waters of Mímir's Well. To retrieve the water, Odin was forced to surrender one of his eyes, and after that, half his sight was dedicated to the inner world and half to the outer world. After wounding himself and hanging from the tree for nine days and nights, he descended to the depths of the well and retrieved the runes, symbolic letters that might serve as tools of communication with transcendent forces, which he brought up as a blessing to his people.[118]

In a Sumerian myth, Inanna the Queen of Heaven descends into the underworld, strips naked adopting a position of vulnerability, and gives up her life. Suspended on a hook for three days and nights, she is rescued by two figures—each both male and female— created by the god Enki. These hermaphrodites (a term that combines the names Hermes and Aphrodite) go to the goddess of the underworld, Erishkigal, tend to her needs, and sooth her pain, and she agrees to give Inanna new life.[119] In Egyptian mythology, we see the death and resurrection of Osiris, and Isis giving birth to Horus; and again a cosmic tree (the Erica Tree) serves as a key image.[120] *Clinging to a sacred tree* while undergoing yet another hellish ordeal, Odysseus experiences a significant moment in his journey of transformation and rebirth. Veterans must learn to appreciate the hardships they encounter in a similar light, understanding that experiences of significant suffering can be defining moments that bring about unprecedented transformation and new life.

The loss of Odysseus's men, while undoubtedly painful, is necessary (if we understand the story symbolically). Eurylochus and the others symbolize the rigid, masculine, warrior-centric aspects of the psyche, the habits that cause Odysseus trouble again and again. These holdovers from war need to perish for deeper transformation to take place. Like the immune system, the unconscious seeks homeostasis (equilibrium, or balance), and it directs its resources where they are needed. Sometimes what we experience as symptoms are necessary for healing. Ultimately, we're subject to the will and wisdom of the unconscious, and there's a price to pay if we attempt to resist it.

If our ego invests energy in unhealthy ways, the unconscious will withdraw energy from our unproductive psychological adaptations and reinvest that energy in the unconscious to spur on our other potentials and healthier adaptations. During this transition, we may feel we have less energy, are less capable of functioning normally, and are more susceptible to overwhelming emotions. If our conscious personality has met its limits, the solution will come from the unconscious.

This necessary reorientation creates an immense upheaval of psychic energy and a host of traumatic symptoms. The image of Odysseus clinging to a fig tree to avoid the life-devouring whirlpool Charybdis mirrors the experiences of many combat veterans who find themselves in crisis, resisting what feels like a potential psychotic break. Overwhelmed by the terror of losing control, they cling to the familiar for dear life. When warriors are in the midst of a regressive experience like this, where the psyche attempts to redirect us, traumatic symptoms are likely, if not inevitable.

In crises like these, veterans need to know *they're undergoing a sacred initiation whereby they're being re-forged from warrior to veteran—to the person they're meant to be—and that fear and pain are a natural part of the process.* We need to normalize suffering as an inherent part of the post-war or post-military transformation process, rather than pathologizing it as brokenness, a disorder, or a sign of weakness.

As this psychic energy runs its course, you may discover a new sense of self that makes healing from war possible. No matter what your strengths, you'll need an experienced guide who knows the territory. That's why therapy is so important—especially therapies of depth, which prioritize fostering a deeper relationship with the unconscious and the soul itself to understand the meaning of symptoms, versus therapies that merely focus on their eradication.

When Charybdis had run her course and the currents returned to normal, Odysseus was able to let go of the fig tree, and he began paddling his raft with his hands until he was out of imminent danger. Imagine this experience—psychologically and emotionally. When Odysseus was no longer at risk of being devoured by a monster or drowned in a vortex, he was alone at sea and utterly alone in the world, without a paddle. All his friends had died. Having endured one hardship after another, he had to have been wondering whether there was any hope at all of making it back to Ithaca. It must have seemed there'd be no end to the suffering, at the same time hoping his raft and the currents of fate might carry him home. Odysseus's raft does indeed bring him closer to home, though not in a direct way. After ten days afloat at sea, he landed on the island of Ogygia, where he would stay the next seven years with the goddess/nymph Calypso.

Calypso explains how she came to meet Odysseus:

> I found the poor creature [Odysseus] sitting, all alone astride of a keel … I got fond of him and cherished him, and had set my heart on making him immortal, so that he should never grow old all his days.[121]

Odysseus describes it this way: "She took me in and treated me with the utmost kindness."[122] Yet, the author makes clear that Calypso's kindness is not enough to soothe the deep pain Odysseus carries within his heart.

> [Calypso] found [Odysseus] sitting upon the beach with his eyes ever filled with tears, and dying of sheer homesickness; for he had got tired of Calypso, and though he was forced to sleep with her in a cave by night, it was she, not he, that would have it so. As for the daytime, he spent it on the rocks and on the seashore, weeping, crying aloud for his despair, and always looking out upon the sea.[123]

This paragraph sums up how Odysseus spent those seven long

years. The lack of eventfulness *is* what makes this experience so impactful from a psychological perspective. For Odysseus, it's torture. But, this is the medicine he needs. A great pause, a break, a kind of extended retreat that might eventually lead to healing and rejuvenation. From the goal-oriented ego's perspective of functional reality, Odysseus's lengthy, unplanned, grief-stricken detour on the island of Ogygia does not seem a reasonable investment of time or energy. But it is a necessary step on Odysseus's journey toward individuation. This apparent stranding is compensatory and is needed so he can learn adaptations more suitable for recovering from war. Odysseus's experience with Calypso is at once painful, necessary, and fruitful. Let's look at Jung's words on the importance of regressive, compensatory experiences.

… regression is not necessarily a retrograde step in the sense of a backwards development or degeneration, but rather represents a necessary phase of development. The individual is, however, not consciously aware that he is developing; he feels himself to be in a compulsive situation that resembles an early infantile state or even an embryonic condition within the womb.[124]

When we experience episodic suffering, there may be a tendency to judge ourselves and our symptoms as negative. This may be especially true among veterans, because military culture is so imbued with the idea that suffering is a sign of weakness. It doesn't help that the field of psychology has labeled post-war suffering as a "disorder." We can take a stand against this notion and declare that suffering can be the soul reaching toward its own goals, oftentimes against the ego's resistance. If we wish to suffer less and reduce the pain of our symptoms, we would be better off taking aim at the ego's position, rather than at the symptoms or suffering. And it's not just veterans and patients whose ego positions need to be challenged. How many professionals in the fields of medicine and psychology focus on symptom reduction without any appreciation for the aim of symptoms or their value? How many therapists attack symptoms under the influence of their own heroic egos, while missing the treasure hiding in the soul's deeper workings?

One former client came to me declaring that he had "uncurable, major chronic depression," and shared that those words were given to him by his former therapist. This client had over fifteen years of therapy under his belt, with a lengthy history of severe childhood and adult trauma, including living with a life-threatening health condition. He said his two previous therapists, who he liked, had tried everything—though they hadn't tried a psychodynamic or psychoanalytic approach. In the early months of our work together, he was so severely depressed that he would sometimes cry about three-quarters of our sessions. Sometimes he hardly spoke with words at all. His grief had plenty to say, and I listened. When he would speak, he would share about how horribly depressed he felt, and communicated that sometimes he would cry almost all day. He hated his job, and his relationship was strained. His sadness continued to deepen the first six months of therapy, and he began to question our approach and its value. He wanted me to make the depression go away, but as our work progressed, it was obvious the sadness was asking for change. The client had adopted a way of being, starting in childhood, that essentially disempowered him to the point of becoming a doormat for others to walk on. He was afraid to stand up for himself, and rarely considered his needs because he had unconsciously adapted to focus on serving the needs of others, and to keep the peace at all costs. Eventually, he became aware of these facts and he started listening to the wisdom of his sadness.

His dreams spoke of a tremendous, quick descent to the bottom of a cavern; a terrible wounding in which he was paralyzed in the desert though I had arrived to help him; his late arrival to a sacred pool at the bottom of a cave; a profound sense of loneliness; and the emergence of a strong, confident man named "Liam," which means "strong-willed warrior" or "protector." In Liam, we saw an unconscious aspect of himself which had been left out of his development, and which had the power to help him protect himself from abuse and exploitation. The imagery in his dreams convinced me—and him—that we were on the right path. He felt it was calling him to put his needs first, so he took an extended leave of absence from work and began to address the inner and outer challenges that surrounded him. He learned to listen to his emotions when he felt frustrated or angry, hurt, sad, or worried, and he spoke on their behalf to make his position known whenever a conflict arose. Before the end of our first year, his horrible, almost life-long depression was all but gone. Once his depression lifted, he continued therapy, and week after week he would show up with a smile on his face, almost like a proud man showing off a big fish he'd caught. A year after his first major breakthrough, major life challenges confronted him again, and this time he faced them with the depth and composure of a spiritual teacher. Once almost helpless in a sea of suffering, he had learned to harness and ride its waves. The cure was in the pain and the images of his unconscious, but he needed the time, space, and a suitable container (a therapy that would listen to—rather than try to extinguish—his pain) to understand its wisdom. That's what Calypso's island afforded Odysseus.

As we imagine Odysseus nearly drowning in his grief with none of his former strength, alone on this island with Calypso, we get a clear sense that this might be the first time his cunning intelligence and heroic strength are not enough. This is true for many warriors. Depression, anxiety, and loneliness can't be powered through. Odysseus lacks the resources to navigate this situation. All he can do is submit to the values of Calypso, a symbolic immersion in the world of the anima. He has no choice but to accept his circumstances. There's no lotus to eat, nowhere to run, and no enemies or monsters to fight. Immersed in suffering, there's nothing to do but allow the suffering to recast his identity. He must turn inward and enter the cave of the unconscious, so the anima can help him reconnect with the gods and goddesses (the archetypes of the collective unconscious), who are the only ones who have the power to set him free and direct him homeward. Revisioning the *Odyssey* in this way can help us understand the Dr. Ed Tick's reflections:

> In my extensive work with vets, another thing I learned is that PTSD is not best understood or treated as a stress

disorder, as it is now characterized. Rather, it is best understood as an identity disorder and soul wound, affecting the personality at the deepest levels. Traditional societies and some modern pioneers have held similar convictions.[125]

Service in a war zone is a descent into the depths of the Underworld of war, psyche, and myth. We dismember— take apart both the civilian identity and that part of the world we fight in. We replace our identity with a new military one. … After the military and war, changes to personhood last our entire lives. Though some returnees ache for a return to the pre-war self and even set it as a goal of their therapy, life and growth are one-way streets; trauma stamps dinosaur footprints into our psyches and the pre-war self cannot be recovered. This constitutes a psychospiritual death. A new self must be constructed that includes the important stories, values, and meanings of military and war experiences. Contemporary psycho-logical diagnoses include identity disorder. War changes who we are … The invisible wound is an identity crisis. … We bring healing to an identity crisis through identity transformation and the creation of life-affirming meaning.[126]

Dr. Tick seems to be suggesting that PTSD is better understood as an identity disorder and soul wound, *rather than* as a stress disorder.

I believe the suffering of most veterans is a result of all these problems at the same time: traumatic stress, identity, *and* soul wound. There's no doubt that the experience of war disorders the nervous system, results in real neurobiological/neuropsychological changes, and creates dynamics of extreme stress that produce the pattern of symptoms we refer to as PTSD. Yet, he is right, we have to appreciate the equally important wounds warriors suffer to their souls and their sense of self or identity.

When we discuss the pattern of symptoms we call *PTSD*, we have to understand that they're a result of hyperarousal (or hyper-vigilance) and dissociation, which are psychological defenses designed to protect us from trauma where the threat of bodily harm feels imminent. Actual, physiological changes in our brains and nervous systems have been detected as a result of trauma, and such changes have been linked to the ways our brains and bodies respond defensively in response to stress.[127] These defenses are essential in combat, but when they continue to affect us long after the trauma has ended, we call them *maladaptive*. Instead of protecting us, they actually cause our suffering. Hyperarousal has us feeling on guard, stressed, afraid, anxious, tense, exhausted, agitated, and irritable pretty much all the time.

Dissociation is a psychological defense that *disconnects us from* our sensations and feelings, and in severe cases, even our identity. It arises to protect us from the pain a trauma might cause, so that if we do happen to get hurt, it won't be so unbearable. But diss-ociation also leaves us feeling disconnected from others, the world, and even from ourselves. It makes it difficult to be in touch with our bodies and our emotions in a fruitful way.

The suffering these defenses cause can be overcome, but it takes work, and usually a fair amount of psychotherapy. As Bessel van der Kolk describes, many experts now consider mindfulness practices like meditation and yoga to be central to transforming these defenses to healthier functioning. These kinds of practices help us form a foundation that increases our capacity for emotional regulation and affect tolerance—our ability to hold ourselves through our pain—in a way that sets the stage for therapy to be successful.[128]

These are not the only psychological defenses that create suffering and disconnection. While hyperarousal and dissociation are attempts to help us bear the threat of physical harm, other defenses protect us from emotional trauma. For example, the psychological defenses associated with narcissism (projection, idealization of self, and devaluation of others) tend to protect us from feeling shame. Some individuals cannot bear to feel flawed or not good enough, and it's intolerable for them to think they might have any imperfections, so these defenses bend reality so they can feel safer in the world. Feeling shame can be intolerable, and if it becomes overwhelming, we might inflate our sense of self to ease our pain, and project our perceived shortcomings or deficiencies onto others. This, too, is a defense against feeling discomfort, in this case the pain of feeling like a failure, or unlovable. Folks who unconsciously rely on this defensive posture don't usually go to therapy because they don't think they need it. They think everyone else has a problem, which is a classic defining feature of *projection*.

On the other hand, individuals who have gone through significant losses (including abandonments or deaths, especially early in life, as well as experiences of rejection or having significant unmet needs) often tend toward a set of defenses that lead to depression. Psychodynamic therapists refer to this pattern of defenses as *introjective dynamics* or depressive character structure (introjection, devaluation of self, and idealization of others). These defenses "*turn against the self*" and are essentially the opposite of the narcissistic position. These individuals believe they (and everything they produce) are flawed, seeing themselves (and their work) as not good enough. Unlike those who take a narcissistic position, depressive individuals aren't so defended against seeing their imperfections. In fact, they hyper-focus on their so-called imperfections and even imagine flaws that don't exist. On the positive side, they're deeply introspective and reflective (which can be part of a superpower), always examining and criticizing themselves, believing that if they could just fix themselves, they might prevent future experiences of loss, abandonment, or rejection.[129] Importantly, most of this is unconscious, so folks tend not to be aware that these things are happening beneath the surface.

I see this trait in those veterans who blame themselves for what went wrong on the battlefield. "It's my fault. If I had just done *something* differently, my friend might still be here." These sorts of experiences are often attributed to moral injury, but as I see it, this sort of bargaining is rooted in introjective tendencies—and those with narcissistic dynamics tend not to blame themselves, but others. This defensive posture is intended to prevent pain and suffering by enforcing an unattainable degree of perfectionism so that something bad doesn't happen *again*, and it also causes a chronic form of suffering where the person turns against himself to the point where it affects their sense of self and identity. They often see themselves as bad, even if they themselves were innocent of wrongdoing.

Veterans who tend to turn against themselves in this manner often carry an exaggerated and unfair sense of guilt. They feel guilty for serving at all, and they sometimes blame themselves for their small part in wars they feel are unjust. Some of my best friends have expressed the guilt they feel just because they witnessed a variety of injustices (from individual events, to broader, systemic problems) in Iraq and Afghanistan. One former member of a past therapy group lamented the horror he felt after seeing dead Iraqis after the first Gulf War, and the fact that he feels so guilty for ever being there—for ever serving or wearing the same uniform as those who dropped the bombs or pulled their triggers.

Another veteran I worked with, who served in Afghanistan, constantly beat himself up about every perceived shortcoming. In childhood, he suffered significant abuse and abandonment, and I believe that set the stages for the depressive dynamics that characterized his personality and influenced how he saw himself and the world. He told me how bad he felt about lobbing M203 rounds toward enemy fighters who took up positions inside a village. They ambushed his platoon, wounding one of his platoonmates, and he was forced to return fire. Then, afterwards, he was haunted by the possibility that he might have hurt or killed someone. He was an exceptionally good person, and yet he saw himself as terrible.

In contrast, there was another veteran I worked with who had been in a remarkably similar situation, but whose emotional and psychological experience was radically different, even though he saw innocent civilians being killed as a result of the firefight he was in. That veteran expressed no sadness or remorse, and in fact, he devalued the civilians and expressed his belief that they were all bad people who deserved what they got. He needed to imagine that the civilians were bad, in order to tolerate such a horrible exper-ience. Each of these veterans' unique perception of their exper-iences—and how they viewed others and themselves—cannot be separated from their character structure and the defenses they used to protect themselves from the pain of these events. When veterans find themselves tortured by feelings of badness or exhibiting dissociated disinterest, we have to appreciate the underlying dynamics within their personality structures. You can call this moral injury if you want, but whatever you call it, you have to understand that this is not just about the violation of morals or norms. This is about the way that unconscious defenses—especially introjection, in this case—bend reality to protect us. It's a trade-off, a devil's bargain, if you will. The acute pain of facing the trauma is substituted by a different form of long-term, chronic suffering as the pain is directed inward.

Again, we have a soul wound that ties in to problems related to our identity, because when we're in this position, *we don't have a clear image of ourselves—it's distorted.* We have a sense something isn't quite right, and we're plagued by suffering that won't go away. Often, those who turn against themselves and beat themselves up like this are the ones who had childhood experiences that set the stage for introjective tendencies or depressive dynamics. That was true for me. My dad left when I was four, and I never realized how much this affected me until almost a decade after I came home from war. For years after coming home from Iraq, I blamed myself for a number of terrible things that happened. I was convinced I could have saved one of my friends if I had done things differently, or that maybe a civilian killed by a platoonmate would still be alive if I had noticed the warning signs that something was wrong. I was haunted by a sense of guilt, sadness, and failure.

For veterans, as with everyone, sometimes psychotherapy has to address the earlier wounds that gave rise to the kinds of suffering we're experiencing now, before work can be done to address more recent concerns. Only when I became aware of the ways in which being abandoned as a child warped my personality, and grieving the pain that was borne out of that experience, was I able to see that the things that went wrong in war were not my fault at all and that I couldn't have changed them. All I could do was accept the pain that came with those traumas and nurture myself through it. Until we face the pain these defenses guard against, they'll just continue to distort reality and cause suffering that appears in a different form. We have to learn from the example of *Odysseus*, appreciating that sometimes it's necessary to revisit painful experiences (as he returned to Charybdis) and allow ourselves to sit with our pain without trying to run from it (as he does while on Calypso's island).

In both these examples of how different types of defenses can distort our personalities and cause suffering (these are just two of countless examples of defenses), we get a sense for the subtle ways in which painful experiences and psychological defenses cause us to lose touch with who we really are. When our true self has been lost because maladaptive defenses get in the way, the unconscious will do what it can to try and restore balance, but often psychotherapy is necessary for real change to occur.

We all have psychological defenses. They are a primary force shaping our personalities and how we experience the world. All these defenses exist on a spectrum from healthy (and flexible) to primitive (and rigid), and ultimately we tend to suffer when our defenses tend toward the primitive, rigid end of the continuum. In times of exhaustion, stress, or hardship, it's inevitable we'll have moments where we'll express ourselves a bit primitively. When you're running on empty, your psyche doesn't have the energy it needs to fuel the defenses in a way that allows them to function "politely," and so our primitive side will show every now and then. That's okay. We're all human. But whenever there are patterns of broken relationships or chronic experiences of suffering, it's a good indicator that psychotherapy would be helpful.

While psychological defenses can cause us to lose touch with who we really are, we can't forget about the characterological imbalances resulting from being possessed by the warrior complex, or from identifying with the warrior archetype. Since military training and service completely reorient the personality and since our culture has no container to facilitate reorientation after war and service toward wholeness, a crisis of identity may be inevitable. After we've been made a warrior and then can no longer serve as one, painful and complicated questions remain: *Who am I, and what do I do now?* For many veterans, all we ever wanted was to serve in the military. From as young an age as I can remember (perhaps four), I had my heart set on joining the Army. But by age twenty-three, a single tour of IED hunting left my psyche ravaged and unable to continue to serve. I was devastated, because I couldn't imagine doing anything but being a soldier. I was cut off from my dream—from the life I'd always longed for—and I wasn't sure who I was anymore.

Many civilians see their dreams realized around midlife and then they have a midlife crisis when disillusionment sets in, and as questions of identity, purpose, and meaning rattle their sense of self. Sometimes accomplishing everything you set out to do and attaining everything you hoped to attain can leave you feeling empty, not fulfilled. What's left when your dreams have been realized—you've got the house, car, job, and family you always wanted—but you're not happy or satisfied? Ultimately, the problem of a midlife crisis leads many folks into a painful, regressive experience where they have to go back and figure out who they really are and what matters most.

When a midlife crisis strikes, the individual is generally already somewhat mature and well-developed, and even then, the experience can be extremely destabilizing. Consider how veterans in their twenties or thirties feel, not only trying to figure out who they really are and where they want to go, but having to do so while carrying the trauma of war and having to navigate a transition to civilian life. It's like going to a new world, while hellish symptoms haunt you like ghosts. Facing any of these problems is not easily resolved through the surface-level, one-size-fits-all therapies. It's why we need the DoD and VA to broaden therapy options for those who serve, other than just offering "trauma-focused" therapies. So many veterans end up wandering lost like Odysseus, chronically suffering through one crisis after another, until eventually a severe crisis forces them to a halt. Nothing short of complete transformation will resolve the issues that lie beneath the suffering that many veterans carry.

As he sits on Calypso's island, Odysseus has no ship, no men, no strength, and no idea who he is or where he's going. He's in a state of extreme uncertainty and suffering. He's stuck. It's a complete and total breakdown—a crisis of immense proportions, and yet staying present with all of this might be exactly what he needs to bring about a change in his personality. Jung reminds us:

> The symptoms of a neurosis are not simply the effects of long-past causes... they are also attempts at a new synthesis of life ... They are seeds that fail to sprout owing to the inclement conditions of life and outer nature ... I myself have known more than one person who owed his entire usefulness and reason for existence to a neurosis, which prevented all the critical follies in his life and forced him to a mode of living that developed his valuable potentialities. These might have been stifled had not the

neurosis, with iron grip, held him to the place where he belonged. There are actually people who have the whole meaning of their life, their true significance, in the unconscious, while the conscious mind is nothing but inveiglement and error.[130]

In the majority of my cases the resources of the conscious mind are exhausted (or in ordinary English, they are "stuck"). It is chiefly this fact that forces me to look for hidden possibilities... I know only one thing: when my conscious mind is stuck, my unconscious psyche will react to the unbearable standstill. This "getting stuck" is a psychic occurrence so often repeated during the course of human history that it has become the theme of many myths and fairy tales.[131]

Odysseus broke down when his men harvested the Sun God's cattle (symbolizing masculine energy) despite the fact that it had been forbidden by the gods and goddesses. Since he already had a propensity to be driven by his so-called masculine faculties and because harvesting more of this energy was expressly forbidden, this violation disrupted the laws of the unconscious and invited a breakdown. The psyche, in its wisdom, has presented a compensatory situation as a solution. Calypso, an embodiment of the anima and the archetypal feminine, invites him into her world.

As a symbol of the anima and the so-called bridge to the

unconscious, Calypso's role is to help Odysseus experience the world from her point of view—from the view of the unconscious. By learning to see the world from this angle, Odysseus transforms and begins to see himself as he really is. In the same way, as we learn to relate to the unconscious, we start to become conscious of the myriad of ways in which our personalities have been distorted, causing us to suffer and wander around lost. As Odysseus comes to understand that he—his ego—is not the center of the psyche, he orients himself toward the psyche's center, which Jung called the *Self* in much of his academic writing—though he referred to *God* in countless other instances. In Greek mythology, all of the gods and goddesses of the pantheon are aspects of the Self—they are the transcendent and divine principles which humans must honor and appreciate.

These various aspects of the *Self* are the archetypes of the collective unconscious, as the likes of Zeus and Athena each embodies unique principles of consciousness that express themselves through us at various times. If I am driven to war, we might say Ares possesses me; If I am driven to love, we might say Aphrodite is inspiring me; If I feel especially heroic, perhaps Heracles has been activated; If I am feeling creative, Hephaestus is acting through me. These are symbolic ways of speaking about the archetypal aspects of consciousness which *move through us.* We do not create them. They exist on their own and have their own life. They are symbols of the forces of consciousness that influence our behavior and our job is to be aware of these energies so that we are not consumed by them or driven to harm. Hillman often encouraged his students to be mindful of what horse they were riding on—in other words, what archetypal form of consciousness is moving through you now? The likes of Circe and Calypso—anima figures —are symbolic embodiments of that aspect of our psyche that makes us aware of what is going on inside of us. Without the inner world perspective afforded us by the anima, we may be oblivious to these spiritual forces that exist in our consciousness and influence us, giving us life. Many of us do not become aware of the spiritual elements of existence until extreme hardship falls upon us, as happened to Odysseus.

Six years after I came home from Iraq, I found myself in a similar situation. I dreamed I was hopping from island to island until I could go no further (like Odysseus), and then I saw the sea turn crimson before me. In that dream, there were two orcas, and there was a vague sense that something happened to one or both of them. The dream had an ominous quality. A few weeks later, a client I worked with through a veterans organization committed suicide, and unfortunately, a couple of mentors at that organization made disparaging comments that suggested something I did, or failed to do, must have contributed to his death. Because of my own depressive dynamics, I was all too ready to accept responsibility and blame myself for his suicide, and this sent me into a tailspin. On one level, I felt as if it was my fault—even though all of the evidence pointed toward the contrary. All of the facts suggested that the limited support I offered him helped him a great deal, while other problems in his life mounted until he couldn't take it anymore.

My own unconscious rejected the unjust and unreasonable position that I was somehow to blame, and it brought about an intense upheaval as it tried to free me from the depressive dynamics that warped my perspective and the tendency to turn against myself. I fell into a terrible, long-lasting episode of anxiety and depression. The emotional demands of navigating the internal conflict between blaming myself and letting in the facts on the ground, along with losing a client, exceeded my capacity to hold it all. Unfortunately, at the time, I didn't understand the deeper reasons for *why* I was suffering. I just thought this was just another PTSD-related crisis, brought on by the suicide. But, there was a lot more happening beneath the surface. Because I was in a complex and my reality was terribly distorted by the workings of maladaptive defenses, I couldn't see I was unfairly blaming myself—and accepting blame that wasn't mine to take.

In the months that followed, other dreams (and symptoms) helped me to become aware that I was unconsciously yielding to these father figures (my colleagues), and that I was taking on emotional baggage that wasn't mine to carry. I think they wanted deeply to believe that their program was infallible—that it was *the* solution to the warrior suicide epidemic. This suicide challenged that notion, upon which rested their belief that they were doing something truly special. The program functioned as an extension of their sense of self. To protect themselves (and their inflated, unrealistic view of the program as being a groundbreaking "cure"), they needed a scapegoat in order to keep their beliefs intact. My perspective of reality was distorted too, and on an unconscious level I felt I needed to be their scapegoat because I (unconsciously) feared another abandonment—like the one I experienced when my dad left when I was four years old. It was a match made in heaven (hell, really), and my unconscious was doing everything it could to free me from the psychological prison I was in.

In the years to follow, I had several big dreams containing orcas, all of which were spiritual in quality and seemed to want to free me from the outdated adaptations that were crippling me. In one of those dreams, an orca in captivity looked sick, like its belly was "boarded up." The dream ended with a woman (an anima figure, like Calypso) coming up out of a stairwell. She pointed at a piece of artwork covered in matted hair, and said, "*Huh, isn't it funny how drunk girls make art?*" Often, dream figures speak in this manner, in accord with their own symbolic language. When I awoke, I immediately associated the matted hair with a horrible trauma I'd experienced where I saw a decapitated woman's body and head. Her matted hair was painfully seared into my memory.

As I reflected on the anima figure's comments, I wondered how drunk girls might make art, and supposed they'd do so quite freely —according to the feeling of the moment rather than the need to be precise or controlled. I took this as a hint, as I had picked up drawing and painting as a hobby, but I tended to create artwork in a controlled, intentional manner. I painted and drew more with my head than my heart. I saw the dream suggesting I try to express my feelings while creating artwork. At the time, I was suffering from severe anxiety—daily panic attacks, intense psychosomatic symptoms, and I often felt my own belly was boarded up, like the orca in the dream. My unconscious was saying, I believe, that my past traumas were causing me to be like this captive orca—in pain and cut off from the world and a life of freedom—and that getting in touch with and expressing my emotions might help set me free. So, I gave it a try.

The next day, when I sat down to paint, I followed the dream's lead, letting my emotions guide me as I settled into my pain, my body, and the memory of the trauma that had been evoked by the dream. I didn't even think about *what* I was painting. I just let the emotion move me. And I wept as I never had before, and for the first time, I happened to paint something I really felt good about. It was one of the most meaningful and therapeutic experiences of my entire life—thanks to the likes of Calypso, the anima figure who led me in the direction I needed to go.

Several years after this, at a point when I was beginning to feel increasingly free from traumatic symptoms, I had another dream that an older woman (another anima figure) took me out on an oceanside pier to see orcas. She invited me down into the water and introduced me to two orcas—the orcas that had been separated years earlier. One of the orcas swam up to me, and when he opened his mouth I saw all of his teeth were broken and he had a metal brace to help him heal. I knew that when orcas are in captivity, they try to chew through their enclosures which breaks their teeth, and so it was clear to me that this was the orca who had been held captive earlier. I felt an enormous sense of compassion and love for this animal, as well as a profound sense of connection. It was as if he was thanking me, and I him. I hugged the huge animal and wept so deeply it woke me from my sleep. This dream didn't need to be interpreted. The experience of the dream was its own medicine—its impact was its purpose and meaning. This dream, in particular, was the single most powerful and important healing experience of my life.

I couldn't have enjoyed these moments of insight and healing if I had not accepted defeat, and learned to surrender—to adopt an attitude of humility and receptivity in relation to the powers of the unconscious. Jung's words below help us to appreciate the need for the ego to endure this sort of death and rebirth. Please note that in this passage, Jung is speaking of the Self as the objective aspect of the psyche, rather than the individual self, or ego personality.

> The self, in its efforts at self-realization, reaches out beyond the ego-personality on all sides; because of its all-encompassing nature it is brighter and darker than the ego, and accordingly confronts it with problems which it would like to avoid. Either one's moral courage fails, or one's insight, or both, until in the end fate decides. … For you only feel yourself on the right road when the conflicts of duty seem to have resolved themselves, and you have become the victim of a decision made over your head or in defiance of the heart. From this we can see the numinous powers of the self, which can hardly be experienced in any other way. For this reason *the experience of the self is always a defeat for the ego.*[132]

In the end, the sum of my experiences during my crisis—in which my symptoms and dreams were guiding me to freedom and the restoration of my true self—amounted to a mystical awakening. In my dreams, such as those with the orcas, I became aware of the wondrous and spiritual realities of the unconscious, as I found myself guided by dreams so poetic and powerful that it was clear their source lay beyond me—that some transcendent force was helping me to heal and transform.

Thanks to Jungian analysis, I was able to make sense of these inner experiences, and they helped to transform my personality. Unhelpful attitudes transformed, wounds healed, defenses fell away, new parts of myself were awakened. Yet, this did not come without hardship. In the midst of my unrelenting grief and sadness on Calypso's island, as it were, I turned to nature, poetry, painting, and journaling, and in the process found that my feelings were ultimately an expression of a longing that could only be satisfied through this sort of inner seeking. I became aware of a whole side of life I'd been ignorant of, and this period of difficulty and challenge amounted to an awakening to and of another half of my soul.

At this point in the story, Odysseus has truly accomplished something. In doing nothing on Calypso's island, he demonstrates his awareness that *action* cannot save him from these circumstances. He accepts his position, stays with his feelings, mourns and grieves. He surrenders to his painful reality, accepting what fate has brought him. And he stays the course, even as days turn to weeks, weeks to months, and months to years. For seven years, he maintains his humility and submits himself to Calypso, allowing himself to be reshaped by her. He does not try to escape, blame, fight, or kill her. The former Odysseus—the pathologically heroic man possessed by the warrior complex—might have delusionally imagined Calypso to be a monster, and might have even tried to kill her, worsening his predicament. Odysseus is a changed man, transformed by the fires of initiation, and finally adapted to successfully make the journey home.

The *Odyssey* is not told in chronological order. It begins with Athena lamenting that Odysseus is stranded with Calypso and her advocating to Zeus for his release. Athena has not been directly involved with Odysseus since his warfighting days in Troy (in the *Iliad*), and she reenters the picture after Odysseus has been on the island with Calypso for seven years.

It is Athena—the goddess associated with wisdom and warfare who was born from the head of Zeus—who initiates Odysseus's release and the final leg of his journey home. She is a prominent counselor to heroes, leading them and assisting them on their journeys, and given this role, she is perhaps the greatest symbol of the anima. Athena waited, I believe, until Odysseus was fully prepared before advocating for his freedom.

From this point on in the chronological unfolding of events, Athena will be a key figure, always offering Odysseus, his wife Penelope, and their son Telemachus whatever help they need. After Athena convinces Zeus to set Odysseus free, she goes to Telemachus to protect him from his mother's suitors who wish to murder him. The two events are related, as Athena must do both to make possible Odysseus's return and reunion with his wife and son.

In response to Athena's request, Zeus sends his messenger, Hermes, to tell Calypso it's time to send Odysseus on his way. This is a defining moment in Odysseus's development, as his stay with Calypso has now brought him into relationship with the gods and goddesses, representing the archetypal powers of the unconscious. Calypso offers Odysseus support so his journey may be fruitful. She shows him the best trees to build his raft and provides the tools to do so. She gives him linen to make the sails and various provisions.

Odysseus sets sail, and all goes well for the first eighteen days, until Poseidon exacts his revenge against Odysseus for blinding his son Polyphemus the Cyclops. Poseidon stirs up a storm, and when Odysseus sees the angry-looking clouds, he says to himself:

> … "what ever will become of me? I am afraid Calypso was right when she said I should have trouble by sea before I got back home. It is all coming true. How black is Zeus making heaven with these clouds, and what a sea the winds are raising from every quarter at once. I am now safe to perish. … Would that I had been killed on the day when the Trojans were pressing me so sorely about the dead body of Achilles, for then I should have had due burial and the Achaeans would have honored my name; but now it seems that I shall come to a most pitiful end."[133]

Calypso warned him, and Odysseus accepted his fate and sailed forth, accepting the potential struggles entailed in answering the call to adventure, to individuation. He is no longer trying to avoid the gods or get around them. He courageously, humbly, and vulnerably places himself at the mercy of Poseidon, to whom he owes a debt for the infraction against his son. Odysseus is accepting responsibility for his previous actions, including the harm he caused, bravely enduring what fate might bring. Poseidon sends a wave that dashes Odysseus's raft.

While Odysseus is being tossed in the waves, the clothes gifted him by Calypso weigh him down, and he's forced to shed them. We have to shed aspects of our old personae when we transition from one situation to another. Our personalities should never be rigid; the attitude that fits one situation may not fit another. Odysseus learned certain ways of being on Calypso's island so he could transform, but he cannot have only one position in all circumstances.

The marine goddess Ino comes to Odysseus's rescue, offering him an enchanted veil that prevents him from drowning. She tells him that as soon as he gets to land, he must throw the veil back into the sea, again stressing the importance of adaptability. As the situation changes, we cannot rely on the same strategy that worked before. While Ino ensures that Odysseus will not drown, Athena actively saves him from being destroyed by the rocks and waves—which serves as evidence that the *Odyssey's* representatives of the archetypal feminine are vital protectors of veterans, which stands in contrast to Shay's position that female figures in the *Odyssey* are all dangerous and untrustworthy.[134]

As Odysseus attentively approaches shore, he feels a current near the mouth of the river, and he prays for the assistance of the god he believes must have some influence over his plight.

"Here me, O king, whoever you may be, and save me from the anger of the sea-god Poseidon, for I approach you prayerfully. Anyone who has lost his way has at all times a claim even upon the gods, wherefore in my distress I draw near to your stream, and cling to your knees of your riverhood. Have mercy upon me, O king, for I declare myself your suppliant." Then the god stayed the stream and stilled the waves, making all calm before him, and bringing him safely into the mouth of the river. Here at last Odysseus' knees and strong hands failed him, for the sea had completely broken him. His body was all swollen, and his mouth and nostrils ran down like a river with sea-water, so that he could neither breathe nor speak, and lay swooning from sheer exhaustion. Presently, when he got his breath and came to himself again, he took off the scarf that Ino had given him and threw it back into the salt stream of the river, whereon Ino received it into her hands ...[135]

Here we have more evidence how far Odysseus has come. He no longer relies only on his own strength, trying to do things by force without consideration of other powers that can sway us. He pays attention to the currents of life, noticing the subtle movements beneath the surface. He is attuned to the unconscious. In noticing there are forces at work he must respect, Odysseus beseeches the gods (archetypes of the unconscious), adopting a position of humility, mindful of whose terrain he's in, and he successfully navigates the currents.

Although completely spent, Odysseus remembers to honor the gods and keep his promises. In former days, he might have run away with Ino's scarf and to use for selfish purposes or bragging rights. He has clearly changed. He now knows how to relate appropriately to the unconscious and is able to endure and suffer through the inevitable hardships that come when we do so. The gods and goddesses have returned and become central forces in his life, evidenced by the emergence of Athena, Hermes, and Zeus in this part of the story. His shipwreck has done him some good, as our suffering sometimes does. Author and Jungian analyst June Singer discussed this vital and common experience in the individuation process:

> When the ego is barred from achieving the task it has set for itself through the intervention of passion, impotence, pain or death, it must realize that it is not the supreme directing force in the human personality; it finds out that it is confronting a more powerful entity. When individuals bow before the awesome order of nature and realize that they cannot subdue it, that the best they can hope for is to discover the ways of learning its laws and functioning in accordance with them, then they know that they are fac-

ing a greater entity.[136]

-9-

REMEMBERING AND THE
RETURN TO ITHACA

It is as though, at the climax of illness, the destructive powers were converted into healing forces. This is brought about by the archetypes awakening to independent life and taking over the guidance of the psychic personality, thus supplanting the ego with its futile willing and striving. … the psyche has awakened to spontaneous activity. … something that is not his ego and is therefore beyond the reach of his personal will. He has regained access to the sources of psychic life, and this marks the beginning of the cure.

— C.G. Jung[137]

When Odysseus arrives on yet another foreign shore, he is cold and naked—laid bare so he must again find clothing that is suitable for yet another situation. Exhausted, he enters into the forest to make a bed for himself in the leaves, and the goddess Athena cares for him as she "shed a sweet sleep upon his eyes, closed his eyelids, and made him lose all memory of his sorrows."[138] Though he does not yet know it, the ever-resilient Odysseus has passed from the realm of mythical creatures, ghosts, gods and goddesses to that of the Phaeacians—a noble *people.* He is in the world of men and women for the first time since he raided the people of Ismarus, suggesting that all his trials since then have been *inner* conflicts and struggles.

Since he angered Zeus with his behavior at Ismarus, he hasn't been among humans. After a long immersion in his inner world, the anima—embodied in Circe and Calypso—has helped him mature and transform enough that is appropriate for him to once again focus on outer goals. Here, we see Athena come to the fore.

Athene began to consider how Odysseus should wake up and see the handsome girl [Princess Nausicaa] who was to conduct him to the city of the Phaeacians. The girl, therefore, threw a ball at one of the maids, which missed her and fell into deep water. On this they all shouted, and the noise they made woke Odysseus, who sat up in his bed of leaves and began to wonder what it might all be.

"Alas," said he to himself, "what kind of people have I come among? Are they cruel, savage, and uncivilized, or hospitable and humane? I seem to hear the voices of young women, and they sound like those of the nymphs that haunt mountain tops, or springs of rivers and meadows of green grass. At any rate I am among a race of men and women. Let me try if I cannot manage to get a look at them." As he said this he crept from under his bush, and broke off a bough covered with thick leaves to hide his nakedness. He looked like some lion of the wilderness that stalks about exulting his strength and defying both wind and rain; his eyes glare as he prowls in quest of oxen, sheep, or deer, for he is famished, and will dare break even into a well-fenced homestead, trying to get at the sheep—even such did Odysseus seem to the young women, as he drew near to them all naked as he was, for he was in great want. On seeing one so unkempt and so begrimed with salt water, the others scampered off along the spits that jutted out into the sea, but the daughter of Alcinous [Princess Nausicaa] stood firm, for Athene had put courage into her heart ...[139]

This initial encounter between Odysseus and Princess Nausicaa is resonant with other mythological motifs. In *The Frog Prince*, a princess drops her precious golden ball (symbolizing psychic energy) into a well, and only a slimy frog (who is actually a handsome prince whose identity is distorted due to a spell) can retrieve it. The frog symbolizes the shadow, the seemingly primitive unconscious and undeveloped contents. Only by relating to the frog (shadow) appropriately is the handsome prince restored to his true state and identity, enriching the princess in the process.

In *Iron John*, a young prince loses his golden ball and only the wild, hairy man, Iron John (another shadow figure), can give it back to him. Iron John is also found in a body of water (symbolizing the unconscious). By the end of the story, Iron John is restored to his true identity as a wealthy baron, and he shares all his wealth with the prince. The message is the same. When we lose our precious psychic energy (via a regressive experience) and find ourselves at an impasse, progress isn't possible until we integrate aspects of shadow, broadening our personality and leading to a new adaptation.

In this part of the *Odyssey*, Odysseus appears as a wild, primitive man—a shadow figure from the viewpoint of Princess Nausicaa. We unkempt, wild, ferocious, rude, and uncivilized veterans may represent shadow for civilians, while tamed and respectable civilians may represent the shadows of veterans.

This story can help veterans navigate our inner worlds as we come home, and it can help civilians navigate their inner worlds and relationships with veterans, because the warriors that civilians must relate with have been immersed in realms of experience they could never adequately imagine. For the relationships between veterans and the civilians in their lives to work (whether spouses, family members, friends, coworkers, or therapists), both parties must do inner work. The relationship cannot afford for either side to fail to see the other by only projecting (and not re-collecting) their own shadows.

Because of our sometimes unruly behavior, veterans can be easy scapegoats that help some civilians avoid their own shadows. In believing veterans are the ones with the problems that need to be fixed, civilians make veterans the *identified patient*, the person in a system (such as a family system) who is the one who has the problem, while the reality is far more complex. This has been the case for a several of my veteran clients, who were in reality rather healthy. When their spouses demanded they get therapy, they did. They made good use of therapy, making tremendous personal strides that resolved a number of challenges they independently faced. What these veterans could not do, however, was fix their spouses, who needed to do a significant amount of personal work —and who, ironically, would not. When these veterans entered into marriage counseling with their partners, the marriage therapists agreed the spouses had their own work to do. One spouse was willing, but two others (who had significant, unresolved issues, including potential personality disorders) would not. The latter two were convinced their husbands were the problem. While these men were (like all of us) imperfect, they were in no way responsible for all the conflict in the family, despite the opinions of their partners. It was unfortunate that these veterans had to carry the burden of their spouses' projections, on top of everything else they carried. Veterans have challenges, plenty of them. And then when others project their own shadows onto us, we're saddled with additional problems.

Marie Louise Von Franz, Jung's student and colleague, wrote, "The projections of our fellow beings onto our selves are by no means harmless affairs that disturb nothing but the adaptation of the people from whom they issue; they also substantially affect the person onto whom the projection falls."[140] As we veterans are forced to carry the burden of civilians' projections, we become prone to *projective identification*—acting out the role that is expected of us, either as "good boy" heroes or "bad boy" dysfunctional vets. It takes a village to sort out what is whose, and to see the gray-scale reality that veterans and civilians are both heroes and villains, functional and dysfunctional.

When veterans carry others' projections, we have several options: We can live out the nasty projections and become scapegoats, carrying the burdens of war and its aftermath, letting civilians off the hook. Or we can accept the hero projection, and play out that role, receiving praise along the way. This can be maintained as long as the unconscious does not subvert the heroic ego and shred the mask. A third option is to rebel and completely disidentify from one's military history. A good friend of mine has chosen this option. He'd rather avoid the possibility of being perceived as a veteran—thus avoiding potential projections for being one. I respect his position and its protective function, though I do believe there's a cost to disowning a part of our history and identity. Whether we like it or not, it will always remain a part of us.

If we can resist the influence of these projections, it can relieve us of burdens that aren't ours to carry. Whether we feel compelled to be the "good boy" hero, or to internalize the feeling of being the "broken" or "bad boy" dysfunctional veteran, we must try to not let ourselves be corrupted by the projections that are hurled our way. Ultimately, this is the work of remembering and learning to own aspects of ourselves we have a hard time being with.

Veterans cannot do all this work on their own. Inner work, transformation, and healing cannot be just the burden of the returning warrior. The society and individuals who sent these veterans away, directly and by proxy, to do their fighting and killing, need to share the burden and responsibility of helping veterans make this transition, and one of the most important aspects of this process is for civilians to own their own shadows and their own suffering.

There are at least two perspectives to consider in the encounter between Odysseus and Princess Nausicaa so that relationships (inner and outer) can be repaired—that of veterans and that of civilians (in this case, women) who must learn how to relate to the likes of Odysseus. Nausicaa not only represents an inner aspect of Odysseus, but she also represents a unique individual who has her own perspective. Likewise, Odysseus is a symbol of the veteran's ego, and he also represents the civilian's shadow. It is critical that veterans don't pathologically project their shadows onto civilians or their wives, and it's equally critical that loved ones and civilians don't project their shadows onto veterans. Inevitably this will happen, and we must be conscious of the tendency and learn to withdraw our projections as we search inside ourselves to see what disavowed qualities in us are being revealed. Odysseus is trying to sort this out when he asks Nausicaa if she is a goddess or a mortal woman. In other words "Am I projecting *goddess* onto you, or are you an actual, human person?"

"O queen," he said, "I implore your aid—but tell me, are you a goddess or are you a mortal woman? … I dare not clasp your knees, but I am in great distress; yesterday made the twentieth day that I had been tossing about upon the sea. … and now fate has flung me upon this coast that I may endure still further suffering; …" To this Nausicaa answered: "Stranger, you appear to be a sensible, well-disposed person. … Now, however, that you have come to this our country, you shall not want for clothes or for anything else that a foreigner in distress may reasonably look for. I will show you the way to the town … I am daughter to [King] Alcinous, in whom the whole power of the state is vested." … They [the maids] made Odysseus sit down in the shelter as Nausicaa had told them, and brought him a shirt and cloak. ... [Nausicaa said,] "If therefore you want my father to give you an escort and to help you home, do as I bid you. ... When you have got past the gates and go through the outer court, go right across the inner court till you come to my mother. You will find her sitting by the fire and spinning her purple wool by firelight. ... Close to her seat stands that of my father, on which he sits and topes like an immortal god. Never mind him, but go up to my mother and lay your hands upon her knees, if you would get home quickly. If you can gain her over, you may hope to see your own country again, no matter how distant it may be."[141]

When Odysseus and his men landed at Telepylos, the city of the Laestrygonians, the same motif unfolded. With both the Laestrygonians and the Phaeacians, the first person Odysseus encounters is a princess, and in both situations, the princess has been sent down to the water on an errand (Nausicaa to wash clothes and linens in the river, the Laestrygonian princess to draw water). And in both cases, the princess tells Odysseus how to get to the home of the king and queen.

Through the lens of Jung's theory, the anima (princess)—with her inherent connection to the unconscious (water)—is the gateway to the Self (the king and queen), the royal union of opposites. The first time 'round, with the Laestrygonians, the imagery suggests something primitive and destructive at work, but this time we see healthier, more promising dynamics. Jungians note that throughout the individuation process, it's common to encounter the same problems as previously, more deeply each time—this is referred to as *circumambulation of the Self* as we circle around the psyche's objective center, working through what we missed the last time around. As we develop and mature, so does our capacity to navigate the tasks before us.

It is significant that the earlier encounter ended disastrously, and Odysseus is now getting a second chance. The first time, he was not yet ready to enter this sacred realm. Now he is. He has become increasingly conscious, and as a result, destructive dynamics are less likely to occur. This motif is reminiscent of *The Grail Myth*. The home of the Laestrygonian king and queen in the *Odyssey* is like the Grail Castle, as presented in Chretien de Troyes' *Perceval ou le Conte du Graael* (*Perceval, the Story of the Grail*), and in Wolfram von Eschenbach's *Parzival*.[142] Parsifal, like Odysseus, is unable to navigate his first encounter at the castle, and like Odysseus, he is forced to wander for many years and undergo many challenges before he can return and have a second chance. To make his return possible, Parsifal must learn to relate to the "Hideous Damsel," an undesirable woman who prescribes an experience of suffering, like Calypso. Unlike the Hideous Damsel, Calypso is beautiful, but to experience either of these women brings suffering, *along with transformation*. Their impact on the two heroes is the same. Parsifal and Odysseus both suffer, are humbled, and continue on solitary paths to individuation.[143]

Like Parsifal, Odysseus is a different man when he arrives at the court of the king and queen for the second time. He has been changed by his experiences, especially through his suffering and through his contact with the archetypal feminine and anima. Now he knows how to relate to the anima (the princess), and he takes a position of vulnerability and humility. Odysseus has been stripped bare. He has no clothing, no strength, and no men beside him. *He's on his own—on his own path, submitting to unconscious via the anima and seeking her direction.* He has been transformed by suffering and learned to follow the direction of the unconscious.

Odysseus is able to progress and meet the king and queen because he has attained familiarity with the demands of his inner world. With Athena's help, he enters the town under a shroud of mist to prevent him from facing additional hardships while he conducts his important task, following Princess Nausicaa's instructions exactly.

[Odysseus] went straight through the court, still hidden by the cloak of darkness in which Athene had enveloped him, till he reached [Queen] Arete and King Alcinous; then he laid his hands upon the knees of the queen, and at that moment the miraculous darkness fell away from him and he became visible. Everyone was speechless with surprise at seeing a man there, but Odysseus began at once with his petition. " ... help me home to my own country as soon as possible; for I have been long in trouble and away from my friends." Then he sat down on the hearth among the ashes [a humble place, where Greek supplicants asked for mercy], and they all held their peace

He must pay homage to and approach the queen, not the king, which is symbolically significant. The queen embodies the feminine principle which had previously been neglected in his former life as a warrior, and she possesses all of those qualities which he had been so desperately lacking before he encountered Circe and Calypso. In kneeling before her and asking for her blessing, he adopts a humble, receptive position that makes possible his return. Veterans must always honor their inner queen, recognizing that the qualities she embodies make them psychologically and emotionally flexible enough to navigate the inherent challenges that come with warriorhood.

In seeing Odysseus's humility, an old hero named Echeneus asks King Alcinous to take Odysseus from his humble place among the ashes and have him seated in a place of honor—in the place of the king's favorite son, which Alcinous does readily. Odysseus is treated as if he were a king, and Alcinous promises to escort him back to Ithaca without further trouble.

After dinner, Queen Arete speaks up, asking Odysseus who he is, where he came from, and how he got his clothes, because she recognizes that her daughter must have given them to him. Does she doubt his character? Is this a test to see if he will reveal what she knows must be true? The former Odysseus may have concealed the reality of things, but this time he tells the truth and *begins* to share his story, starting with Calypso and ending with Princess Nausicaa helping him and giving him the clothes. Odysseus passes the trial, earning the respect, concern, and care of both queen and king. Importantly, Odysseus never discloses his name. He remains an unidentified traveler.

The following day, King Alcinous orders a ship be made ready for Odysseus's voyage home, and he presents the bard Demodocus, who entertains all present by singing great tales—tales Odysseus knows because he has lived them.

The company then laid their hands upon the good things that were before them, but as soon as they had had enough to eat and drink, the muse inspired Demodocus to sing the feats of heroes, and more especially a matter that was then in the mouths of all men, to wit, the quarrel between Odysseus and Achilles, and the fierce words they heaped on one another as they sat together at a banquet. But Agamemnon was glad when he heard his chieftains quarreling with one another, for Apollo had foretold him this at Pytho when he crossed the stone floor to consult the oracle. Here was the beginning of the evil that by the will of Zeus fell both upon Danaans [the Greeks] and Trojans.

> Thus sang the bard, but Odysseus drew his purple mantle over his head and covered his face, for he was ashamed to let the Phaeacians see that he was weeping. When the bard left off singing, he wiped the tears from his eyes, uncovered his face, and, taking his cup, made a drink offering to the gods ... then Odysseus again drew his mantle over his head and wept bitterly. No one noticed his distress except Alcinous, who was sitting near him, and

heard the heavy sighs that he was heaving.[145]

Alcinous sees that the story is affecting the stranger, and so he calls off Demodocus and redirects all his guests toward games and sports. Odysseus initially refuses to join in, although he is taunted. He responds:

> Laodamas, why do you taunt me in this way? My mind is set rather on cares than contests; I have been through infinite trouble, and am come among you now as a supplicant, praying your king and people to further me on my return home.[146]

Odysseus is not the prideful, competitive soul he once was; his heart is focused on his inner world, and returning home. A man named Euryalus approaches and insults Odysseus, saying he is probably not skilled in athletics anyway. Euryalus assumes Odysseus to be a weak and spoiled merchant or trader. This offensive comment brings old fighting Odysseus out of the unconscious, where he sits ready in case he is needed—and given the offense here, it seems more than appropriate for Odysseus to stand up for himself. This is important, because it is a mistake to assume that an initiation into the realm of the feminine means we are now cut off from our masculinity, our capacity to be firm and even violent if we are attacked. Odysseus does not turn violent, however. He responds intelligently, though firmly, holding the tension between opposites.

> "For shame, sir!" answered Odysseus, fiercely. "You are an insolent fellow! … Your ill-judged remarks have made me exceedingly angry, and you are quite mistaken, for I excel in a great many athletic exercises. Indeed, so long as I had youth and strength, I was among the first athletes of the age. Now, however, I am worn out by labor and sorrow, for I have gone through much both on the field of battle and by the waves of the weary sea. Still, in spite of all this I will compete, for your taunts have strung me to the quick."[147]

Odysseus asserts himself and competes, refusing to be disrespected or belittled. He defeats the competition easily, proving that although he's been immersed in the realm of the feminine, he can still be a hard-ass when necessary. Veterans need to know this: *Balance* is essential. No energy—feminine or masculine—is healthy in either its repressed or its unrestrained state. We need access to both; each must be balanced by its opposite. Psychological adaptability and flexibility are the foundations of resilience, making us capable of enduring difficulties and navigating a wide variety of different types of challenges. Mature warriors can fight *and* mourn, act with violence *and* compassion, overcome *and* surrender. However, warriors must also be wise enough and emotionally mature enough to know when it is time to take one approach rather than another. Here, Odysseus expresses his masculinity in a mature form, versus just lashing out in rage, as he likely would have had such an encounter occurred earlier on in his journey.

You might ask, how do we know when we've found the balance? As always in matters of the psyche, ego's judgment is subjective, so we must look to messages from dreams. "Hermes" conveys objective, psychic reality. Consider this dream:

The Tension Between Opposites

I'm driving in the country and see a dust devil coming from a power line, where there is a positive and negative charge. Then I see a small tornado followed by a second one. Both have descended from clouds where half the cloud is in shadow and half in sunlight. Thus, the balance of light and shadow creates a vortex and rotation. … Soon I'm with my father-in-law [who is quite rugged and masculine]. He gathers some primitive weapons and tools, spears and such, to go hunting. I am to help him. As we go outside, we see a female lion. I check behind us and a big male lion threatens us from the rear. As I turn to face the male lion, it backs off. We're stuck between the male and the female.

We retreat back to the house which the female has entered, and I try to keep the male out but it barges in despite my best efforts. I arm myself with a knife and I plan to kill the big male with my bare hands if I must. Instead, I end up in an unexpected struggle with the female lion. It has transformed into a small brown brindle-coated animal, like a dog or a pig—very ambiguous, as if it were both at once. It seems mythical, and reminds me of my brother-in-law's dog. In any case it seems it must be killed. *It is what we must do*, even though I do not want to. I grab a knife and stab the animal in the throat, delivering a terrible wound, but it's not enough and I do it again. Deep and terrible but still not enough. I tell my father-in-law that I need his help. He coaches me and tells me I can do it. "Lower, and slide the knife across," he tells me. I dig in and make the long deep cut, opening up the animal's throat. Blood is spilling out. It'll be over soon. I begin to cry. I hate killing. I am so upset. I put the knife down and walk away. At the end of the dream, there's a keen awareness that the male lion is now loose in the house, but this doesn't necessarily seem like a bad thing.

I was deeply upset when I had this dream, but a synchronicity (a meaningful coincidence which Jung notes tend to happen at key moments, as if by design, rather than mere chance) occurred that same day that brought a great deal of relief. I was reading a book by Joseph Campbell, and happened upon a passage in which he discussed the initiation rights for males in Melanesia. In this particular culture, boys are made to raise a pet pig (hence, the ambiguity between the pig and dog in the dream) which they must eventually sacrifice. Throughout their lives, these men repeat the same initiation rite at various life stages, sacrificing another pet pig at each stage.[148] This dream, and the synchronicity of stumbling onto this passage in which the dream's meaning was brought to me, made clear that I had undergone an initiation rite, passing from one stage to the next.

Appropriately, this dream happened to come at the exact time I was completing my master's program, which was in itself an initiation into the realm of the feminine and unconscious, given the nature of the curriculum, the challenges I faced in my life throughout that period, and the fact that nearly all my classmates were mature, supportive women. These women had an enormous impact on me because of the ways in which they challenged my view of things and showed me another way of seeing and being in the world. Because of the experiential nature of this program and its focus in depth psychology, my female classmates also taught me how to hold my suffering in ways that would have been difficult to learn without their support and modeling. A lot of it was subtle— the way they spoke softly when I was hurting, which taught me how to speak to myself, and how they wept and surrendered to their own pain with such courage. Now, when I feel anxious or afraid, it's often their voices I hear.

Two other key and related aspects of the dream are the balance of the opposites (positive and negative, light and shadow, male and female) and a rotation of energy. In the dream, I am with my rugged and masculine father-in-law, who represents an aspect of shadow within me—the once dominant masculine qualities in my personality that had been relegated to the unconscious during my lengthy and necessary initiation into the world of the feminine (my stay on Calypso's island, as it were). In the dream, I initially target the male lion, thinking he is the threat, which mirrored my own suspicion toward what I perceived as hypermasculine males—something I had been myself. Yet, in the dream, I'm unexpectedly forced to face and sacrifice the female lion, as it was time for me to step out of the realm of the feminine and take up a more balanced position. Though difficult for me and extremely sad because of its significant positive impact on my life, it was apparently necessary. The dream's *lysis* or end comes with the male lion—the masculine principle—free in the house. A shift of energy has occurred, leading to the next stage of my individuation process.

This is where we find Odysseus—newly emerged from the world of the feminine but happily reclaiming his masculine prowess, easily overcoming the other men who stand in competition against him. He goes so far as to proclaim, "I am a good hand at every kind of athletic sport known among mankind. I am an excellent archer. In battle I am always the first to bring a man down with my arrow… when we Achaeans were before Troy …"[149] Odysseus makes this bold claim in the presence of the king *and* the queen—the sacred, royal unity of the opposites. This undoubtedly captures the attention and curiosity of King Alcinous, who after the games helps the party transition back to the tales sung by the bard, Demodocus.

Fittingly, Demodocus sings about "the loves of Ares and Aph-rodite"—the rage-filled god of war and the sensuous, beauty-loving goddess of love. Again, we have a union of opposites. This story progresses with limping Hephaestus, Aphrodite's husband (who has a terrible leg wound—like both Odysseus and the Fisher King whom Parsifal encounters in his quest for the Holy Grail), capturing the lovers. This prompts Apollo to declare, "Ill deeds do not prosper, and the weak confound the strong. See how limping Hephaestus, lame as he is, has caught Ares, who is the fleetest god in heaven …"[150] This seems to suggest that one who is in touch with his wounds can overcome the influence of the god of war.

Remember, Odysseus, like Hephaestus (and the Fisher King), has a leg wound. Odysseus's wound does not cause him to literally limp, though his wounds of war have caused him to hobble figuratively from place to place for the better part of a decade. Thus, Odysseus is identified with Hephaestus in this part of the myth, suggesting he is finally grasping the nature of the dichotomic and yet united relationship between Aphrodite, the goddess of love, and Ares, the god of war. Hephaestus—despite his woundedness—has been able to grasp both of these powerful opposites and produce a resolution, restoring justice. Since Odysseus is identified with Hephaestus through his own qualities (the leg wound, his cunning nature, and his own difficulties with love and war), this suggests he is coming into a deep awareness of how these forces and his own experiences have influenced him. Ultimately, this is a task for all veterans, as we seek to understand the nature of our passion and desire for war, love, and finding meaning in the wounds we carry.

Love and war exist hand-in-hand—some of the greatest acts of love I have ever witnessed occurred in the midst of hellish battles, and remembering these beautiful but painful moments brings tears to my eyes, even now. One does not offer his life up as a sacrifice, exposing himself to the risk of death, for a platoonmate, comrade, or country, unless love is present and profound. And we cannot forget the role love played in starting the Trojan War, as Aphrodite lured Paris to choose her over Athena and Hera, and she did so by promising Paris the love of Helen of Troy. In singing "the loves of Ares and Aphrodite," Demodocus evokes the memory of how Aphrodite (love) led Odysseus and the other Trojans into the realm of Ares (war), whose influence reshaped Odysseus's psyche.

I want to amplify the leg wound motif a bit further, because it leads us deeper into this portion of the *Odyssey*. As I've mentioned, in the tales of Parsifal and the Grail, the Fisher King also has a leg wound. The Fisher King's wound has left him infirm and emasculated, without the ability to produce new life. Like him his land is also infertile, a wasteland—as Odysseus's kingdom is becoming in his absence with the suitors threatening to overtake his kingdom. There is a curious thing about the Fisher King's wound, though— if someone would just be compassionate enough to ask about the king's sorrow, the king's wound and his land would be healed. This is the Grail Knight's task—and this is the fate of young Parsifal, *perce le val* (in French), which means through the middle—in other words, between the pairs of opposites.[151]

There come times when we must be prepared to step into one world or the other, the masculine or the feminine, knowing which energy is called for in a given situation. Odysseus has now achieved this capacity, and appropriately, at this point in the story he receives important gifts from both masculine and feminine figures. The first gift is from Euryalus, the man who offended him and drew him into competition, luring out his unconscious capacity for masculine ferocity, and therefore Euryalus can be understood as a shadow figure. Euryalus gifts Odysseus with a beautiful sword, a symbol of masculinity, which can be used not only to assert power, but also to delineate, separate, and discern as needed. We might remember that he hasn't had a sword since his ship wrecked on Calypso's island, so this might represent a retrieval of a masculine aspect of the psyche that had become dormant.

The second gift comes from King Alcinous, who presents Odysseus with a golden goblet, not unlike later medieval conceptions of the grail—which Campbell says is that which "can transmute the life of the world into the golden life of the spirit. ... the vessel of plenty, a symbol of the spiritual conduit that carries the inexhaustible of the eternal into the inexhaustible forms of the temporal world."[152] Meanwhile, Queen Arete prepares a chest of gifts and a warm bath. Like his bath on Circe's island, it comes at a time when a union between opposites is needed, or perhaps being affirmed, and Homer evokes the names of both Circe and Calypso as Odysseus is bathed. As noted, the bath is present in other mythological motifs of returning warriors, including the Celtic hero Cúchulainn, and in alchemical imagery. It's also fitting that just after Odysseus's bath, Princess Nausicaa greets him and they exchange pleasantries and a farewell.

After bathing, Odysseus takes his seat next to King Alcinous, and when dinner is served, Odysseus cuts off a piece of pork from his own plate and has a servant take it to the bard Demodocus. After they've finished eating, Odysseus goes to Demodocus and tells him how much he appreciates his tales, praising him for his accuracy. Odysseus then makes a special request, asking Demodocus if he will sing of the final battle of the Trojan War and Trojan Horse (which the Greeks used to sneak into Troy to defeat the Trojans), as well as Odysseus's role in this adventure. While everyone at the dinner is familiar with this tale and its heroes, no one knows that their guest is Odysseus himself, a major combatant in the Trojan War and especially that final battle. So, "the bard inspired of heaven," Demodocus, sings of Odysseus's quest that led to the end of the war. This is perhaps one of the most important, powerful, and emotionally evocative segments of the myth:

Anon he sang how the songs of the Achaeans issued from the horse, and sacked the town, breaking out from their ambuscade. He sang how they overran the city hither and tither and ravaged it, and how Odysseus went raging like Ares along with Menelaus to the house of Deïphobus. It was there that the fight raged most furiously, nevertheless by Athene's help he was victorious.

All this he told, but Odysseus was overcome as he heard him, and his cheeks were wet with tears. He wept as a woman weeps when she throws herself on the body of her husband who has fallen before his own city and people, fighting bravely in defense of his home and children. She screams aloud and flings her arms about him as he lies gasping for breath and dying, but her enemies beat her from behind about the back and shoulders, and carry her off into slavery, to a life of labor and sorrow, and the beauty fades from her cheeks. Even so piteously did Odysseus weep, but none of those present perceived his tears except Alcinous, who was sitting near him, and could hear the sobs and sighs that he was heaving.[153]

Hearing his exploits in battle sung by the bard, Odysseus weeps—like the women whose grief and devastation he caused. Before, while at war, he raged like Ares, bringing an end to the sacred, precious connection of love between the Trojan men and women. He took away a divine gift that only Aphrodite can grant, and there can be no doubt that this haunts and tortures him. Odysseus saw the pain his actions caused, perhaps for the first time at this banquet, and he mourns the burden he has been carrying all this time. It's significant that he was the one who requested this tale be told. This sacred setting presented an opportunity that he felt he had to lean into.

This is a profoundly important part of his healing process. From a therapeutic perspective, this is a potent image of remembering (re-membering), reexperiencing, and catharsis. It is a painful but important expression of grief, as the past is pieced back together and evoked in the present moment, full of the feeling that was necessarily absent in the moment of trauma. This kind of healing—remembering the past—necessitates a remembering of all the sensations and emotions that had to be split off and dissociated to protect Odysseus from the unbearable pain and terror of the event itself. Odysseus is cathartically finding himself in his own personal myth, undergoing an ancient form of psychotherapy.

Odysseus's suffering touches King Alcinous, causing him to call off Demodocus again. Rather than ignoring Odysseus's pain and pretending he doesn't see it (as many people would and do when they see warriors who are experiencing sadness), Alcinous turns to address the entire party, drawing attention to the pain of their guest. We might imagine that Odysseus was terrified, even mortified, to have the king point out that he's weeping. But, perhaps he was tired of having to hide his pain and true identity. Perhaps he was glad to have someone *finally* acknowledge the pain he's been carrying in secret, and to have it brought into the room where he can be joined by others who can help him bear it. As long as combat veterans hide their pain while they're pitied or extolled by emotionally avoidant communities, we remain isolated. Civilians must not shy away from the pain we carry on their behalf. They bear a responsibility for the war itself, they sent us to war, and they are in a position to help those who served heal.

Alcinous does something brave and necessary by acknowledging that Odysseus is carrying a burden all of them ought to be carrying with him, and at this point he asks Odysseus what connection he has to the story. He asks for his name, where he is from, where he has been, and what he has endured. He makes it clear that he asks to know his guest's story because he cares, not just out of curiosity. These are the things Alcinous and his people must know, so they can support Odysseus better and help him get home. This action by Alcinous is reminiscent of what Parsifal does—and must do—in order to heal the Grail King of his chronic pain and suffering—he has the courage and compassion to ask the wounded hero about his sorrow.

Part of Odysseus's homecoming—and that of today's veterans—requires an exchange like this, where civilians hold their fair share of war's costs by bearing witness to the tales of war and suffering. In our society, this happens primarily in private, secretly, behind closed doors, between patient and therapist. However, there are some venues where veterans are invited to do this, and in my opinion, the more intimate they are, the better. The manner in which one's story is told is vitally important. We have to find ways to get therapy out of the therapy room and into the world, as James Hillman advocated for, so that veterans can truly be unburdened. So long as their suffering remains *their personal problem* to be worked out in private, reintegration and homecoming remains a solo task that leave veterans isolated, bearing all of the projections and burdens heaped upon them by civilians. Whether they are seen as baby killers or heroes, veterans are harmed by the shadow projections they are forced to carry, nasty or positive. While veterans have received a distinctive mark that will never leave them, it is also essential that they become peers to civilians and be seen as merely human, like everyone else, full of paradox, with hard and soft spots, and in need of love, caring, and support.

At this vital point in his journey, Odysseus finally shares his identity —his name and his story of loss, heartache, mistakes, longing, and transformation, from Ismarus to Calypso and finally to his shipwreck on their shore. As mentioned, I've been sharing

Odysseus's tale in this book chronologically, in the order that Odysseus lived these events, but the reader of the *Odyssey* only learns these details of his life's journey in Book 8, when Odysseus recounts them to the Phaeacians. Sharing one's story is an essential part of every veteran's homecoming, and it is a story that cannot completely be told until the veteran learns to see his or her trials as part of a coherent narrative, weaving together inner and outer experiences to find their meaning and purpose. Being able to see one's experiences in this way is only possible after an initiation into the world of the feminine—the anima—who makes inner sight possible. Without the perspective of our inner dimensions, our *story* is just a shadow of the reality. Odysseus's narrative brings the realities of his inner world into the waking one, tying the two together in a way that makes his return home possible.

Marlantes notes the same themes—the importance of civilians welcoming warriors home and hearing their stories to help them return and heal.

Metaphorically, veterans should be encouraged to sing. [Jungian analyst] Joseph Henderson once showed me a collection of paintings in his home that were copied from pollen drawings made by a Navajo shaman. He walked me through the story of two brothers who went on a journey to find their father, the Sun. Their father armed them, and they became warriors and fought the wild monsters threatening their tribe. The paintings showed bolts of lightning and vibrant energy coming off the brothers when they returned to their village. The villagers were afraid of them and told them to leave. Sky Woman took them in and taught them to sing of their adventures. When they had made up their songs and sang them to the people, the people were no longer afraid. This book is my song. Each and every one of us veterans must have a song to sing about our war before we can walk back into the community without everyone, including the king, quaking behind the walls. Perhaps it is drawing pictures or reciting poetry about the war. Perhaps it is getting together with a small group and telling stories. Perhaps it is dreaming about it and writing dreams down and then telling people your dreams. But it isn't enough just to do the art in solitude and sing the song alone. You must sing it to other people. Those who are afraid and uneasy must hear it. They must see the art. They must lose their fear. When the child asks, "What is it like to go to war?" to remain silent keeps you from coming home.[154]

In Marlantes's recounting of the Navajo twin brother motif, we see again an example of the archetype of the warrior's return, where an anima figure makes it possible for painful inner realities to be seen, understood, and translated into expression. Without her assistance, no return is possible. As the Sky Mother helped the Navajo twin brothers through this process from isolation to connection, so do the many female figures in the Odyssey, including Circe, Calypso, Athena, Princess Nausicaa, and Queen Arete, to whom he had to appeal in order to find acceptance with the Phaeacians.

After hearing Odysseus's story, where he is open and honest about his pain and suffering, the Phaeacians load him up with gifts and prepare to send him sailing home. *There are golden gifts in our wounds, if we have the courage to face them and share them with the world.* As the ship departed, Odysseus fell asleep—"into a deep, sweet, almost deathlike slumber."[155] Alcinous told Odysseus that their ships have no pilots and no rudders, and that the ships are guided by an inner knowledge that senses what its passengers think and want, and that when traveling on these ships, there is no danger of being wrecked or coming to harm.[156]

Similarly, a client of mine once shared a dream where he was being driven across the sea on a boat, just like this—without sails or rowers. The magical ship drew him over the ocean and into a cave, where he entered into what he described as an atrium. He used the word according to its architectural definition, but being a former medic, I had to point out that the atrium is also a chamber of the heart. This man was being led by a transcendent force in the unconscious to the sacred core of his soul.

The Phaeacians take the sleeping Odysseus and all of the treasures gifted to him and place him on the shore at the base of an olive tree in a harbor near where a merman named Phorcys and nymphs called the Naiads live. The presence of the olive tree again evokes the archetype of the cosmic tree or *axis mundi*. As Jungian psychotherapist C. Michael Smith noted, this symbol is common in motifs related to healing and soul retrieval, and that is exactly where this story is going.[157]

-10-

FREEDOM FROM THE SUITORS & RESTORATION OF THE KINGDOM

Sailing *home*, understood psychologically, is not a matter of effort as much as something that takes place when particular inner conditions are met. Earlier in the tale, after receiving the bag of winds from Aeolus, Odysseus tried his damnedest to get back to Ithaca, but it did him no good. He fell asleep, and destructive, unconscious elements of his own psyche (symbolized by his men) thwarted his efforts. This time, leaving Phaeacia, he has abandoned his former ways of heroic and compulsive *efforting* to complete tasks, and he simply surrenders to the realm of dreams while the Phaeacians sail him home. He has learned to trust in the guidance of the unconscious to lead him where he needs to be.

His inner world is now characterized by a far greater degree of wholeness and balance, and as a result, when he opens his eyes again *he is home*. In Jungian psychology, it is widely observed that people will often dream of trying to get home. This is a fitting metaphor for our efforts to heal and realize our true selves—to *come home* to who we really are, beneath our maladaptive defenses, complexes, and other barriers that prevent us from living as the person we would be if these things weren't in the way. Over the years, I've had dozens of such dreams; in many of them I find myself stranded in a foreign, hostile land, not unlike Odysseus experienced along his journey. At a critical place in my healing process, I had the following dream.

The Flight Home

I'm talking to a veteran friend of mine who is a therapist and I'm crying. I'm scared and sad, because I am trying to get home but I have to visit Iraq again. Part of me wants to go back, but then again I don't. Later I am trying to fly home with a Vietnam veteran who was a Marine Corps pilot. The Viet Cong are tracking him on their radar so he is flying low to avoid them, and his plane is running out of power because it has already been hit. As we sputter through the air, just barely flying, we see the place where we must land—a beautiful little bay where my classmates are awaiting our arrival to welcome me. I have been waiting for this for so long. We softly crash-land, almost perfectly, right in the quiet surf. I am laughing. It is perfect. I'm finally safe. My friends are there to hug me the moment I arrive.

In this dream, my veteran-therapist friend is a fitting embodiment of the wounded-healer archetype—a shadow figure—who tells me that in order to get home I must first visit Iraq again. The wounded-healer in me knew that in order to heal and "get home," I needed to face the painful memories of war. During this period, I spoke about my experiences in combat rather frequently in weekly therapy, and questioned its usefulness because it was quite distressing at times. This dream encouraged me, letting me know it was indeed necessary. The Vietnam veteran/pilot is another helpful shadow figure, or perhaps a *Self* figure, who—like the Phaeacian sailors—has the skill to overcome challenges (*navigating the terrain of hostile figures*) to carry me home. It is fitting that in my dream I arrive in a bay, while Odysseus arrives in a harbor. This parallel imagery came to me years before I had ever read the story. Lastly, I am greeted by my friends (who were all classmates of mine) who played a significant role of my healing process, and these supportive individuals were ultimately internalized, becoming aspects of my own psyche, as you see here. As I awoke from the dream, I wept. It felt like a real homecoming—and this inner homecoming was far more significant than any outer homecoming I experienced.

Odysseus arrives in Ithaca while still asleep, first thing in the morning as the sun is beginning to rise. It's a new day, yet there is still trouble ahead. He awakes confused, not sure where he is. He doesn't recognize his home, probably for two reasons. First, it's been twenty years since he left, but also he arrives on the part of Ithaca where mythical beings live and he doesn't recognize this place because *he didn't previously know this part of his home.* The harbor and caverns of the merman and nymphs represent a sacred part of his own soul that he never knew before the war. When he returns, this is the first place he experiences, and it's here that he is greeted by Athena.

Athena is disguised, and Odysseus lies to her, not realizing who she is. He keeps his identity hidden. When she reveals herself to him, she rebukes him for being such a trickster. Odysseus has not seen her since they left Troy, and so it comes as quite a surprise to meet her again. As they talk, Athena makes it possible for Odysseus to see his home clearly, and upon recognizing his homeland, he rejoices and kisses the soil. Athena—symbol of the anima, who faces the *inner* half of the psyche—is the one who gives us sight to see our souls as they truly are.

Next, Athena helps Odysseus hide and protect his treasure in a cave. Then they sit at the base of an olive tree to discuss how they will overcome the "wicked suitors." The suitors, who number 108 in total, are each competing to win over Odysseus's wife, Penelope, in hopes one of them might make her his own. In the process, they've essentially hijacked his estate, and since Odysseus's son, Telemachus, is the only one to challenge them, they've plotted to murder him. When Odysseus gets home, Telemachus is gone— Athena (in disguise) sent him away to see Menelaus in Sparta to see if he could get word of Odysseus's whereabouts, but in actuality, this was a protective move. Had Telemachus stayed, the suitors would have killed him, and Odysseus's homecoming would not have been a happy one. The psychoanalyst Carol Leader wrote about the suitors in a way that helps us appreciate their nature and imagine what they might symbolize psychologically.

> The suitors know nothing of mindful human relating. They are continuing to live parasitically off the bounty of the host while showing sadistic contempt towards the stranger, the beggar that Odysseus appears to be.[158]

The suitors are symbols of dark, shadowy aspects of the psyche (*like maladaptive psychological defenses that cause our suffering*) that must be overcome, because otherwise they will drain our inner kingdoms of life. To help him overcome the suitors, Athena disguises Odysseus as an old beggar so no one will recognize him. As we'll see, these themes are resonant with the dreams of trauma survivors—groups of hostile men, a youth and/or woman in danger, separation from one's home, and the distortion of one's identity.[159]

Odysseus finds his way to the hut of his servant Eumaeus, who does not recognize him because Odysseus's identity is distorted by his disguise. Eumaeus is a swineherd, a lowly man who cares for pigs. Odysseus had received a childhood wound from a boar, and his men were turned into pigs temporarily on Circe's island. Now (and later), the man who cares for and tends pigs offers Odysseus critical support. As discussed earlier, in the ancient world pigs were often associated with the archetypal feminine and goddesses, including in ancient Greece, so Eumaeus is identified as having a relationship with this principle.

We learn from Eumaeus that Odysseus was a good master who Eumaeus loved and praises, saying that he would not even find such caring from his own parents. A second significant detail has to do with Eumaeus's origins. In keeping with Jungian perspectives on working with dreams and myths, all figures can be understood as primarily inner ones. Eumeaus, who represents an aspect of Odysseus, was kidnapped and taken from his home as a young boy. Eumeaus was a prince and his father was king of an island called Syra, which apparently was a sort of paradise. Eumeaus says of his homeland, "The soil is good, with much pasture fit for cattle and sheep, and it abounds with wine and wheat. Dearth never comes there, nor are the people plagued by any sickness."[160]

Syra is like a *Garden of Eden*, a lost utopia—as youth is often thought of, at least before significant traumas or trials find us. Eumaeus shares that when he was a boy, he was kidnapped by Taphian pirates, who took him and sold him Odysseus's father, Laertes. Importantly, the motif of the lost, abandoned, or exiled child plays itself out elsewhere in the *Iliad*, the *Odyssey*, in dozens of other myths around the world, and in the dreams of trauma survivors, so we will explore it in detail shortly.

At the exact same time that Odysseus is dwelling with Eumaeus—a man separated from his royal parents as a young child—Athena transports herself to Sparta to retrieve Telemachus, Odysseus's child, who he has been separated from for twenty years. Telemachus and Eumaeus have similar beginnings—both were traumatically separated from their fathers and from the peaceful innocence of youth. Fittingly, at the moment Eumaeus's tale of his traumatic childhood comes to a close, Telemachus arrives! Odysseus's son, Telemachus can be viewed as a symbol of what Jungians refer to as the archetype of the divine child, and can be understood to represent the innocent, unique, and vital core of the personality and one's future potential.

Eumaeus' and Telemachus' shared experience of traumatic separation from their parents is something that they also have in common with Paris, whose elopement with Helen, queen of Sparta, was one of the proximate causes of the Trojan War. Classicist Eric H. Cline describes:

> Although Alexander/Paris was the son of Priam, king of Troy, he had been banished from the royal court as a newborn infant. Apparently, Priam had a dream in which his wife Hecuba gave birth not to a son but to a torch of flaming snakes. Sparks from the torch lit the tall grass surrounding the city of Troy on fire and burned the city to the ground. When Priam summoned the dream interpreters, they declared the unborn child would be a curse upon the city and to his father. They recommended that he be left in the forest to die, so that the prophecy might come to pass. As soon as he was born, the child [Paris] was given to Priam's herdsman, who took the infant to Mount Ida and left him out in the open to die. He was saved, however, by a bear, which nurtured him until the

herdsman returned and found the boy still alive. The herdsman then took the boy home and raised him as his own son. When making his great decision as to who was the most beautiful of the three goddesses, Alexander/ Paris was unaware that he himself was of royal birth. It was only later that he went to Troy, discovered his true identity, and was reunited with his father, mother, and entire family. It may be for this reason that he has two names: the one given to him either at birth or after rejoining his family and the one given to him by the herdsman.[161]

Paris, Eumaeus, and Telemachus all seem to be symbols of the same thing—a vital aspect of the psyche which was abandoned, rejected, or left behind, and in the midst of a painful, developmental trauma. The war began with one rejected by his parents, Paris, who was cast out into the wilderness to die when he was only a baby. When he made the decision that triggered the Trojan War, *he did not even know his true identity.* As a young man, Paris did not yet know who he really was, and Hermes presented him with a dilemma, to choose among the three goddesses, Aphrodite, Hera, and Athena. He chose Aphrodite, and she promised Paris *Helen of Sparta*, the most beautiful woman in the world. Helen, of course, was married to Menelaus, the brother of the Greek King Agamemnon, and thus by choosing her, the war began. It is a well-known fact that unresolved trauma can create serious problems later in life, as we unconsciously make mistakes that can repeat our traumas in new ways. Freud called this the *repetition compulsion*, and believed that we do this accidentally (unconsciously) because it gives us a fresh chance to work out what is still unresolved. Paris was not only unconscious of his true identity, but of the trauma of losing his home in Troy and his family. Sadly, he makes an unconscious decision that will cause him to lose his home and family again. Paris's tale, like that of the Greek Oedipus, is a caution to *know thyself* and to do one's inner work so that one does not unconsciously repeat one's traumas.

Levine relates a story of a Vietnam veteran client of Bessel van der Kolk's, where the veteran fell victim to repetition compulsion in a way that endangered his life. This vet pretended to have a weapon and held up a gas station six times over a period of fifteen years, *each time at 6:30am on July 5th*. The police brought the veteran to the VA hospital, and shared this information with van der Kolk, and so he explored it with the client. What the client came to realize was that he was unconsciously reenacting a trauma from Vietnam. On July 4th, when he was in Vietnam, his entire platoon was killed except for his friend Jim, who was wounded in the chest. The two huddled together all night hiding from the Viet Cong, until at 6:30am Jim died in this man's arms. Levine writes:

> In the therapy session with Dr. van der Kolk, the vet experienced grief over the loss of his friend. He then made the connection between Jim's death and the compulsion he felt to commit the robberies. Once he became aware of his feelings and the role in the original

event had played in driving his compulsion, the man was able to stop re-enacting this tragic incident. What was the connection between the robberies and the Vietnam experience? By staging the robberies, the man was re-enacting the firefight that had resulted in the death of his friend (as well as the rest of his platoon). By provoking police to join in the re-enactment, the vet had orchestrated the cast of characters needed to play the role of the Viet Cong. … He then brought the situation to a climax and was able to elicit the help he needed to heal his psychic wounds. The act enabled him to resolve his anguish, grief, and guilt about his buddy's violent death and the horrors of war. Admittedly, the story of the man staging robberies every year on the same day is a rather extreme example. It serves the purpose of illustrating the fact that we can go to great lengths to create situations that will force us to confront and deal with our unresolved trauma.[162]

Obviously, the ancient Greeks seemed to be keenly aware that we are prone to unconsciously enact unresolved traumas, at the risk of great personal harm, or else they would not relate such stories such as that of Paris or Oedipus. Moreover, it's worth wondering if the author of the *Odyssey* saw such risks for returning veterans, but it seems likely there was at least an awareness of the need to be in relationship with certain elements of psychic experience (symbolized by particular archetypal figures in the myth) in order to avoid catastrophe.

Campbell believed the three goddesses whom Paris had to choose between presented themselves to Odysseus in different forms—Aphrodite as Circe, Hera as Calypso, and Athena as Nausicaa (the associations in each pair closely align), and thus in learning to relate to each of these three feminine aspects of consciousness in the course of his journey home, Odysseus accomplished something vital.[163] Young Paris, on the other hand, was forced to make a choice he was not yet prepared for because he lacked sufficient consciousness, and he paid for it dearly. I believe many veterans expose themselves to harm unconsciously, simply by joining the military before they're aware of what unconscious forces steer them to do so—and that part of our recovery requires an examination of what led us to where we are today.

How many of us volunteer for military service and go off to war before our brains are done developing and before we even know who we really are? How many of us carry childhood wounds that distort our personalities, causing us to make decisions that are not in keeping with who we really are? I cannot count the number of veterans I've worked with who admit their childhood trauma was an influential factor in their decision to join the military and to go to war. One combat veteran I worked with not only experienced abandonment by his father, but neglect by his mother, and was raped by another family member for several years beginning at a very young age. He expressed his sadness of feeling like he didn't know what it was to experience loving relationships with others, and felt that the comradery he experienced in the military was the closest thing he had to a family—for a time—until certain events transpired and he came to feel used and abandoned by the military too. His childhood trauma played out in a new form, and it was extremely painful for him, considering how much he sacrificed during intense fighting in Afghanistan. The depth of his suffering was so profound that he attempted suicide on multiple occasions, lamenting that he felt like his soul was irreparably damaged. His tasks in therapy were many, among them being the need to explore why he joined the military in the first place, to understand what he was really longing for, and to process the profound pain he carried in a void he'd had since early childhood.

I want to stress that Eumaeus, now a servant and swineherd, was (like Paris) born a prince and the son of a king. *He is living disconnected from his inborn potential because he was kidnapped as a child and stolen from his royal parents, and this is a risk Telemachus still faces because of the suitors, unless Odysseus can deal with them accordingly. We can interpret this as a statement of a psychological fact: a vital aspect of Odysseus's psyche remains in peril because unaddressed issues from long-past traumas remain.* Despite all the work Odysseus has done up to this point, he hasn't yet been in a position to address the most profound threat to the integrity of his home—or his soul. Though critical tasks lie ahead, it is fitting that Odysseus finally reunites with his precious son in the home of Eumaeus. The description of the meeting of these two figures strikes one to the core.

And Odysseus said, "I am your father, on whose account you grieve and suffer so much at the hands of lawless men." As he spoke he kissed his son, and a tear fell from his cheek onto the ground, for he had restrained all tears till now. ... As he spoke he sat down, and Telemachus threw his arms about his father and wept. They were both so much moved that they cried aloud like eagles or vultures with crooked talons that have been robbed of their half-fledged young by peasants. Thus piteously did they weep, and the sun would have gone down by mourning ...[164]

The symbolic reunion of Odysseus with his son is nothing less than the recovery of a vital aspect of his own soul. Yet, danger still lies ahead. The suitors are actively plotting to kill Telemachus, and they have considerable control over Odysseus's estate. The suitors are to Telemachus what the Taphian pirates were to Eumaeus. In both cases, these dark, hostile elements represent vitality-stealing aspects of the psyche, and as we shall see, these figures are abundant in the dreams of trauma survivors.[165]

From here, let's skip forward to Odysseus's return to his home, who is still disguised as a beggar. Because there is so much psychological meaning to the events that follow, which requires an in-depth discussion, I will share the story in whole, then elaborate on its meaning. When he arrives, his old dog Argo recognizes him and then, immediately after seeing his master, heart-wrenchingly passes away. This serves as a poignant reminder that while we are away, life at home goes on—that everything is impermanent, and all that we hold most dear is vulnerable to aging, death, and loss.

Odysseus's homecoming is by no means easy for him, an experience most war veterans share no matter how welcome they are made to feel. We find not only that we have changed, but so has everything that is most precious. The life we once had has died, and there is no getting it back. A new life will have to be discovered.

Odysseus is not at all welcome when he returns home, which must resonate deeply with most Vietnam veterans. The suitors treat him like a piece of garbage in his own house because they take him for a beggar, despite the cultural norm in ancient Greece of treating guests and travelers with respect. While this part of the story may parallel our actual, outer experiences, it also reminds us the hostile elements of our psyches will continue their destructive tendencies even though we've physically come home.

Preparing to reclaim their kingdom, Odysseus and Telemachus remove all the weapons and armor from the court to the storeroom, so when Odysseus takes on the suitors, they won't be able to defend themselves against him. Soon after, Odysseus talks to Penelope, though she doesn't recognize him because of the magical disguise Athena has placed upon him. Athena made him appear as an old man, completely unrecognizable. While they're together, Penelope tells him about a contest she has arranged for the following day.

> … I am about to hold a tournament of axes. My husband used to set up twelve axes in the court, one in front of the other, like the stays upon which a ship is built; he would go

back from them and shoot an arrow through the whole twelve. I shall make the suitors try to do the same thing, and whichever of them can string the bow most easily, and send his arrow through all the twelve axes, him will I follow, and quit this house of my lawful husband, so goodly and so abounding in wealth.[166]

The next day, Telemachus hosts a banquet and sits Odysseus in a place of honor, and again, he is abused and mistreated by the suitors. When the feast is finished, Penelope brings down Odysseus's bow for the contest. Telemachus tries to string it and cannot. Then, the suitors begin to try and string it and cannot, despite warming it in a fire to make it easier. While this is going on, Odysseus shows his leg wound to his servants, Eumaeus and Philoetius, to reveal his true identity to them and enlist their support. This symbolism speaks to the reality that our wounds can serve a purpose—ultimately they can help us reclaim our identity and our kingdom, when we have the courage to share them. Odysseus charges his friends with containing the court so no suitors can escape when the onslaught begins.

When Odysseus finally gets his bow in his hands, he strings it easily, while at the same time Zeus sends a boom of thunder through the sky as a sign from the heavens. Whereas once the gods resisted Odysseus's misguided aims, now Odysseus is aligned with the Self, the unconscious, and his calling. He takes an arrow and sends it flying through each of the holes in the handles of the twelve axes. He fulfills a task that only he can fulfill. It's a symbolic act signifying that we must *own* our uniqueness, that this is where our power comes from.

As Odysseus claims victory over the tournament and his own kingdom, Telemachus rises with spear and sword, standing next to his father. Suddenly, Odysseus tears off his rags and sends an arrow straight into the throat of the suitor Antinous. The others suitors shout back that he will pay, not yet recognizing who he is. He then rebukes them all, sheds his disguise, and reveals his true identity, saying:

> Dogs, did you think that I should not come back from Troy? You have wasted my substance, have forced my womanservants to lie with you, and have wooed my wife while I was still living. You have feared neither God nor man, and now you shall die.[167]

At this, the suitors run for their lives. Some manage to arm themselves, but despite their best efforts to fight back or run, Odysseus and Telemachus kill them all. The only ones spared are Phemius (a bard) and Medon (a herald), who were good to Telemachus. It's meaningful that they are spared. Odysseus shows restraint and the ability to distinguish where the line ought to be drawn. This is important for veterans and other trauma survivors, as we endure our own transformational processes.

At this point, I want to pause and present a dream of my own which mirrors this part of the *Odyssey* closely, and again it is a dream I had before ever reading this story:

Dispatching Hostile Figures

I am trying to get home. I arrive in a room with three or four workers who are initially afraid when I enter, then they realize I am good. One of them gives me an M4 with a M203 grenade launcher. There is a room full of gangsters in the other room who are all really bad guys it seems, and the workers need me to get rid of them because they are extremely dangerous. Though afraid, I walk in there and kill them all. It is a bloodbath and it is very disturbing. One man is shot in the head and is still fully alive, which allows his heart to function and his head to get out of the way, and now he is a decent guy. We tell him to go find an old woman, a witch doctor, who can fix him up.

This dream, like the imagery from the *Odyssey*, reflects a psychological task many veterans and trauma survivors must complete as they free their psyches from hostile, life-robbing elements that must be confronted. The disturbing nature of this imagery reflects how a person feels in the midst of this brutal, transformative experience. It's an unpleasant affair to be in such an intense inner conflict with those toxic parts of yourself that rob you of life and prevent you from reclaiming your inner kingdom, and hence the imagery of such dreams and the myth portrays the harsh situation as it is—a horrifying and unsettling experience.

 While the imagery of my dream is modernized and differs from the myth (as is often the case), the basic elements are all there. There are three or four men who seek my assistance and who help me, just as Odysseus was helped by Telemachus, Eumaeus, and Philoetius. I receive a weapon from one of the helpful shadow figures, just as Odysseus receives his bow from Eumaeus. Next, I enter a room full of bad guys to dispatch them, just as Odysseus slaughters the suitors who are trapped in the courtyard. Yet, one is left alive—a man whose head was apparently getting in the way of his heart, which is symbolism that speaks to some of my own challenges from this time. This is not so different from the corresponding episode of the *Odyssey,* as Phemius and Medon are left to escape with their lives. It's significant that these men are a bard and a herald—men who share stories from the heart and proclaim important news, *just as Odysseus must do when his own return is complete, according to the prophecy of Tiresias.* The men who were spared represent necessary and helpful shadow elements of Odysseus that he must preserve and learn to live with.

When the fighting is over, Odysseus asks Euryclea to identify the women who were disloyal. These women are forced to clean up the mess from the slaughter, and then they are put to death by hanging. This is particularly challenging to digest. Yet if taken symbolically, we might understand that there are some seemingly innocent qualities in our psyches that work in conjunction with unhealthy and destructive aspects of the psyche (which the suitors represent). For example, one might have a pattern of peoplepleasing that is rooted in maladaptive defenses, such as introjection, and this seemingly innocent behavior might need to die along with the maladaptive defenses if we are to restore our sense of power and vitality. It is the wise old Euryclea, Odysseus's nurse and maid—a symbol of the mature feminine—who must distinguish which of these aspects must perish, and again, it is only those that are aligned with destructive elements of the psyche.

After the bloodbath, Euryclea and Odysseus purify the area, then all of the remaining women of his household greet him cheerfully. Euryclea then goes to wake Penelope and shares the news that Odysseus has returned and that all of the suitors are dead. At first, Penelope is in denial, but then she embraces Euryclea and weeps with joy. When Odysseus and Penelope are finally reunited, she's in shock and denial and finds it difficult to believe he's finally home. We have to appreciate that Penelope has also been through a prolonged traumatic experience, wondering if her husband was alive, and if she would be forced into a marriage she didn't want. It's worth considering how Penelope's hardships mirror those of military spouses, and also how this might fit the perspective of the anima—as our soul desperately longs for us to return to it, and for our inner kingdom to be restored and freed from the hostile influences that threaten it. Odysseus is then washed and anointed with oil in his own home, given a shirt and cloak, and at this point Athena restores his appearance, even taller and stronger than before. He has been transformed and made new through his trials. This is an image of *Post Traumatic Growth*.

After Odysseus is repaired to an even more impressive state than before, he goes before Penelope, who tests him to ensure he really is Odysseus. She orders Euryclea to move his bed. Odysseus protests saying this would be impossible, because he made the bed and he knows that it cannot be moved. He shares details about the bed that only he could know, and when she realizes it truly is Odysseus, she breaks down in tears and throws her arms around him, kissing him and saying, "We have suffered, both of us. Heaven has denied us the happiness of spending our youth and growing old together."[168]

… [Odysseus] melted, and wept as he clasped his dear and faithful wife to his bosom. As the sight of land is welcome to men who are swimming toward the shore, when Poseidon has wrecked their ship with the fury of his winds and waves … are thankful when they find themselves on firm ground and out of danger—even so was her husband welcome to her as she looked upon him.[169]

Odysseus shares with Penelope that his work is not done, that *he must still travel to a land where people do not know the sea*, and then he tells her about the long and painful journey he endured on his way home. Then, at last, they fall asleep.

When they awake in the morning, Odysseus tells Penelope that he must go to see his father, Laertes, while at the same time warning that news will soon spread about his killing the suitors. Odysseus, Telemachus, Philoetius, and Eumaeus put on their armor and head to see Laertes, while Athena conceals their presence from others. When they arrive at the home of Laertes, there is a tearful reunion. Soon, though, rumor spreads that Odysseus killed all of the suitors, angering the people, many of whom are family and friends of the dead. While some want revenge, others remind the men of Ithaca that they had been warned of their sons' ill-doings and had been asked to keep their sons in check, which they did not. Nevertheless, many of the townsmen come for Odysseus, seeking retribution.

Athena goes to Zeus asking what should be done about the situation, and he encourages her to create a covenant of peace. As Odysseus and his comrades finish dinner at his father's house, they learn that the men of the town are heading their way, so they put on their armor and go out to meet them. Odysseus is joined by his father, son, and two men, as well as Dolius (Penelope's man-servant) and his six sons—twelve men in total (a number we have heard throughout the story). Additionally, Athena stands by their side. The battle begins when Odysseus strikes a man in the helmet with his spear, and then Odysseus and Telemachus crash into the front line of the men of Ithaca, striking them down with their swords and spears:

> Indeed, they would have killed every one of them, and prevented them from ever getting home again, only Athene raised her voice aloud, and made everyone pause. 'Men of Ithaca,' she cried, 'cease this dreadful war, and settle the matter at once without further bloodshed.' On this pale fear seized everyone; they were so frightened that

their arms dropped from their hands and fell upon the ground at the sound of the goddess' voice, and they fled back to the city for their lives. But Odysseus gave a great cry, and gathering himself together swooped down like a soaring eagle. Then the son of Cronus [Zeus] sent a thunderbolt of fire that fell just in front of Athene, so she said to Odysseus, 'Odysseus, noble son of Laertes, stop this warful strife, or Zeus will be angry with you.' Thus spoke Athene, and Odysseus obeyed her gladly. … and presently made a covenant of peace between the two contending parties.[170]

It is fitting that the *Odyssey* ends with the resolution of a great tension between opposites, the creation of peace, and a direct, personal experience of the divine in a desperate moment of need. It is also fitting that our stubborn friend, Odysseus, initially ignored Athena and "like an eagle" (or one who is inflated, since flying is associated with inflation) he attempted to continue the forbidden fight. Fortunately, Zeus sends a convincing warning rather than striking him dead for his insolence, and Athena makes it clear that Odysseus cannot afford to repeat the mistakes of the past. Here, Odysseus is shaken from his old warrior-centric habits and brought back to his humanity.

To have such an experience of these gods and goddesses is in itself a mystical awakening to the transcendent realities of human experience—becoming aware that we are in relationship with psychic and spiritual forces that far exceed our egos, and that we must heed them and live in alignment with them. The journey home (transformation process) from war or military service requires that we submit to individuation and rediscover our place in relation to the powerful forces of the unconscious. Only through this can we truly transform and be healed in a way that brings with it a new sense of identity and the restoration of a profound sense of meaning.

Without Odysseus's transformative adventure, he never would have reached home. Without his battle with the suitors (the maladaptive and destructive aspects of the psyche), which threatened his relationship with Telemachus (divine child) and Penelope (anima), he would have never been completed the journey. And through his powerful encounter with gods and goddesses (the Self and archetypes of the collective unconscious), he makes the unconscious conscious, and the ego comes into proper relationship with the Self. Jungian analyst Edward Edinger called this the *reunion of the ego-Self axis,* as our relationship with the divine, spiritual nature of the Self is rediscovered and repaired.[171] While still capable of asserting himself and exercising his heroic, warrior energy in situations that demand it, Odysseus is now also capable of restraint, and he knows he must heed the demands of the gods and goddesses (the archetypes of the collective unconscious). He is not the man he was when he left Troy. He has been made new, and his hardships have brought him into relationship with sacred realms of experience.

Although the term *Post Traumatic Growth* (PTG) is catchy and likeable, the concept is hardly new. Obviously, whoever created the

Odyssey understood this notion. Also, Jung's entire psychology is rooted in the idea that our wounds can lead us to transformation, meaning, and wholeness, and thus we might consider the term PTG as a new label for the inherent outcome of the individuation process. I also suspect Jung might have resisted the term *growth*, because becoming more mature or *deepening* our wisdom does not necessarily mean we have grown. Cancer is a growth that knows no limits, and so obviously not all growth is a good thing. A psychology that focuses on "growth" can be cancerous, and keep its patients sick.

Odysseus was not a man whose ego needed to grow. It needed shrinking so it might restrain itself against impulsive or inflated acts, like raiding Ismarus, or attacking Polyphemus, the son of a god. Had Odysseus oriented himself toward humility and wholeness, he would have gotten home faster and without so much hardship. Odysseus needed to *become more whole*, to find himself in relationship to the likes of Circe, Calypso, Athena, Eumaeus, Telemachus, and Penelope, and this he could not do until his ego was relativized by the likes of Polyphemus, the Laestrygonians, Zeus, and Poseidon. The same is true for veterans and many trauma survivors today.

At this point, I want to step back and amplify key aspects of the final books of the *Odyssey*, as there are some critical lessons here that should not be overlooked. Previous examiners of the *Odyssey* have not had the vantage point we have today, provided in part by recent research from the Jungian analyst Donald Kalsched, who examined the dreams of trauma survivors.[172] Kalsched's work helps us better understand the nature of trauma and recovery, and it also helps us understand key themes in Odysseus's return to Ithaca. If we consider Kalsched's findings, we will recognize that the symbolism in the events we have explored in this book closely matches the inner drama that all trauma survivors must endure and hopefully—with good support—overcome. My interpretation of Kalsched's work is that there are three primary phases of the recovery process.

In the first phase, when trauma occurs, psychological defenses arise to protect the person from unbearable pain, and all these defenses distort reality to some degree to make the pain more manageable. The activation of the psyche's defensive system is accompanied by dreams or imaginal experiences where the dreamer receives archetypal support in some form. Kalsched demonstrated that often, in the dreams, fantasies, or other imaginal experiences of children who experience severe trauma, they encounter a guardian angel, imaginary friend, or special animal that assists them through their terrible experience. Such figures are the equivalent of what is referred to in depth-oriented literature as *a spirit or totem animal.*

In traumatic circumstances, survivors may dream that a special soul-child fitting the divine child archetype is lost (like Telemachus, Eumaeus, and Paris). Paris, after being abandoned in the wilderness as an infant, was saved by a bear. In the midst of trauma, life-preserving elements of the unconscious (sometimes symbolized by mythic creatures) step in to provide critical support that sustains our well-being to some degree. Our psychological defenses are the same; they intervene so that life's blows are not catastrophic. Unfortunately, when their work is done, our neural pathways have difficulty not holding onto them. As our defensive strategies become a foundational part our new reality, where we focus on protecting ourselves from pain, they can also deprive us of our vitality. At this point, we call these defenses *maladaptive*. For example, dissociation helps protect us from the pain that is inherent in the heat of combat, but in the long run, if dissociation persists and kicks in during times where we are not in danger, it also robs us of the ability to feel real and present in our body. Similarly, hyperarousal may help us to become keenly aware of threats while we are at war, but when we are back home, having a night out to dinner with our families, hyperarousal can leave us feeling tortured by paranoia, a fear of threats, anxiety, and tension.

Kalsched argues that there is a wisdom and purpose in the "loss" of the divine child, a critical aspect of the psyche. He believes that in especially threatening or traumatic situations, the soul intentionally "splits off" the vital core of the self to keep this aspect of the psyche out of suffering—as Athena sends Telemachus someplace safe until Odysseus is in a position to deal with the suitors.[173] If we had to endure the full impact of extreme suffering without such defensive responses from the psyche, it could lead to a psychotic break and perhaps permanent damage to the psyche. If Telemachus was killed before Odysseus returned, his homecoming might've been empty. Kalsched says this splitting off of a vital part of ourselves is generally *not* permanent, which I have come to agree with through my own lived experience. Later, when the unconscious senses it's safe enough for the innocent core of the self to reemerge, it seeks to correct the injustice and bring about healing and restoration of the personality, dislodging maladaptive defenses that have worn out their usefulness. Kalsched calls the psyche's defensive system the *self-care system*, and summarizes its purpose:

Trauma constitutes an interruption of the normal processes through which an embodied, true self comes into being. . . . The unfolding process of the soul's incarnation is temporarily suspended, and a second world is pressed into service to provide a mytho-poetic matrix for the soul. But the relationship to the outer world is compromised. The trauma survivor will often describe this experience as being "broken" or as "losing my innocence forever" . . . the person's sense of animation and aliveness is mostly gone. This is because the soul *is* by definition, this very animation and aliveness—the center of our God-given spirit—the vital spark in us that "wants" to incarnate in the empirical personality but needs help from supportive persons in the environment to do so— help that is often not available. Without this help the psyche provides a partial cure of trauma so that life can go on, but there is a great price for this self-cure—loss of soul. Through dreams we can see how the innocence-identified soul has been sacrificed and given up to another world and we can see the spiritual powers that protect and persecute it there. ... Having experienced the unbearable pain of trauma, the intelligence that seems to inform the defensive system wants to avoid the suffering necessary to come into being.[174]

The divine child or human/divine soul within us is not an artifact of the defensive process, but the very thing the defensive process is protecting. And it is protecting it because it is sacred—the very core of our aliveness.[175]

My own experiences confirm Kalsched's assertions, in large part. Interestingly, and unfortunately, while I was studying this specific topic to write my thesis in graduate school, my wife and I were innocent bystanders who got caught up in a shootout among gang members, and our lives were in serious danger. This is the dream I had the night of the shooting.

My Child in Danger

I am outside my body and see myself sitting on the couch next to my wife holding our child. A dark man is there and he wants to take our baby. The dark man has us say a prayer that sends our baby into death. The baby falls limp and lifeless. He asks us to hand the baby over so he can take it. I am considering his request. I go back into my body and sit down in it, and I am holding my lifeless child. I see how beautiful he is. I am not going to give away my child, even if things might be easier. I say a healing prayer to bring life back into the child. The child is okay. I respectfully tell the dark man that I love my baby too much, and I am keeping my child at all costs, even if that means he has to drag me through hell. The dark man seems disappointed. I reassure the dark man that he took every care to make things pleasant and comfortable, but that nothing in the world could replace our child.

At the time I had this dream, I had already undergone three years of Jungian analysis, two years of other therapies, and spent almost a decade dedicated to recovering from trauma, practicing meditation, yoga, and other forms of inner work daily. I had sufficient inner resources to hold myself through the experience in a way I would not have been able to earlier in my recovery. Also, the night of this trauma, I was surrounded by friends and family, whose support was critical because I was devastated by the horror of the experience. Without both the inner resources and outer support, I might have been overwhelmed to a degree that was especially traumatic and the dream might have been different. If the traumatic encounter had been worse or the inner and outer conditions less advantageous, I might have dreamed that this dark man was taking my child away from me—an image of the loss of something vital in the psyche. In the initial stage of the psyche's defense system, splitting within is aimed at protecting the vital core of the self and keeping it out of suffering. In later stages of the journey to wholeness, we are ready to reclaim these abandoned parts of ourselves.

We see the loss or exodus of a divine child figure three times in the

Iliad, the *Odyssey*, and related tales. First in Paris's abandonment, second in Eumaeus's kidnapping, and third when Odysseus has to leave Telemachus to go to war (in order to prevent him from being murdered). Being disconnected from the divine child aspect of our psyche is a real loss, and is common among those who go to war. For us to heal, this aspect of the soul must be recovered, or perhaps it's the other way around—for this aspect to be recovered, we must heal.

After the initial stage when trauma occurs, there may be a period when symptoms are latent and the survivor is able to function despite their lives having been interrupted. They may not even be aware of the degree to which they've changed. The new adaptation is generally a necessary, unconscious, defensive reaction where reality is distorted in one way or another, yet this adaptive strategy allows them to keep their pain at bay. Long after trauma, however, in situations where maladaptive defenses are no longer helpful or appropriate, they create suffering and rob the person of life. When defenses become maladaptive, in order to heal, our psychic energy needs to be redirected in ways that lead to new, appropriate strategies and a greater variety and maturity of defenses.

Importantly, I believe Odysseus's suffering (and that of many veterans) gets "stuck" for prolonged periods of time because the inner conditions are not sufficient for the defenses to be challenged. If a person's inner attitude is not conducive to doing inner, therapeutic work—if we are resistant or avoidant of emotions, if we lack the capacity to hold ourselves through our pain, if we shame ourselves for suffering, or if we are too busy to care for ourselves—then we cannot do the work that must be done to rid ourselves of our inner suitors, or the maladaptive psychological defenses which torment us. We cannot complete this step in the recovery process before we've done the necessary preparatory work that makes it possible. Odysseus had a number of tasks he had to complete just to get back to Ithaca, where he could face the suitors.

As our old defensive adaptations begin to fail and unconscious activity increases, so do dreams, as the psyche tries to help us understand what we're up against and help us heal. Kalsched illustrates how the survivor may be haunted by dreams in which hostile, authoritarian figures threaten the dreamer, a woman, a child, or a special animal.[176] These hostile figures may appear as demons, Nazis, the Viet Cong, the Taliban, members of Al Qaeda, ISIS, the Jaysh Al Mahdi, domestic terrorists, dictators, corrupt police officers or businessmen, men in black, gang members, Odysseus's suitors, or any number of similarly threatening and abusive symbols. Below is an example of such a dream, which shows how a Vietnam veteran was haunted by hostile elements of the psyche which kept his trauma alive.

> I am carrying a baby in my arms. I think it is my little boy. I don't remember seeing his face. I am inside this building trying to get shelter. We are under attack. I can hear the bombing, *Poom! Poom! Poom!* I am scared and running and running, carrying the baby. I don't recognize the other people. I don't know who it is trying to drop bombs on us

and kill us. All of a sudden I am running scared when I get hit. One of those things lands right next me to. I can feel the pain that the baby and I are going through. It is really real. I have this weird feeling like dying, man and the baby, and I say, "Oh my god, this is it." It seems like the real thing until I find myself shaking in bed. That is when I realize it is a dream.[177]

In this particular dream, the hostile elements of the psyche are relatively impersonal and unknown, perhaps reflecting the dreamer's own confusion that he doesn't understand *what* exactly is causing his suffering—all he knows is that he can feel the pain it causes. Other dreams of this sort tend to feature a "bad guy," along with his hostile cronies.

I'm running and being pursued by this evil force. *I use many identities and names* and barely get away. Now I'm separate from the guy running away … like I've met my double. I'm sympathetic with his plight … I wish he could have a fuller life. I feel a lot of compassion for him as we talk. Then the scene changes. Somehow, through this compassion we've become one again. I'm now the man on the run, but I now know I have to go back to where this running all began—to find its source. I enter a large courtyard with many buildings. I approach the central headquarters from which all this is directed. I start feeling anxious—like I'm walking into the lion's den! All around me are computers and circuit-boards and huge files and then I see a central figure—a Nazi. He's demonic and intense. He's spent his whole life pursuing me and I've been running... We start to talk about how our whole life has been about the chase. I say to him, "I know how much meaning this chase has given to your life" ... he says "yes, but now I've got you!"[178] (emphasis added)

Kalsched and other psychoanalysts refer to this dark, shadowy figure in dreams as *Dis*, and note that he (it's usually a male figure, although not always) tends to present himself along with his abusive cronies. Whatever mask these figures wear, they are dark forces who create a state of distress in the kingdom and must be overthrown so that peace can return. In the *Odyssey*, these figures appear as the suitors, who siphon off the resources belonging to Odysseus and want to kill his son and take his wife as their own. Dreams of being tormented by Dis are symbolic of what *continues to happen* in the inner world of trauma survivors.

Whitmont's work contains an example of a dream that hints at a solution, where the dreamer has to travel to "the Holy Land" to escape the situation.[179] Traveling to the Holy Land is a symbol of individuation, in which one might experience something divine. In the dream, the dreamer dresses as a beggar (as Odysseus did), hinting at the need for humility so the ego can be transformed.

I was in a place surrounded by old buildings. Suddenly

there were explosions on all sides, the buildings began to crumble and fall, steel beams and molten steel were falling all around—a most dangerous, deadly situation. The only relatively safe spot was a small area with a floodlight shining on it. But there I was a slave and prisoner of the Nazis and death from their hands would be my lot. The only ones to whom the Nazi regime permitted free travel and who would not be killed by beams of steel were pilgrims and beggars traveling to the Holy Land. As it was obvious that we were meant to assume the role we began to crouch and limp like beggars and, though I could hardly believe it, I saw that we were actually leaving that evil place and no harm was befalling us.[180]

We see the same imagery in the *Odyssey*. As long as the suitors are present, Odysseus is forced to stay in disguise as a beggar, taking the humble path so eventually he can restore justice to his kingdom. At the same time, as long as he appears as a beggar, his identity is distorted and he cannot claim his true self. Another example from Kalsched's work portrays this theme more clearly:

I've gone to visit a young female friend who's a member of a convent or cult of some kind. *She's using an alias and has created a whole false impression* of who she is, for protection. Now somehow I come to understand that she wants to "come clean" i.e., use her real name, and tell people who she really is ... Now "Pam" is being led upstairs to a gallows ... I put on a monk's robe *to conceal my own identity* so I can rescue her. I feel her life is now my responsibility... They put the noose around her neck. The guards all have submachine guns. I don't have a chance. But there's gotta be a way. Tension is building... In this dilemma I wake up with my heart pounding.[181] (emphasis added)

In these dreams, there is a real need and purpose for taking a humble, lowly position as the dreamer seeks to overcome these threatening aspects of the psyche. Indeed, for the personality to be flexible enough to transform and heal, humility is a necessity. Those who are too rigid and defensive will not be able to overcome what haunts them. At the same time, perhaps there is a protective function in disowning one's true identity, at least for a time.

Certain maladaptive defenses can lead to a distortion in the personality. The true self is lost, and one lives according to the guidance of a false self. For example, one might fall into a pattern of disavowing one's true nature or needs in an effort to please others in order to maintain relationships or prevent feared abandonment. This might imply there is a greater need to assert oneself against the powerful unconscious forces (especially maladaptive defenses) that cause the kingdom to become a wasteland, but this isn't possible until one's inner resources (such as ego strength and one's capacity for emotional regulation and affect tolerance) are strengthened to a point where transforming one's defenses to a healthier state becomes possible.

Again, this connects to the experience of combat veterans. Recall Jason Kander's dream shared early in this book, where intruders were trying to kidnap his wife and child, which is not unlike the threats facing Odysseus and his family. I had the same sort of dreams for the first several years after I returned from Iraq, despite the fact that I had no literal children at the time (I've not had such a dream since I have had children, however, I believe because I have addressed the issues that led to such dreams). Often in my early dreams, the Jaysh al-Mahdi, a terrorist militia I fought in Iraq, would invade my home and I'd do my best to fight them off— often without much success. Later, the dreams took a more archetypal turn. The following dream came about six months into my Jungian analysis and after two years of other therapies. I knew very little about dream symbolism and was unaware of Kalsched's work when I had it:

The Divine Child

It's 1936 and I know Hitler is coming soon. I have a child who is being kept safe by a man in downtown Parkville (Missouri), near where the Battle of Deadwood took place. My child is unusual, a Native American Indian. Within a few days, he has grown tremendously. He is already walking, and he has blonde hair. He is huge. I know I must take my child and leave before Hitler comes, so I tell the attendant to prepare him so I can go. While I am waiting for him to prepare the child, a man takes my wife and me to a boardwalk above the ocean. I don't feel safe, and I don't trust him. I think he's trying to keep my wife and me from our child. We notice that the wood on the boardwalk is rotten. I know the boardwalk is going to fall through, and we run as fast as we can to get back to land. We barely manage to escape the collapse.

This dream imagery and the features of the divine child are consistent with what Jung observed:

But the clearest and most significant manifestation of the child motif in the therapy neuroses is in the maturation process of personality induced by the analysis of the unconscious, which I have termed the process of individuation. . . . In dreams, [the child] often appears as the dreamer's son or daughter as a boy, youth, or young girl; occasionally it seems to be of exotic origin, Indian or Chinese, with a dusky skin, or, appearing more cosmically. . . . Seen as a special instance of "the treasure hard to attain" motif.[182]

It is therefore not surprising that so many of the mythological saviours are child gods. This agrees exactly with our experience of the psychology of the individual, which shows that the "child" paves the way for a future change of personality. In the individuation process, it anticipates the figure that comes from the synthesis of conscious and unconscious elements of the personality. It is therefore a symbol which unites the opposites, a mediator, a bringer of healing, that is, the one who makes whole.[183]

Abandonment, exposure, danger, etc. are all elaborations of the "child's" insignificant beginnings and of its mysterious and miraculous birth. . . . In the psychology of the individual there is always, at such moments, an agonizing situation of conflict from which there seems to be no way out—at least for the conscious mind. . . . But out of this collision of opposites the unconscious always creates a third thing of irrational nature, which the conscious mind neither expects nor understands. . . . Out of this situation the "child" emerges as a symbolic content manifestly separated or even isolated . . . threatened on one hand by the negative attitude of the conscious mind and on the other by the *horror vacui* of the unconscious, which is quite ready to swallow up. . . . Nothing in all the world welcomes this new birth, although it is the most precious fruit of Mother Nature herself, the most pregnant with the future, signifying a higher stage of self-realization. That is why Nature, the world of instincts, takes the "child" under its wing: it is nourished or protected by animals.[184]

In reading these descriptions and dreams, I am reminded of myths where a child is forced into hiding to avoid some evil king, though he is destined to make a triumphant return later. For example, we see this in the stories of Moses and Christ. Moses was sent away in a reed basket to avoid being murdered by Pharaoh, and Christ had to flee the wrath of Herod to avoid infanticide. The same theme appears in Disney's *The Lion King*. In all these instances, divine children are pursued by hostile figures that seek to maintain a rigid control over the kingdom, resulting in a sort of wasteland, while preventing transformation or justice. Yet, it is these divine children (images of the true self) who eventually bring about renewal and restoration. Otto Rank, a colleague of Jung and Freud, penned *The Myth of the Birth of the Hero*, which documents seventy similar myths for comparison.[185] June Singer summarized Rank's findings:

In brief: the hero is the son of parents of the highest station, his conception takes place under difficulties, and there is a portent in a dream or oracle connected with the child's birth. The child is then sent away or exposed to extreme danger. He is rescued by people of humble station, or by helpful animals, and reared by them. When grown he rediscovers his noble parentage after many adventures and, overcoming all obstacles in his path, becomes at last recognized as a hero and attains fame and greatness. The best known, as mentioned in the series, are Sargon of Agade, Moses, Cyrus, and Romulus . . . Oedipus, Karna, Paris, Telephos, Perseus, Heracles, and Gilgamesh. To the list we would surely add Sri Krishna and Christ.[186]

The true self (like an exiled prince or princess) wants to return home and create prosperous, peaceful dynamics in its kingdom, the psyche. But it cannot do so until maladaptive defenses (represented in dreams and myths by hostile or authoritarian forces—the suitors of the *Odyssey*) are transformed into healthier functioning, which necessitates a great deal of preparatory therapeutic work and an attitude that is sufficient for such work to take place. The image of the divine child hints toward a lifegiving future where we are in touch with our objective personality, and maladaptive defenses are the primary obstacle standing in the way.

In the third and final stage of the healing process, the soul-child (or perhaps part of the soul itself) is retrieved or recovered. This reunion does not mean all problems are solved. It is not the end of suffering, but rather signifies that a precious, vital aspect of the personality has been recovered and we are once again in touch with the true self or objective personality. Maladaptive or primitive defenses are no longer as pervasive, distorting, or disruptive as they were. The following dream reflects my own "soul-retrieval experience," and was the first in a series of dreams in which I was once again in touch with my own soul-child:

The Retrieval

I am with three women and we go up a hill. One is pregnant. At the top of the hill is a beautiful tree with a circle of roots around it. The roots have Celtic-style knots throughout them. The tree stands in front of a very old house. I go up the stairs to the second floor. It seems someone important lived here, but it's empty now. I go to the master bedroom, where a darkness is present. In this room, there's a master bed and at the foot of the bed, a baby crib. I sense evil, and I use magic to hold the evil at bay and I try to escape. As I get to the door, an invisible force tries to slam the door to shut me out, but I sense a tiny presence trying to come with me. I ask this invisible presence, "Do you want to come with me?" and it says yes. I pick up the invisible creature, and the door slams behind us. The tiniest, cutest puppy appears in my arms. It's a pug, just like I had before Dad left.

This dream begins with three women, not unlike the trials of Paris and Odysseus, with Aphrodite, Hera, and Athena. The fact that one is pregnant suggests new life is on the way. We go up a hill, making an archetypal ascent, where we find a special or cosmic tree, the *axis mundi*, which tends to be symbolic of the fact that one is in a position to encounter something transcendent and experience transformation (such symbols, like the cross of Christianity or Yggdrasil of Nordic mythology, are the means by which one ascends to an upper or lower realm, such as heaven or the underworld, in the midst of a transformative act). Here I come into contact with some unknown, dark, and hostile force that seems to be keeping a small, invisible creature hostage—a puppy that's just like the one I had before my dad left when I was four years old. As Kalsched notes, the divine child often appears as a special animal, and thus, this puppy is the equivalent of the divine child, just as Telemachus is the divine child in the *Odyssey*. This figure resembles something innocent, precious, and life-giving and brings happiness. In my case, the dream suggests this particular aspect of my soul is something I lost when my father left, which serves as a reminder that many of us carry wounds that did not originate in war. At this stage, the hostile forces remain invisible. I couldn't see (nor was I conscious of) the sources of my suffering. Not long after this dream, I had another:

Dis Is Swept Away

Brad Pitt is a Nazi submariner hiding underground. Raging floodwaters are forcing all the rusty, old submarines out of the water. The Nazi submariner is swept away by it, too. I am floating out of the cave as well. The waters are unbelievably rough, and I'm doing my best to ride this extremely strong current. I want to end up on the other side of the river, so I can go home. But the current is too strong, and it's not possible for me to reach the other shore. I have to remain in Germany, for now.

The Nazi submariner in my dream—*the one who controls these rusty, outdated, unconscious defenses that lurk beneath the surface*—is Dis, the equivalent of the suitors in the *Odyssey*. At this point in my life, the hostile defenses that were most disruptive were those that give rise to depressive or introjective dynamics. I believe they forced me to become like an actor, like Brad Pitt—hence the meaning of this symbolism in the dream. During my analysis, I realized that I was *acting* like someone I'm not in order to earn others' approval and to prevent potential experiences of rejection or abandonment. This defensive complex had an authoritarian grip over my ego that I couldn't see, which caused a great deal of suffering and prevented my true self from being expressed. This dream happened to come shortly after a breakthrough experience in analysis, where I became conscious of how depressive dynamics had caused me to suffer. Kalsched focuses largely on dissociation in his work, but in this dream (because of its known relationship to a specific daytime therapeutic discovery) we become aware that (in this case) the hostile forces are associated with defenses other than dissociation. Thus, we must appreciate that a full range and variety of different maladaptive defenses and complexes can inflict psychological harm, and can show up as these sorts of hostile figures in nightmares.

The dream portrays Dis and his outdated defenses being washed away by a flood, which seems to correspond with a cathartic discovery relating to the origins of my symptoms that came the day before while I was in therapy. The flood of emotion and psychic energy brought these harmful elements up to the surface where I could see them, and allowed me to become aware of why I was suffering as I was. This dream, however, suggests that the cathartic discovery resolved only part of the problem, because I was still stuck in Germany, *not home*. This is reminiscent of Odysseus's journey; he gets through one problem only to find another.

The next dream came a few months later, presenting a similar but different challenge as dynamics in my psyche had evolved.

The Transformation of Dis: Becoming an Ally

A woman and her baby are separated from me. Their plane crash-landed in Russia and they are trapped inside. I board a helicopter with a few other men on a rescue mission. When we arrive, the other guys rescue the woman and the baby, but I notice a little boy and I help him. We are rummaging through stuff on the plane to find objects we need to take back with us, including some of my personal belongings from childhood. The whole time, the KGB is watching us, and they're putting out all kinds of misinformation and propaganda. As we dig up things to recover them, several men are helping, including Brad Pitt and other men in World War II clothing. Their clothes are torn and dirty. They've been living a rough, underground life.

The scene has shifted from Nazi Germany to Russia, hinting that the problems I was facing now were less threatening and of a different nature than those I faced previously. Like Odysseus's mythic journey, my own shifted from place to place, from one challenge to the next. In this dream, a woman and a baby—an aspect of the archetypal feminine and the divine child—are being rescued from this hostile territory. This is the equivalent of Penelope and Telemachus, who are threatened by the suitors. At the same time, I am recovering important items related to my own childhood, which suggests the beginning of the retrieval of my own woundedness, and by extension (through tending to this pain), my vitality and liveliness.

Interestingly, the Brad Pitt figure is no longer an adversary but is now an ally, fitting the shapeshifter archetype. This suggests that his identity was distorted and that the defensive aspect of my psyche he represents is not *all* bad, that in certain situations he can be helpful. This is reminiscent of Iron John, the imposing, primitive figure covered in hair who lives underwater, like Brad Pitt in my previous dream. By the end of the tale, Iron John is revealed to be a wealthy prince and his support is critical to helping the prince overcome his challenges. In this dream, Brad Pitt has been a Prisoner of War (POW) living underground, and now he is emerging to offer me support.

When I first had this dream and reflected on the dirty, disheveled POW, I felt an enormous sense of sadness. It was a fitting metaphor of my experience at the time. Because of my severe war trauma, especially while clearing bombs off the roads of Sadr City, I had not felt comfortable driving back home, and as a result I rarely left my house unless it was necessary. I had become, in certain respects, a prisoner in my own home—symbolically portrayed in the dream as a POW. As helpful figures emerge from underground (from the unconscious), I am assisted in recovering other items that are symbolically significant as they hint toward the recovery of aspects of my own innocence—lost both in childhood and during war. This suggests once again the necessity of regression and suffering on the journey to wholeness. If we pay attention to symptoms and dreams, they can be valuable guides.

In this dream, we see that the hostile elements of my psyche are still active, despite the transformation of "Brad Pitt" from adversary to ally. The KGB is not threatening me or the divine child with the same hostility (or the same defenses) the Nazis did, but I'm being confronted with disinformation. I attribute this to hyperarousal; my traumatized psyche was still producing thoughts and feelings that threats could be anywhere. This misinformation from Dis, propaganda or distortions of reality, were the result of defenses aimed at protecting me by limiting what activities I engaged in.

Harry Wilmer was a psychoanalyst in both the Freudian and Jungian traditions and a Navy veteran who worked with Vietnam veterans, studying their dreams. The following dream is from one of his Vietnam veteran patients, and it also includes the symbolism of one being a "Prisoner of War."

The Americans have turned on me. It is as if I am the enemy. They tied me to a tree and threw axes at me. Sometimes I dream I am a POW being captured by the Americans.[187]

It seems this dreamer had also become like a Prisoner of War, unable to escape the torture imposed on him by aspects of his psyche that had turned against him. The fact that the hostile elements of the psyche are Americans speaks powerfully to the reality that once-helpful defenses have become maladaptive, causing rather than preventing suffering, like an autoimmune disease attacking healthy tissue. This dream also highlights that the toxic elements of the psyche are legion and can appear in many symbolic disguises.

If we consider my dreams shared here (largely reflecting the healing of childhood trauma) and the Vietnam veteran's dreams (reflecting combat trauma), we see that all our wounds can threaten essential, lifegiving elements of our personalities and must be treated with the utmost care. Coming home and experiencing a reunion with the divine child and true self requires nothing less than a healing of the entire personality. In Jungian psychotherapy, we focus on cultivating wholeness, bringing together the totality of the personality by considering all our life experiences and following the guidance of the unconscious. As we follow our dreams through our own inner odysseys and as we sacrifice our lifeblood by dedicating our care and attention to our dreams, symptoms, and wounds, we find ourselves on a path of transformation.

Veterans (and most of the rest of our society, including many therapists) must learn to see suffering differently. It is less an indication of pathology or disorder, than it is the soul's way of calling out to us and dragging us onward and downward into remembering who we really are. By heeding suffering's call, we're drawn into the realm of the unconscious so we might tend our wounds and be transformed. Facing our pain—when we can do so safely—is the pathway to freedom from the hostile elements of the psyche that threaten our connection to the true self and keep our inner kingdoms a wasteland. This is not something we do in just a few weeks of therapy. Odysseus's journey home takes him ten *intentional* years of striving—seven of which were spent humbly on Calypso's island as he learned to relate to the anima and his inner world. As we seek the way home, we must do so patiently, focusing on the present moment and the tasks that lie immediately before us, one breath at a time.

ODYSSEUS AND THE OAR:
LIFE BEYOND TRAUMA

Knowing is not enough; we must apply what we know. Willing is not enough; we must also act.
— Johann von Goethe (1749-1832)

When Odysseus was in the underworld, this is what Tiresias said to him:

When you get home you will take revenge on these suitors; and after you have killed them by force or fraud in your own house, *you must take a well-made oar and carry it on and on, till you come to a country where the people have never heard of the sea and do not even mix salt with their food, nor do they know anything about ships, and oars that are as the wings of a ship.* I will give you this certain token which cannot escape your notice. A wayfarer will meet you and will say it must be a winnowing shovel that you have got upon your shoulder; on this you must fix the oar in the ground and sacrifice a ram, a bull, and a boar to Poseidon. Then go home and offer hecatombs to all the gods in heaven one after the other. As for yourself, death shall come to you from the sea, and your life shall ebb away very gently when you are full of years and peace of mind, and your people shall bless you. All that I have said will come true.[188] (emphasis added)

The end of Odysseus's odyssey is the beginning of the rest of his life. The symbolism here strikes me as something that has relevance for many veterans. Once he has completed his homecoming and reached a point of security and stability, he is asked to do something very peculiar: to carry an oar (a tool gifted to him in the underworld by Tiresias that allowed him to navigate the journey home) to a people who are unfamiliar the sea (a symbol of the unconscious), and who do not mix salt with their food (whose lives lack flavor). Anyone who lives a one-sided life, without a connection to the unconscious, will have a stale, flavorless life. But, to navigate the seas of the unconscious you need tools and mentorship from someone who is familiar with this realm. Odysseus is being asked to step into a role where he is passing on the lessons he has learned through his return home from war—to pay it forward.

While Shay sees this prophecy in a negative light (accusing Odysseus of "running off again"), I believe its implications for returning combat veterans is quite meaningful and important.[189] Odysseus leaves his family for a new journey—or a completion of his long journey—because he has to. Yet, I don't take this literally, but see it as a symbolic inner process. It is his fate, and it cannot be denied. Hillman writes:

> Fathers have been far away for centuries: on military campaigns; as sailors on distant seas for years at a time; as cattle drivers, travelers, trappers, prospectors, messengers, prisoners, jobbers, peddlers, slavers, pirates, missionaries, migrant workers. … we need to ask where Dad might be when he's "not at home." When he is absent, to what else might be present? What calls him away? Rilke has an answer:

> Sometimes a man stands up during supper
> and walks outdoors, and keeps on walking,
> because of a church that stands somewhere in the East.
> And his children say blessings on him as if he were dead.
> And another man, who remains inside his house,
> dies there, inside the dishes and in the glasses,
> so that his children have to go far out into the world
> toward that same church, which he forgot.[190]

> [The father] must keep one foot in another space, one ear cocked for other messages. He must not lose his calling or forget obligations to the heart's desire and the image that he embodies.[191]

Hillman, Rilke, and Homer all saw that fathers—or all mature adults, for that matter—have a responsibility to answer the spiritual call of their inner lives. As Campbell's work centering around the hero's journey, which echoed Jung's understanding of the individuation process, made clear: the great task of our lives is to heed our inner calling—to go on our own odyssey, to transform through our exploration of the underworld, and then to bring the gifts that come with our transformation to those who need what we can offer. None of these wise writers is actually suggesting that a father's physical absence is good or necessary—and I certainly am not either. They're saying that if you don't answer your inner calling and share your gifts with a world that needs them, you have not completed your task. The soul demands the expression of its essence because that is its purpose. If you do not allow your soul to complete its journey, you will live a flavorless, frustrating life. I believe taking this inner journey reduces the likelihood that we'll feel tempted to literally run off, causing harm to our families and those who depend most on us. Odysseus completed his task because his soul demanded it, because a world that is not in touch with the unconscious is one where transformation and healing become difficult if not impossible.

Odysseus's journey is a story-map through individuation. When myths are reduced to mere allegories or, worse, literal statements about something that actually happened, the psyche loses the framework it needs to navigate transformation, which gives rise to symptoms that refuse to be solved as rational problems or with meds. When the inner significance is lost, so is the opportunity for transformation, and then, as Jung said, *the gods become diseases*:

> We think we can congratulate ourselves on having already reached such a pinnacle of clarity, imagining that we have left all these phantasmal gods far behind. But what we have left behind are only verbal specters, not the psychic facts that were responsible for the birth of the gods. We are still as much possessed today by autonomous psychic contents as if they were Olympians. Today they are called phobias, obsessions, and so forth; in a word, neurotic symptoms. *The gods have become diseases;* Zeus no longer rules Olympus but rather the solar plexus, and produces curious specimens for the doctor's consulting room, or disorders the brains of politicians and journalists who unwittingly let loose psychic epidemics on the world.[192]

When we lose touch with the unconscious and the archetypes of the collective unconscious—the gods and goddesses, so to speak— we lose touch with the soul and so it has no choice but to speak to us through suffering. After war, if we have no map and no myths to guide us, the soul has no choice but to bend us toward it through dreams or pain. When dreams and symptoms are diagnosed as pathological disturbances without a purpose and without a mythological trellis upon which they find their shape, everyone remains sick, except for those like Odysseus who come to see the unconscious and the symbolic suffering it produces as a guide. If we can learn to relate to our inner worlds in a satisfying way, the flow of life will proceed from the unconscious to the ego without being thwarted.

Myths like the *Odyssey* can restore the sacredness of our symptoms by helping us be transformed by them. These things help us find ourselves in relation to the psychological forces symbolized by the likes of Athena, Zeus, and all the gods and goddesses who still populate our inner worlds. The Odysseus figure that lives inside of and possesses combat veterans must find himself relativized by these psychological forces, or else the veterans he possesses will live unhappy lives, like those of the "heroes" Odysseus encounters in the underworld.

If veterans can *live their own Odysseys* and encounter *others* in a way that is transformative and healing, the ego-Self axis—the relationship between I and Thou—can be repaired, along with our sense that we're held and supported by the divine. Meaning is less created than discovered, and with its discovery we come away with a sense of life and home that transcends the physical realm. Jung wrote:

> Life has always seemed to me like a plant that lives on its rhizome. Its true life is invisible, hidden in the rhizome. The part that appears above ground lasts only a single summer. Then it withers away—an ephemeral apparition. When we think of the unending growth and decay of life and civilizations, we cannot escape the impression of absolute nullity. Yet I have never lost a sense of something

that lives and endures underneath the eternal flux. What we see is the blossom, which passes. The rhizome remains.[193]

In the end, I am left with an image of an elderly Odysseus sitting on a hillside just outside the gates of his home island of Ithaca. Penelope is sitting next to him, and Telemachus and his wife are playing with their own children nearby. The giggles of Odysseus's little granddaughter light up his once-frozen heart. The sun is setting over the sea, and Odysseus is blinking through the happy tears that fill his eyes and spill out on the ground, because the beauty of the moment is too powerful to contain. The peaceful old man looks over at the stunning blossoms in his garden, whose days are few in number because their time, like his and that of the sunset, are passing. With thankfulness, he drinks in this precious moment— quite the contrast from the trials and tribulations of his past.

Not far offshore are sails marked with the symbols of the country where he traveled with his oar. Their ships are pulling in an impressive haul of fish that will feed the hungry. Everywhere Odysseus looks, he sees the fruit of his soulful life. The moment is ripe with happiness, most especially in the eyes of his loving wife. Somewhere in the courtyard behind them, friends make music so wonderful it must have been born in heaven. Being stiff and elderly doesn't keep the old man from asking his dear Penelope if she would like to dance. The scene is so vibrant and full of love that even cool-headed Athena is moved to tears. No treasure could be more valuable than being able to *feel* life deeply enough to really live it, and to see through it well enough to know that the source of life goes deeper than we can ever understand.

My hope for the veterans who read this book is that they too may be transformed as I have been, and as Odysseus has, and that all of us will continue to heal as we grow in age. The last decade has taught me that recovery is possible, even if we still suffer at times. I am a different person because of the therapeutic process I underwent, even though I (like every human being) still experience pain. But suffering has a different meaning for me now—instead of being felt as a sign of something wrong, I now experience it as a sacred message, a voice of the soul that can teach me the next lesson I need to hear. Suffering is what led me through my own odyssey, and that journey led me into what I would call a mystical experience of the transcendent realities of life. I consider pain my greatest teacher, along with my dreams.

Writing this book has not been easy. It's been a Herculean task, taking the perseverance and no-quit attitude of Odysseus. As troublesome as this attitude can be when unchecked and out of control, Heracles and Odysseus still have vital roles to play in our lives. The life-saving actions of those veterans who took part in "Digital Dunkirk," to help innocent people escape the wrath of the Taliban, were ultimately inspired by the archetypal warrior finding its place within the psyche of the veterans involved. Odysseus still lives in me, and I let him take the wheel when necessary, steering the way home, taking turns with the likes of Athena, Circe, Calypso, Eumaeus, Telemachus, Penelope, and all the rest.

My sincerest hope is that our generation of warriors will carve out a new way of being for warriors of the future—that perhaps the next generation of warriors will not have to suffer as we and so many before us have, nor feel so lost. It is inevitable there will be other wars, because war itself is archetypal, and the archetypal warrior who lives in all of us and who will live in every person of the future is always looking for a fight. I fear it is likely that our children, or children's children will have to shed their blood as our generation did. And as I think of my now three-year-old son, I ache considering the possibility that my innocent, tender little boy should ever see such horrors as I have. I pray he does not. I pray none of our children or grandchildren do. And yet, it seems conflict and war have become an ever-present reality, and the consequences of war permanent and everlasting. Let it be our commitment, then, that we shall deepen our inner journeys not just for ourselves and our families, but to normalize deep, inner work as an inherent feature of warriorhood itself. If our descendants must share in our painful journey, let us aid them through our work and by *dreaming the myth onwards* (as Jung put it[194]), so we might be the good, and loving ancestors we now need.

APPENDIX I:

HOMER AND THE ORIGINS OF THE *ODYSSEY*

Much of what we know about the life of Odysseus comes from the so-called Homeric hymns, the *Iliad* and the *Odyssey*, which are among the oldest extant works of Western literature. Its written version is usually dated to somewhere between the 7th and 6th centuries BCE. We learn a bit more about Odysseus in other sources, which were recorded in other times, by different authors. Such sources include the *Aethiopis*, the *Little Iliad*, the *Iliupersis* (*Sack of Troy*) and Sophocles' play, *Ajax*.[195] Therefore, our imagination of Odysseus and his character is colored by stories other than the *Iliad* and the *Odyssey*. The *Iliad*, for example, contains no mention of the episode with the Trojan Horse (a story which Odysseus was a primary figure in), while the *Odyssey* refers to it only briefly (when the bard Demodocus sings of this event during a banquet in the palace of the Phaeacians). We learn of this event through the *Little Iliad* and the *Iliupersis*. The *Iliad* itself covers only fifty days of the ten-year-long Trojan War, focusing on a host of Greek and Trojan figures (of which Odysseus is a relatively minor figure), whereas the *Odyssey* focuses on Odysseus's journey home from the war.[196]

It should be noted that while the *Iliad* and the *Odyssey* are attributed to Homer, he is likely not their source. In fact, many scholars doubt a single person recorded these two poems, as the record appears to suggest they were composed too far apart. There are a variety of linguistic, material, and archaeological clues that inform this be-lief.[197, 198] Interestingly, scholars don't even agree that there was someone named Homer. *Some* suggest that Homer might have been a title rather than a person's name.

The poems were recorded in what is referred to as *Homeric Greek*, an artificial language composed of several different dialects that were never spoken by any actual group of individuals. It was developed to *sing* myths and tales according to the rhythm of the hexameter, so that the stories could be memorized and passed along orally.[199]

Scholars believe that the Trojan War, if there really was one, happened before the twelfth century BCE, before the early Greek (Mycenaean) civilization was wiped out by mysterious invaders, sending the region into a period referred to as the dark ages. After Mycenaean cities and fortresses were destroyed, no monumental constructions were built in Greece for more than four hundred years, and the archaeological record is nearly blank through this period.[200] The decimation was so severe that the system of writing (*Linear B*) used during that time by small coteries of tablet-writers was forgotten, and they did not recover a writing system for another four centuries. When writing reemerged and the region began to flourish again (in the eighth century BCE), it was an entirely new system of writing (an alphabetic system).[201] The ancient Greeks also lost some of the technologies, expertise, and wisdom held by earlier Greeks. For example, later Greeks—those of Homer's time (estimated between 800 and 700 BCE)—could not fathom how their earlier ancestors had built such impressive cities with gigantic stones. It was supposed that a race of gigantic cyclopes must have built earlier cities and their walls, and hence such walls have been referred to as "cyclopean walls."[202] The Greeks of Homer's time idealized their ancestors, imagining them in an especially heroic light, which is evident in the tales.[203]

A variety of clues support the conclusion that the *Iliad* and the *Odyssey* could not have been composed long before the eighth century BCE (which was approximately four centuries after the events they describe), as they contain references that those from earlier times simply couldn't have known.[204] At the same time, textual and archaeological evidence shows that the poems contain details that had to have been handed down from the time of the Trojan War, and thus the tales must have been passed on orally to have survived. They appear to have accumulated some new details over the centuries, evolving with the culture.[205, 206]

While we are indebted to Homer for recording these stories, it seems highly unlikely that the tales originated from his imagination. Therefore, we also owe a gratitude to all of the oral storytellers who kept this tale alive, generation after generation, through the dark ages of ancient Greece. These people likely looked to this tale as a way of coping with the collective *dark night of the soul* their culture was undergoing, and as a way of illuminating the inner challenges they must have faced in the midst of so much hardship.

APPENDIX II:

A CHRONOLOGICAL SUMMARY OF ODYSSEUS'S JOURNEY

Below is a summary of the key events that affected Odysseus, in the order they happened, from the *Iliad*, the *Odyssey*, and fragments of related tales.[207] In Homer's telling of the *Odyssey*, events are presented in a different sequence, so we learn about what Odysseus endured only when he recounts them later in time.

1. The Trojan War begins after Helen, Queen of Sparta, went away with Paris, Prince of Troy. In some accounts Helen went willingly, in others she was stolen and taken against her will. According to the mythological depiction of *The Judgement of Paris* (to which there is only a brief reference at the end of the *Iliad*), Paris was forced by Hermes, the messenger of the gods, to choose between the goddesses Aphrodite, Hera, and Athena. Aphrodite promised Paris that if he chose her, she would grant him Helen of Sparta (the wife of Menelaus—

Odysseus's friend and ally), the most beautiful woman in the world, and so Paris made that choice and thus began the Trojan War. Paris, Prince of Troy, *did not know his true identity* when he made this decision, because he had been rejected and abandoned in the wilderness as an infant after his parents, King Priam and Queen Hekuba, received a vision that he would cause the destruction of Troy.

2. According to the post-Homeric writer Pseudo-Apollodorus (writing sometime in the first or second century CE), Odysseus heard from a seer that if he were to go to war, he would have a difficult time getting home. Wanting to stay home with his wife, Penelope, and their infant son, Telemachus, when his allies came to beckon him to war, he pretended to be crazy to avoid the deployment. His (apparently brutal) allies then snatched his son and threatened to murder him, and thus, according to this later-written account, this is what impelled him to leave home and go to war.[208] During the Trojan War itself (only the final months of the war are recounted in the *Iliad.*), Odysseus was a prominent figure, known for his fierceness, level-headedness, wisdom, and cunning. Compared to other high-ranking figures, Odysseus is among the highest of character.

3. After the end of the ten-year Trojan War, Odysseus sets sail from Troy with twelve boats full of his men. The wind carries him to Ismarus, the city of the Cicones. There he and his men sack the town, killing many of its people, taking women and riches. In the process, Odysseus loses six men from each of his

twelve boats, or seventy-two men, symbolizing a significant loss of his power.

4. The actions of Odysseus and his men at Ismarus anger the Greek god, Zeus, who generates a storm that lasts for nine days. The storm drives them to the land of the Lotus Eaters, who eat food from a delicious flower that causes those who ingest it to forget about their homes. Fortunately, Odysseus is wise enough to drive his men back to his boat, and they sail on in great distress.

5. Next they arrive in the land of the Cyclopes (Cyclopes is plural, Cyclops is singular), a race of giant, one-eyed creatures. Soon they enter the cave of Polyphemus the Cyclops, who traps them in his cave and eats several of Odysseus's men. Eventually, Odysseus tricks the Cyclops, blinds him by stabbing him in his only eye, and he and his men escape. After escaping, Odysseus foolishly and repeatedly taunts Polyphemus, which imperils Odysseus and his men further. Odysseus proudly discloses his name to the monster as he seeks bragging rights, before learning Polyphemus is the son of Poseidon—the god of the sea—the very god no sailor can offend if he wishes to travel safely on the water.

6. As Odysseus and his men sail on, they arrive at the Aeolian island, where King Aeolus greets them kindly, sharing luxuries and feasts. They stay for a month and as they are departing, King Aeolus grants Odysseus a bag of winds to assist them on their journey home to Ithaca. For nine days and nights they sail, while Odysseus commands the rudder without sleeping in

hopes they will get home faster. He does it all himself, not including his men, nor does he use the bag of winds, just his own labor as helmsman. His neglected men begin to feel jealous of all Odysseus has acquired along their journey, and wonder what's inside the bag. On the tenth day, after Odysseus has fallen asleep his men open the bag of winds, and the winds blow them all the way back to Aeolia. Odysseus begs Aeolus for help, but Aeolus rejects him.

7. Without wind, Odysseus's men row for seven days until they reach Telephylus, the city of the giant Laestrygonians. A princess greets them as she is drawing water and directs Odysseus's men toward the home of her parents, the king and queen. Odysseus and his men are unwelcome, and the giants attack, killing and gobbling up most of Odysseus's men. Eleven of Odysseus's twelve ships are annihilated, leaving only the men on Odysseus's single remaining ship.

8. Odysseus and his remaining men (perhaps forty-six of the approximately 550 men who left Troy together) arrive at the Aeaean island where the goddess Circe lives. They are disoriented and terrified, given all they've now endured. Half of Odysseus's remaining men, led by Eurylochus, venture out to explore. They hear Circe singing and are invited into her home, where she feeds them a potion that turns them all into pigs. Eurylochus is suspicious, so he watches from afar and returns to the ship to tell Odysseus and the others what has happened. Odysseus heads out to Circe's home, and meets Hermes, the messenger of the gods, on the way. Hermes gifts

Odysseus a herbal talisman to protect him against Circe, then tells him exactly what he must do to navigate his encounter with her. Odysseus heeds Hermes's advice, and his experience with Circe becomes fruitful. Odysseus sleeps with Circe, and then her four servants bathe Odysseus with holy waters. Next, Odysseus requests that Circe restore his men, which she does and they become stronger and better-looking than they were before. Circe provides them with food and drink until they are restored to the level of health and strength they had when they left Ithaca. This all takes a year. When Odysseus feels ready to continue his journey, Circe says that he may leave but in order to be successful in his return home to Ithaca, he must first go to the house of Hades and Persephone in the underworld to consult with the ghost of the blind prophet Tiresias. This causes Odysseus and his men to weep.

9. Odysseus sails on as advised until he reaches the fertile shores of Persephone's country, where he finds the house of Hades. There, he makes a drink offering and sacrifice to the dead. First, he encounters the ghosts of one of his men and his mother, as well as the blind prophet Tiresias, who tells him *not* to harvest any of the sheep or cattle belonging to the Sun God on the Thrinacian island where they will land next. Tiresias also tells Odysseus that in Ithaca suitors are trying to steal his wife and his estate, and threatening his son's life, while he also issues a prophecy about Odysseus's future, explaining what he must do after he overcomes the suitors. After that, Odysseus sees and meets with the ghosts of many powerful and important wives and daughters of famous men, as well as

warriors and heroes (including many who were doomed because of overly heroic tendencies and a lack of respect for the gods), including Agamemnon, Achilles, Antilochus, Ajax, Minos, Tityus, Tantalus, Sisyphus, and Heracles.

10. Odysseus returns to his ship and men and sails onward, while a fair wind helps them along as they return to Circe's island to bury the body of their comrade properly (as Odysseus promised his ghost in the underworld). Circe tells Odysseus of the troubles that lie ahead and how to overcome them: the Sirens (he must be bound to the mast and command his men to stuff their ears with wax); the six-headed monster Scylla who devours any who come near (he must rush past her, not even bothering to put on his armor); and finally the whirlpool of Charybdis who sucks the surrounding waters into her abyss thrice daily (he must hug the side near Scylla and drive past quickly). Finally, she tells Odysseus not to touch the cattle and flocks of sheep that belong to the Sun God on the Thrinacian island (as Tiresias also advised).

11. As they sail on, Odysseus tells his men exactly what they are supposed to do. First, they successfully navigate past the Sirens, and then as soon as they are past the their islands, Odysseus spots a great wave arising from Charybdis, which causes his men to panic. As Odysseus recounts this part of the story, he noted that he made only one mistake: *He put on his armor.* This error of judgment puts him and his men in harm's way, as they come desperately close to Charybdis while Scylla devours six of Odysseus's men—a sight he finds the most sickening of all

that he experiences. Yet they do manage to get past this set of trials.

12. Next, Odysseus and his remaining men (now about thirty-nine) reach the island of the Sun God, Hyperion. Odysseus warns his men that they must absolutely not harvest any of the cattle or sheep belonging to the Sun God. After they arrive and begin to rest, they weep the loss of their comrades, and then Zeus produces a storm with unfavorable winds that lasts a month, causing them to remain there, stranded. Over the course of a month, they eat all their provisions, then try to get food by fishing, catching birds, and whatever else they can get their hands on because they're starving. Then, one day while Odysseus is sleeping, Eurylochus convinces the rest of the men to kill the Sun God's cattle. When Odysseus awakens to the smell of meat cooking, he cries out in anguish and prayer to the gods because of his men's failure to obey their orders. When the gods learn of their violation, Zeus promises to exact revenge.

13. As soon as favorable weather sat in, Odysseus and his men board their ship and continue on their journey. Once they are far from land, Zeus produces a terrible storm that begins to break the ship apart, and then a lightning bolt strikes and tears it to pieces. When this happens, all of Odysseus's men perish, leaving him the sole survivor clinging to a piece of wreckage. Odysseus is dragged back into an encounter with the Charybdis and only manages to escape its pull because of a fig tree, which he clings to in desperation. When Charybdis runs her

course and quits sucking in the waters, Odysseus paddles with his hands until he is out of danger. He's then carried by the sea for ten days and nights, when he is washed up onto the Ogygian island where the goddess Calypso lives.

14. Odysseus stays with the goddess Calypso for seven years, sleeping with her in her cave. While with her, he is filled with grief. He spends much of his time sitting along the shore, weeping and thinking of home. After seven years, the goddess Athena implores Zeus to ask for his release, and he does. Hermes, on behalf of the gods and goddesses, asks Calypso to let Odysseus go. She does so willingly, and provides a great deal of support to prepare Odysseus for his journey home. When Odysseus is ready, he sets sail, and all goes well for eighteen days, though more trouble lies ahead.

15. After eighteen days of smooth sailing, Poseidon raises a storm against Odysseus in an act of revenge, since Odysseus had blinded his son, Polyphemus the Cyclops. In the storm, Odysseus's ship is dashed to bits, and in order to avoid drowning, he has to ditch the clothes gifted him by Calypso. In a moment of desperation, he is saved by the marine goddess Ino, who gifts him her enchanted veil to protect him from harm, as long as he promises to return it once he reaches land. Athena also steps in to provide assistance, stilling the winds and helping guide him to shore near the city of the Phaeacians. As promised, he throws the Ino's magical veil back into the sea.

16. Athena goes to Princess Nausicaa, the daughter of King Alcinous and Queen Arete of the Phaeacians, in a dream, and

inspires Nausicaa to leave the palace to venture out in the countryside where she will find Odysseus. After they meet, Nausicaa directs Odysseus to her parents' palace, instructing him to approach the queen in order to earn her compassion. Odysseus follows her advice precisely and delivers his petition, explaining his situation and asking for help. His royal hosts treat him favorably, offering their full support. During his stay there, they throw banquets in his honor, and a bard sings a number of meaningful tales that have a cathartic and therapeutic effect on Odysseus. Before sending Odysseus home, they adorn him with gifts and riches.

17. As soon as Odysseus is aboard the Phaeacian ship, he lays down and falls into a deep sleep. Odysseus sleeps the entire way home to Ithaca, and their voyage is without incident. When they arrive in Ithaca, the Phaeacians lift Odysseus up with his rug and linen sheet, and place him down upon the sand of his native shores while he is still sleeping. Then, they take all of the presents Athena had persuaded the Phaeacians to give him, and gather them around the root of an olive tree next to where they've placed him. When Odysseus wakes up, he doesn't even recognize his homeland, and he's worried what he should do with all the riches given him. Soon Athena approaches (at first in disguise and then reveals her true identity) and explains how she has helped him thus far, and gives him additional assistance. They hide all of the treasure in a cave, then sit at the base of an olive tree to discuss how Odysseus will overcome the suitors. To assist his efforts to reclaim his kingdom, Athena disguises Odysseus as a poor, old

beggar.

18. While Odysseus finds his way to his old friend and swineherd, Eumaeus, Athena transports herself to Sparta to retrieve Odysseus's son, Telemachus. Odysseus remains in disguise so that Eumaeus doesn't know who he is. While they're together, Odysseus makes up a tale, telling Eumaeus that Odysseus will return home soon. Eumaeus then shares his own story with Odysseus: Eumaeus is from an island called Syra, a land free of pestilence or illness. When he was a boy, he was kidnapped by Taphian pirates who took him away over the sea and then sold him to Odysseus' father, Laertes. As Eumaeus completes the story about how he was separated from his family, it just so happens that Telemachus returns and is reunited with his father.

19. After Telemachus and Odysseus are reunited, they lay out a plan to overcome the 108 suitors who are threatening Telemachus's life and threatening to steal Penelope and Odysseus's estate. Odysseus will remain in disguise until the suitors are overcome. Meanwhile, the suitors get word that Telemachus has returned to Ithaca (despite their attempt to ambush and kill him while he was at sea), and now they consider how they might kill him before he gets back to his home. The next day, Telemachus returns home and shares with his mother all that Menelaus has shared with him about Odysseus, and then Odysseus returns to his home too (though disguised as a beggar). When Odysseus comes inside, he is mistreated and abused by the suitors. Next, Telemachus and

Odysseus prepare to kill the suitors, and then Odysseus has a chance to speak with Penelope, though he is still in disguise and she does not realize it is her husband. She shares about how she will host a tournament of axes the following day, where the suitors will be given the opportunity to win her hand. All they have to do is string Odysseus's bow and shoot an arrow through twelve axe handles, just as Odysseus used to do.

20. The next day, Telemachus hosts a feast and sits Odysseus in a place of honor, but he is abused by the suitors yet again. When the feast is finished, Penelope brings down Odysseus's bow for the tournament of axes. Telemachus tries to string it and cannot. Then, the suitors begin to try, and they cannot either, even after warming it in a fire to make the task easier. Finally, Odysseus gets the bow in his hands, and he kills all of the suitors, leaving only a bard and a herald alive.

21. When Odysseus and Penelope are finally reunited, she is in shock and finds it difficult to believe he is finally home. Odysseus is then washed and anointed in his own home, given a shirt and cloak, and Athena restores him as even taller and stronger than before. When he is restored, he goes before Penelope, who tests him to ensure he really is Odysseus. Penelope orders Euryclea to move his bed, which causes Odysseus to protest saying this would be impossible, because he made it and he knows that it cannot be moved. He shares details about the bed that only Odysseus could know, and when Penelope hears this, she breaks down in tears and throws her arms

around Odysseus, kissing him, as he embraces her.

22. When they awake in the morning, Odysseus tells Penelope that he must go see his father, Laertes, while at the same time he warns that news will soon spread about his killing of the suitors. Odysseus, Telemachus, Philoetius, and Eumaeus put on their armor and head to see Laertes, while Athena conceals their presence from others. When Odysseus and the others arrive at the home of Laertes, there is a tearful reunion. While Odysseus and the others are in the home of Laertes, rumor spreads around the town that Odysseus has killed all of the suitors, angering the people, many of whom are family and friends of the dead. Athena looks on, noting that trouble is on the way. She goes to Zeus asking what should be done in this situation. Zeus encourages her to provoke them to swear a covenant of peace. As Odysseus and the others finish dinner, the men of the town are close by seeking them out, so they put on their armor and go out to meet them. Odysseus is joined by his son, father, and two men, as well as Dolius (Penelope's servant) and his six sons—twelve men in total. Additionally, Athena is with him. Just after the battle begins, Athena and Zeus intervene, bringing the battle to an immediate halt, and they force the townspeople to establish a bond of peace with Odysseus.

23. Though not in the *Odyssey*, we know that after the story ends, Odysseus had to carry an oar on his shoulder and travel to a land where people did not know the sea, or use salt with their food. Evidently this was a symbolic act whereby Odysseus was

meant to share his story, making people aware of the ocean realm he had come to know so intimately. We know this came to pass, because Tiresias prophesied that it would, while he also declared that Odysseus would live a long life.

APPENDIX III:
PRIMARY CHARACTERS AND FIGURES IN THE *ODYSSEY*

Gods and Goddesses

Athena (Athene in some accounts; in Rome, Minerva): daughter of Zeus; goddess of

wisdom and war; divine guide of Odysseus

Aphrodite (in Rome, Venus): daughter of Zeus and Dione; goddess of love; she promises Paris of Troy the love of Helen of Sparta, which ignites the Trojan War. Though she is married to the creative god, Hephaestus the builder, she had an affair with Ares, the god of war.

Ares (in Rome, Mars): son of Zeus; god of war who fell in love with Aphrodite.

Hades (in Rome, Pluto): son of Cronus (in Rome, Saturn); brother of Zeus and Poseidon; god of the dead and king of the under-world.

Hera (in Rome, Juno): wife of Zeus; goddess of women, marriage, family, and childbirth. While not present in the Odyssey, she is one of the three goddesses who Paris of Troy must choose from (the other two are Aphrodite and Athena).

Hermes (in Rome, Mercury): son of Zeus; the messenger of the gods.

Persephone (also called Kore/in Rome Proserpina): daughter of Demeter; wife of Hades and queen of the underworld.

Poseidon (in Rome, Neptune): son of Cronus (Saturn); brother of Zeus and Hades; king of the sea. He is also the father of Polyphemus the Cyclops, who Odysseus encounters and offends, thus provoking Poseidon's revenge.

Zeus (in Rome, Jupiter): son of Cronus (Saturn); king of gods and goddesses and ruler of the sky, thunder, and lightning.

Lesser Gods and Goddesses, as well as Demigods and Mythic Figures

Aeolus: divine keeper of the winds; he grants Odysseus a bag of winds to help him on his journey home, but when Odysseus's men open the bag, their ship is blown back to the place they had just left.

Antiphates: king of the Laestrygonian giants. The Laestrygonians attack Odysseus's men, wiping out eleven of twelve ships, killing most of his men.

Calypso: daughter of Atlas; island goddess and nymph of Ogygia; Odysseus is shipwrecked on her island, and he is forced to stay with her for seven years.

Circe: daughter of the sun; enchantress and goddess of the wild. She is the first female figure Odysseus encounters on his journey home, and he stays with her for a year. She directs Odysseus to the underworld to find Tiresias and tells him how to navigate various challenges.

Charybdis: a whirlpool Odysseus must sail past that threatens to devour any who come too near (near the six-headed monster, Scylla).

Heracles (in Rome, Hercules): son of Zeus who (in the *Odyssey*) is dead and lives in the underworld, where Odysseus meets him. He was the greatest of the Greek heroes and a model of masculinity, so his lowly station in the underworld is a symbol of the limits of unrestrained heroism.

Idothea (Eidothea in some accounts): sea nymph and daughter of Proteus, the old man of the sea. She helps Menelaus navigate his journey home, directing him to descend to the bottom of the sea to find Proteus, much like Odysseus having to descend into the underworld to find Tiresias.

Polyphemus: son of Poseidon; giant Cyclops who Odysseus has a nearly disastrous encounter with early on in his journey home.

Proteus: old man who lives at the bottom of the sea, who Menelaus must descend to in order to get home.

Scylla: six-headed monster who dwells on a cliff, whom Odysseus must pass by, while the whirlpool Charybdis sits nearby.

Tiresias (Teiresias in some accounts): the blind prophet of Thebes who dwells in the underworld. He tells Odysseus how to get home and what he must do, while offering a prophesy about Odysseus's future.

Human Figures

Aeolus: keeper of the winds; he grants Odysseus a bag of winds to help him on his journey home, but when Odysseus's men open the bag, their efforts are undone. In the *Odyssey*, Aeolus is presented as a mortal, though later Greek writers regarded him as a god.

Agamemnon: brother of Menelaus, king of the Greeks, and commander of the Greek army at Troy. He is known for his abysmal character, poor judgement, and offensive behavior.

Alcinous: King of the Phaeacians; husband of Queen Arete and father of Princess Nausicaa; Alcinous is particularly supportive of Odysseus and assists him in his journey home to Ithaca.

Anticleia (Anticlea in some accounts): Odysseus's mother, who committed suicide. Odysseus meets her in the underworld during his return.

Arete: Queen of the Phaeacians; wife of Alcinous; Arete has compassion for Odysseus and she plays a key role in helping him to return to Ithaca.

Eumaeus: Odysseus's swineherd and a faithful servant. He was stolen from his homeland, Syra, when he was a young child. When Odysseus returns to Ithaca, Eumaeus gives him shelter and assists him in his efforts to overthrow the hostile suitors.

Euryclea (Eurycleia in some accounts): head housemaid for Odysseus and Penelope, who was also the wet-nurse of both Odysseus and Telemachus.

Helen of Sparta: daughter of Zeus and Leta; wife of Menelaus, King of Sparta; the Trojan War began after Helen was either abducted or ran away with Paris, Prince of Troy.

Menelaus: King of Sparta (brother of Agamemnon), who fought alongside Odysseus in Troy. The war began when his wife, Helen, was taken by Paris of Troy. Menelaus undergoes his own adventure to get home, which mirrors that of Odysseus. Menelaus hosts Telemachus after Athena sends Telemachus to Sparta in search of news of his father.

Nausicaa: Princess of the Phaeacians; daughter of King Alcinous and Queen Arete; Athena inspires Nausicaa to seek out Odysseus and lead him to her parents, who assist him on his homeward journey.

Laertes: father of Odysseus.

Odysseus (Ulysses, in Rome): son of Laertes; king of Ithaca who serves as a commander of Greek troops during the Trojan War, and who is the focus of the Odyssey.

Paris, Prince of Troy: son of King Priam and Queen Hekuba of Troy, who abandoned him in the wilderness as an infant after they received a prophecy that he would cause the destruction of Troy. Paris was later forced by Hermes to choose between Aphrodite, Hera, and Athena, and Aphrodite promised Paris Helen of Troy, which led to the beginning of the Trojan War.

Penelope: Odysseus's faithful wife, who waits for him for twenty years. She is known for deceiving the suitors by spending her days weaving a pall (a burial cloth) for Laertes, Odysseus's father, then unweaving it every night. She promised them she would choose a new husband once she finished the task, but delayed completing it to buy time as she waited for Odysseus's return.

Philoetius: Odysseus's cowherd and faithful servant who assists Odysseus as he battles against the suitors.

Telemachus: Odysseus's son, who is about twenty years old at the time of the Odyssey. He was an infant when Odysseus left for the Trojan War. His life is threatened by the suitors, and he plays a key role helping his father to dispatch them.

APPENDIX IV:
GLOSSARY OF JUNGIAN TERMS

The following definitions are presented according to my own interpretation of Jung's concepts, while taking into consideration the critiques of other Jungian and depth psychological writers. Readers are encouraged to explore Jung's own definitions of these terms, which can be found in his essay *Psychological Types*, in the dedicated chapter, *Definitions.*[209]

Anima (Greek and Latin for "soul"): The symbolic personification of the unconscious aspect of the male psyche (according to Jung's conception), which appears in men's dreams (and male-centric myths) as a female figure, sometimes referred to as the feminine aspect of the male personality.[210] Others have challenged the notion that the anima is unique to the male psyche, asserting the anima is active in females as well.[211] However, Jung asserted that "In every case where the individuality (q.v.) is unconscious, and therefore associated with the soul, the soul-image has the character of the same sex."[212] This difference of interpretation is a matter of significant controversy in the Jungian community. The anima (and corresponding animus in females, according to Jung's conception) exists in a compensatory nature to the persona, therefore whatever is absent from the persona is then constellated in the inward-facing anima (or animus). Jung conceived the anima as the mediator or "bridge to the unconscious," guiding the ego through transformative experiences.[213, 214, 215]

Animus (Greek and Latin for "spirit"): The symbolic personification of the unconscious aspect of the female psyche (according to Jung), which appears in women's dreams (and female-centric myths) as a male figure, the masculine aspect of the female personality. Some Jungian analysts and depth psychologists, including Hillman and Downing have challenged the notion that women have any less need of "soul" (anima) than men, or that their nature implies a need for "animus" or "spirit." [216, 217] Given cultural differences between Jung's time and our own, and how culture influences our personalities (and personae), we have to appreciate that what Jung observed about the animus (and anima) is likely a bit different from what we observe today. Again, both animus and anima exist in a compensatory relationship with the persona; whatever is missing from the persona will appear in the animus (or anima).[218]

Archetypes: underlying patterns of psychological experience which are reflected as images, symbols, or ideas that repeat themselves in dreams, myths, fairytales, stories, religions, artwork, and other human creations. There are a wide variety of archetypes which present themselves in certain situations. For example, story patterns themselves are archetypal, one of which the mythologist Joseph Campbell called "the hero's journey," and within stories we see archetypal events like the call to adventure, crossing the threshold, the decent, ascent, and return with the boon, and these correspond to stages or events within the individuation process. There are also archetypal figures that correspond with elements of the psyche, such as the shadow, anima/animus, wise old man, wise old woman, *puer aeternus* (eternal male child), *puella* (eternal female child), trickster, Self, and many others. A few other examples of archetypes include the *axis mundi*, cosmic tree, or world navel; the archetype of initiation; mandalas; the quaternity; and as presented in this book, *the archetype of the warrior's return*.

Complex: an unconscious, emotionally charged collection of images, which has an archetypal (or collective) core, and a personal shell composed of personal associations. When certain images are evoked, it activates a complex and its associated images, emotions, or ideas, and initiates a psychological response which can (if strong enough) disrupt the flow of consciousness and the ego's control over the psyche. Thus, it behaves as if it were a foreign element within the psyche that has its own power.[219]

Ego: the central complex within the personality and our field of consciousness. We tend to identify with the ego and experience it as "I" or "me." A person with a strong ego can experience himself or herself securely and independently of other contents (such as emotions or archetypal images) within the unconscious, rather than finding himself or herself completely overwhelmed and at the mercy of them.

Individuation: the natural process of development through which individuals are formed and differentiated as unique or distinct. Given that our personalities are often and rather easily distorted by a variety of influences, such as complexes and maladaptive psychological defenses, the true self (the personality as it would be if not for the interference of these influences) can be lost. Individuation can therefore be understood as the developmental process that restores, heals, and transforms the personality so that the individual can experience him/herself in the truest and most vital state. In this state, the person experiences him/herself as consciously being in touch with the unconscious, the Self, and the inherently spiritual forces of nature.

Inflation: a state in which the individual's ego perceives itself to be unrealistically high (or low, as in negative inflation or deflation). In such a state, the individual may not recognize his/her bounds or limitations, coming across as grandiose. Usually, this occurs when the ego is too one-sided, or when the person fails to recognize him/herself as being in relationship with other aspects of consciousness.

Persona (Latin for "mask"): a functional complex that exists for the purpose of helping the individual serve a role in society. The persona is merely the mask or the role one plays. *Identifying with* one's persona inhibits one's development, as it is merely a shell of the personality meant to help one relate with the world.

Projection: a psychological process where we cast out our inner, psychological contents (certain qualities or emotions that belong to us) and experience them as belonging to another person or object. When we project our own contents onto another, it is generally because those contents are unconscious within us. Unable to "own" our inner realities, we project them onto others. So, if for some reason we are defended against feeling anger and do not realize we are angry, we might project our anger onto another person and believe they are angry. We can project positive or negative characteristics, qualities, emotions, or other psychic contents onto others.

Psyche (Greek and Latin for "soul"): the ancient Greeks referred to psyche as "the breath of life." We can understand the psyche as that ineffable, conscious presence that expresses itself through our symptoms, emotions, longings, creative endeavors, and all that we create or that comes from us, intentionally or not. Jung wrote, "by psyche I understand the totality of all psychic processes, conscious as well as unconscious. By soul, on the other hand, I understand a clearly demarcated functional complex that can best be described as a "personality.""[220]

Self: in Jungian literature, the term *self* (with a lowercase *s*), and *Self* (with a capital *S*), are understood as distinct psychic elements. Shamdasani noted that Jung equated his term *Self* to the Hindu notion of Brahman and Atman.[221] Whereas the concept of Brahman refers to the cosmic soul—the soul of the universe of which we are all an inseparable part—Atman is conceived to be the personal, indwelling soul that experiences itself as separate from the rest. Likewise, the individual *self* is not a lone, independent entity that is governed exclusively by the *ego* and its will, but seems to be subject to a greater ordering principle, the *Self*, which is the archetype of unity and totality. Jung believed the *Self* seems to direct one's development toward a certain goal through the process of individuation. Often, in Jungian literature, when referring to the individual ego, the term *self* is used, whereas references to the *Self* are to the archetypal, superordinate, organizing principle of the psyche.[222]

Shadow: Unconscious aspects of the personality, either positive or negative, which the conscious ego remains unaware of, rejects, or ignores. Shadow elements are personified in dreams by "non-ego" images or other persons.

Symbol: an imagistic expression representing an otherwise inexpressible or unknown thing, idea, or quality.

Appendix V:
General Guidelines for Therapists

1. **Appreciate individuality:** While all veterans may have some shared experiences, each veteran remains unique with their own experiences, histories, challenges, and qualities. Two veterans who have similar symptoms and trauma histories may require entirely different approaches in therapy, and their symptoms may have their own unique meaning to be uncovered and understood.

2. **Respect the mystery:** While there are a variety of reasons we assign diagnoses and formulate specific treatment approaches to treat problems that clients experience, another, less obvious, reason we do this is to give us a sense of control—to help manage our own anxiety in the presence of the great unknowns of any therapeutic process. This may be especially true when we aren't sure how to help someone, and because of the steep challenges many veterans face, it's understandable that we therapists sometimes feel unsure and even insecure. We can try to be honest with ourselves about

our own feelings relating to this process and be prepared to be a good student, not just a good teacher. We can respect the mystery that comes with being in the unknown with our veteran clients, acknowledging that there are many unknowns of any therapeutic experience, including what the ultimate outcomes will be and how we will get there. In my experience, many veterans benefit from unstructured approaches where their experiences can unfold organically. This means we have to trust their process, as opposed to the other way around, where we ask veterans to follow a predetermined path laid out for them by the therapist.

3.Develop competence in multiple theories and thera-peutic approaches: Because each veteran—like all clients— is a unique individual with unique needs, we should be ready for anything. Our clients will benefit if we are flexible and multipronged in our approach. It is unwise to assume any specific theory, approach, or therapy will be a fit for *all* veterans. Being prepared for whatever comes up enhances our ability to serve veterans. One day the client may benefit from learning emotional regulation skills or receiving help understanding how certain behaviors might fuel certain symptoms, while in another session the client might present a dream we can explore with them, perhaps focusing on some of the archetypal images that have mythological parallels. Another session might require the skills to process a specific trauma that arises; and yet another might invite us to explore characterological challenges arising from childhood traumas or military experiences. I've yet to work with a veteran where the treatment process was straightforward, allowing me to utilize any single therapeutic approach. When you find yourself in territory that is unfamiliar, seek consultation with another professional who can help you develop new capacities.

4. <u>Do your own work</u>: To paraphrase C.G. Jung, "You cannot take your patients any further than you have been yourself." I agree with this perspective wholeheartedly, and I've seen how true it is in my work on both ends of the therapy room—as a patient and as a therapist. In fact, my experiences as a patient allows me to experience this reality as a therapist, and it would be impossible for understand this had I not learned so much about myself while sitting on my analyst's couch. Therapists who have done a significant amount of their own personal therapy are a tremendous asset to their veteran-clients; and those who have not tend to be limited in what help they can provide. If you haven't undergone at least a year of weekly therapy, I highly recommend it. It will be a gift to you and to your clients. And, if possible, consider working for a few years with a Jungian Analyst or depth psychologist, as an approach that works with unconscious material is likely to evoke a greater awareness of challenges and gifts you may not be conscious of.

Finally, taking good care of yourself is essential when working with veterans, especially if they have experienced horrific combat traumas and/or if you've experienced trauma yourself. Having unresolved trauma of your own makes you vulnerable to vicarious traumatization and burnout—and if you're struggling to hold the traumatic material of your veteran-patient, they are going to know it and it could negatively impact them. Countless veterans have told me stories where their therapist admitted or demonstrated they could not adequately hold their veteran-client through their process. When therapists' responses make veterans feel like their trauma is "too much," it leaves them feeling even more hopeless and adds to their pre-existing distrust of therapists and therapy. So, if you haven't been intentional in tending to your own inner world in a therapeutic context, please do not take on clients with combat trauma. This is not a population to experiment with.

5. Develop veteran-specific cultural competency: It is widely believed that a lack of cultural competency relating to veterans is an impediment to their treatment process, so please do anything and everything you can to better understand veterans' experiences from multiple perspectives. Reading books, like this one, is a good place to start. Other professionals in the field including Edward Tick (*War and the Soul* and *Warrior's Return*), Jonathan Shay (*Achilles in Vietnam* and *Odysseus in America*), Roger Brooke (*An Archetypal Approach to Treating Combat PTSD*), Joseph Bobrow (*Waking Up from War*), and Shauna Springer (*Warrior*) have written great books and articles that will enhance your understanding of working with veterans in a therapeutic context. Other important books about war and veterans include Karl Marlantes (*What It Is Like to Go to War*), James Hillman (*A Terrible Love of War*), and Sebastian Junger (*Tribe*). In my opinion, these are must-reads. I also recommend reading memoirs and poetry by veterans of different wars, and watching movies (including documentaries) that accurately depict veterans' experiences, such as *Saving Private Ryan, The Hornet's Nest*, Sebastian Junger's *Restrepo* and *Korengal*. These show in granular detail some of the reality your clients have lived through. Finally, if possible, attend trainings that focus on this topic.

6. <u>Remember, it's not all about trauma:</u> If there's anything therapists take away from this book, I hope it's the awareness that veterans' suffering can have a variety of possible roots. It's not all about trauma, and diving straight into trauma is usually not the best starting point. Jung's psychology helps us understand that the unconscious doesn't like it when we are living a false life or identified with a narrow aspect of ourselves. If we're out of touch with our true nature, the unconscious will try to buck the false personality by any means necessary to bring us back to ourselves. Don't forget, the whole of military life—from basic training, to military culture, to war itself—pulls veterans deeper and deeper into one's identity as a warrior, and this in itself is a major barrier to healing and transformation. Ultimately, many veterans' therapeutic processes will invite them to navigate a transitional challenge wherein they become conscious of different aspects of their personality with competing influences: An old warrior self must retire and give way to the emergence of a new self. Much of the time, this is a prerequisite to doing deeper trauma work, because otherwise the old, overly rigid warrior self imposes barriers that make it difficult for the veteran to accept their emotional experiences and hold themselves in a way that is supportive and healing. In the end, the more flexible and open-minded we can be, the better—and adopting this attitude and way of being helps the veterans we serve to do the same. In the end, I believe veterans would be much better served by therapies that tend to their whole souls, as opposed to rigid, trauma-focused therapies that take aim at specific symptoms.

ABOUT THE AUTHOR

Adam Magers is a Licensed Professional Counselor who served in the US Army as a combat medic and "IED (Improvised Explosive Device) Hunter" in Baghdad during the Iraq War. He was awarded the Army Commendation Medal with Valor and Combat Action Badge for his actions during the Battle of Sadr City. He is an alumnus of Pacifica Graduate Institute and a recipient of the Joseph Campbell Scholarship. Since 2014, he has worked with hundreds of veterans in a variety of capacities. He is the architect of *The Battle Within's* five-day *Revenant Journey* program, and the co-architect of their *Frontline Therapy Network*, which connects veterans, first responders, and frontline medical professionals to psychotherapists at no cost. In addition to a Master's Degree in Counseling Psychology with an emphasis in Depth Psychology, he also possesses a Master's Degree in the cognate fields of International Relations and Comparative Politics from Missouri State University.

ABOUT *THE BATTLE WITHIN*

The Battle Within is a 501(c)(3) nonprofit organization that provides veterans and first responders with quality therapeutic programs and services, including the five-day Revenant Journey program, and the Frontline Therapy Network. The five-day Revenant Journey program is, in essence, the application of the lessons laid out in this book, following *the archetype of the warrior's return* as the roadmap to the healing and transformation process. The Frontline Therapy Network is a psychotherapy referral network that seeks to create the best possible client-therapist match so that veterans and first responders can receive treatments that are catered to their unique needs.

ENDNOTES

[1] Steenkamp, M. M., Litz, B. T., Marmar, C. R. (2020). First-line psychotherapies for military-
related PTSD. *Journal of the American Medical Association*, Vol. 323, Issue 7, pp. 656-
657.

[2] Shedler, J. (2018). Where is the evidence for "evidence-based" therapy? *Psychiatric Clinics of North America*, Vol. 41, pp. 319-329.

[3] Shedler, J. (2017). Selling bad therapy to trauma victims: Patients and therapists should ignore
new guidelines for treating trauma. *Psychology Today*, November 19, 2017. Retrieved from https://www.psychologytoday.com/us/blog/psychologically-minded/201711/selling-bad-therapy-trauma-victims

[4] Jung, C. G. (1964). Approaching the unconscious. In C. G. Jung & M-L. von Franz (Eds.), *Man and his symbols* (pp. 18-103). London, England: Aldus Books, p. 64.

[5] Jung, C. G. (1967). Psychoanalysis and neurosis. In H. Read et al. (Eds.), *The collected works of C. G. Jung: Vol. 4. Freud and psychoanalysis* (pp. 243-251). Princeton University Press. (Original work published 1916), para. 574.

[6] Kalsched, D. (2013). *Trauma and the soul: A psycho-spiritual approach to human development and its interruption.* Hove, East Sussex, England: Routledge.

⁷ Jung, Approaching the unconscious, p. 64.

⁸ Jung, C. G. (1967). Commentary on The secret of the golden flower (R. F. C. Hull, Trans.). In H. Read et al. (Eds.), *The collected works of C. G. Jung* (Vol. 13, pp. 1-56). Princeton, NJ: Princeton University Press. (Original work published 1929), para. 62.

⁹ Moore, R. L. (2001). *The archetype of initiation: Sacred space, ritual process, and personal transformation: Lectures and essays* (M. J. Havlick Jr., Ed.). Philadelphia: Xlibris Corporation.

¹⁰ Haile, B. (2019). *Origin Legend of the Navajo enemy way: Text and translation*. Flagstaff, AZ: Native Child Dinétah. (Originial work published 1938).

¹¹ Jung, C. G. (1998). *Jung's seminar on Nietzsche's Zarathustra*. (J. L. Jarret, Ed.) Princeton, NJ: Princeton University Press, p. 27.

¹² Marlantes, K. (2011). *What it is like to go to war*. New York: Atlantic Monthly Press, pp. 184-186.

¹³ Jung, C. G. (1971). Psychological types. In H. Read et al. (Eds.), *The collected works of C. G. Jung* (Vol. 6, 2nd ed.). Princeton, NJ: Princeton University Press. (Original work published 1921), paras. 806-808.

¹⁴Jung, C. G. (1968). Aion: Researches into the phenomenology of the self (R. F. C. Hull, Trans.) In H. Read et al. (Eds.), *The collected works of C.G. Jung* (Vol. 9i) Princeton University Press. (Original work published 1951) https://doi.org/10.1515/9781400851058, pp. 11-22.

¹⁵ Jung, Psychological types. para. 805.

¹⁶ Jung, Psychological types, para. 808.

¹⁷ Jung, C. G. (1966). The relations between the ego and the unconscious (R. F. C. Hull, Trans.). In H. Read et al. (Eds.), *The collected works of C. G. Jung* (Vol. 7, 2nd ed., pp. 121–241). Princeton, NJ: Princeton University Press. (Original work published 1928), paras. 303-304.

[18] Kerven, R. (2017). *Viking myths & sagas: Retold from ancient Norse texts.* New York, NY: Chartwell Books, pp. 37-39.

[19] Wilmer, H. A. (1986a). Combat nightmares: Toward a therapy of violence. *Spring,* p. 133.

[20] McWilliams, N. (2011). *Psychoanalytic diagnosis: Understanding personality structure in the clinical process* (2nd ed.). New York, NY: Guilford Press.

[21] Siemaszko, C. (2019). Former Democratic rising star and Afghanistan war veteran speaks out for
first time about PTSD treatment. *NBC News,* June 13, 2019. Retrieved from https://www.nbcnews.com/news/us-news/former-democractic-rising-star-afghanistan-war-veteran-speaks-out-first-n1017406

[22] Marlantes, *What it is like to go to war,* pp. 236-237.

[23] Shay, J. (2002). *Odysseus in America: Combat Trauma and the Trials of Homecoming.* New York: Scribner, p. 20.

[24] Smith, C. M. (1997). *Jung and shamanism in dialogue: Retrieving the soul, retrieving the sacred.* New York, NY: Paulist Press, p. 123.

[25] Stevens, A. (1982). *Archetypes: A natural history of the Self.* New York: Quill, p. 262.

[26] Jung, C. G. (1969). A review of the complex theory (R. F. C. Hull, Trans.). In H. Read et al. (Eds.), *The collected works of C. G. Jung* (Vol. 8, 2nd ed., pp. 92-104). Princeton, NJ: Princeton University Press. (Original work published 1948), paras. 18-19.

[27] Jung, A review of the complex theory, paras. 200-201.

[28] Singer, J. (1994). *Boundaries of the soul: The practice of Jung's psychology.* New York, NY: Anchor Books. (Original work published 1972), p. 44,

[29] van der Kolk, B. A. (2014). *The body keeps the score: Brain, mind, and body in the healing of trauma.* Viking.

[30] Whitmont, E. C. (1991). *The symbolic quest: Basic concepts in analytical psychology.* Princeton, NJ: Princeton University Press. (Original work published in 1969), p. 69.

[31] Jung, A review of the complex theory, paras. 387, 582, 611-616.

[32] Jung, A review of the complex theory, para. 611.

[33] Stevens, *Archetypes*, p. 262.

[34] Shay, J. (1994). *Achilles in Vietnam combat trauma and the undoing of character*. New York: Scribner.

[35] Shay, *Odysseus in America*, p. 20.

[36] Homer. (2014). The Odyssey. (Samuel Butler, Trans.). In *The Iliad and the Odyssey.* New York, NY: Fall River Press. (Translation published 1900/Original work circa 8th century BCE), p. 527; Book 9, lines 39-41).

[37] Shay, *Achilles in Vietnam combat trauma and the undoing of character*.

[38] Shay, *Odysseus in America*, p. 20.

[39] Marlantes, *What it is like to go to war*, pp. 206-207.

[40] Eickhoff, R. L. (1997). *The raid: A dramatic retelling of Ireland's epic tale.* New York, NY: Forge: Tom Doherty Associates, Inc., p. 98.

[41] Jung, *Jung's seminar on Nietzsche's Zarathustra*, p. 27.

[42] Jung, A review of the complex theory, para. 18

[43] Whitmont, *The symbolic quest*, pp. 65-66

[44] Homer, The Odyssey. (Samuel Butler, Trans.). In *The Iliad and the Odyssey*, p. 528.

[45] Shay, *Odysseus in America*, p. 39.

[46] Berking, M., Margraf, M., Ebert, D., Wuppermann, P., Hofman, S.G., & Junghanns, K. (2011). Deficits in emotional-regulation skills predict alcohol use during and after cognitive behavioral therapy for alcohol dependence. Journal of Consulting and Clinical Psychology, 79(3): pp. 307-318.

[47] Magers, A. (2021). The Battle Within: Impact Evaluation, p. 14. Retrieved from https://www.canva.com/design/DAExaryd9iQ/augpE4P8PiJB7SVX2zBDMA/view?utm_content=DAExaryd9iQ&utm_campaign=designshare&utm_medium=link&utm_source=homepage_design_menu#16

[48] Magers, The Battle Within: Impact Evaluation.

[49] Doll, A., Holzel, B., Bratec, S. M., Boucard, C., Xie, X., Wohlschlager, A., & Sorg, C. (2016). Mindful attention to breath regulates emotions via increased amygdala-prefrontal cortex connectivity. NeuroImage, 134, March 2016. DOI: 10.1016/jneuroimage.2016.03.041

[50] Tick, E. (2014). Warrior's return: Restoring the soul after war. Boulder, CO: Sounds True, Inc., pp. 178-179.

[51] Brooke, R. (2017). An archetypal approach to treating combat post-traumatic stress disorder. In D. Downing & J. Mills (Eds.), Outpatient treatment of psychosis: psychodynamic approaches to evidence-based practice (pp. 171-195). London: Karmac., p. 179.

[52] Tick, War and the soul, p. 266.

[53] Homer, The Odyssey. (Samuel Butler, Trans.). In The Iliad and the Odyssey, p. 528-529.

[54] Homer, The Odyssey. (Samuel Butler, Trans.). In The Iliad and the Odyssey, p. 531.

[55] Shay, Odysseus in America, p. 47.

[56] Mitchell, S. (2004). Gilgamesh: A new English version. New York: Free Press.

57 Jung, The relations between the ego and the unconscious, para. 314.

58 Downing, C. (2007). *The Goddess: Mythological images of the feminine*. Lincoln, NE: Authors Choice Press. (Original work published 1981), p. 77.

59 Jung, C. G. (1968). Concerning rebirth (R. F. C. Hull, Trans.). In H. Read et al. (Eds.), *The collected works of C. G. Jung* (Vol. 9i, 2nd ed., pp. 113-147). Princeton, NJ: Princeton University Press. (Original work published 1950), para. 240-241.

60 Jung, C. G. (1968). Archetypes of the collective unconscious (R. F. C. Hull, Trans.). In H. Read et al. (Eds.), *The collected works of C. G. Jung* (Vol. 9i, 2nd ed., pp. 3-41). Princeton, NJ: Princeton University Press. (Original work published 1954), paras. 40, 298.

61 Jung, C. G. (1968). Introduction to the religious and psychological problems of alchemy (R. F. C. Hull, Trans.). In H. Read et al. (Eds.), *The collected works of C. G. Jung* (Vol. 12, 2nd ed., pp. 1-38). Princeton, NJ: Princeton University Press. (Original work published 1943), para. 31.

62 Campbell, J. (1991). *The masks of God: Occidental mythology*. New York: The Viking Press. (Original work published 1964), p. 167.

63 Homer, The Odyssey. (Samuel Butler, Trans.). In *The Iliad and the Odyssey*, p. 542.

64 Homer, The Odyssey. (Samuel Butler, Trans.). In *The Iliad and the Odyssey*, p. 543.

65 Woodman, M. (1985). *The pregnant virgin: A process of psychological transformation*. Toronto, Canada: Inner City Books, p. 23.

66 Whitmont, *The symbolic quest*, p. 102.

67 Whitmont, *The symbolic quest*, p. 88.

68 Shay, *Odysseus in America*, pp. 56-59.

69 Shay, *Odysseus in America*, pp. 57-58.

[70] Bobrow, J. (2015). *Waking up from war: A better way home for veterans and nations.* Durham, NC: Pitchstone Publishing, p. 78.

[71] Woodman, *The pregnant virgin*, pp. 21-22.

[72] Hillman, J. (1976). *Re-visioning psychology*. New York, NY: Harper & Row, pp. 32-33.

[73] Levine, P. A. (1997). *Waking the tiger: Healing Trauma.* Berkley, CA: North Atlantic Books, p. 29.

[74] Levine, *Waking the tiger,* p. 31.

[75] Jung, Archetypes of the collective unconscious, para. 55

[76] Jung, Archetypes of the collective unconscious, para. 56

[77] Hillman, J. (1997). *Suicide and the soul.* Woodstock, CT: Spring Publications. (Original work published 1965)

[78] Jung, Commentary on The secret of the golden flower, para. 62.

[79] Homer. (2007). The Odyssey. (Richmond Lattimore, Trans.). New York, NY: HarperCollins Publishers. (Translation published 1967/Original work circa 8th century BCE), p. 156, line 143.

[80] Homer, The Odyssey. (Samuel Butler, Trans.). In *The Iliad and the Odyssey*, pp. 545-546.

[81] Jung, C. G. (1966). The aims of psychotherapy (R. F. C. Hull, Trans.). In H. Read et al. (Eds.), *The collected works of C. G. Jung* (Vol. 16, 2nd ed., pp. 36-52). Princeton, NJ: Princeton University Press. (Original work published 1931), para. 84).

[82] Hillman, J. (1985). *Anima: An Anatomy of a Personified Notion.* Dallas, TX: Spring Publications, Inc., p. 137.

[83] Ronnberg, A. & Martin, K. (2010). *The book of symbols: Reflections on Archetypal Images.* Archive for Research in Archetypal Symbolism. Cologne, Germany: Taschen, pp. 324-327.

[84] Jung, The relations between the ego and the unconscious, para. 304.

85 Stein, M. (1998). *Jung's map of the soul: An introduction.* Peru, IL: Open Court, p. 128.

86 Jung, Psychological types, para. 806.

87 Johnson, R. A. (2016). *Inner Gold: Understanding Psychological Projection.* Kihei, Hawaii: Koa Books.

88 Jung, C. G. (1963). *Memories, dreams, reflections* (A. Jaffé, Ed.) (R. Winston & C. Winston, Trans.). New York, NY: Vintage Books. (Original work published 1961)

89 Jung, The relations between the ego and the unconscious, para. 314.

90 O'Bryan, A. (2014). *Navajo Indian myths.* New York: Dover Publications, Inc. (Original work published 1993), pp. 1-13.

91 Homer. (2007). The Odyssey. (Richmond Lattimore, Trans.), p. 161, lines 363-364.

92 Homer, The Odyssey. (Samuel Butler, Trans.). In *The Iliad and the Odyssey*, p. 550.

93 Eickhoff, *The raid*, p. 98.

94 Jung, Archetypes of the collective unconscious, para. 40.

95 Jung, C. G. (1966). The psychology of the transference (R. F. C. Hull, Trans.). In H. Read et al. (Eds.), *The collected works of C. G. Jung* (Vol. 16, 2nd ed., pp. 163-323). Princeton, NJ: Princeton University Press. (Original work published 1946), paras. 453-454.

96 Jung, C. G. (1968). Individual dream symbolism in relation to alchemy (R. F. C. Hull, Trans.). In H. Read et al. (Eds.), *The collected works of C. G. Jung* (Vol. 12, 2nd ed., pp. 39-224). Princeton, NJ: Princeton University Press. (Original work published 1936)

97 Shay, *Odysseus in America*, p. 70.

98 Homer. (2007). The Odyssey. (Richmond Lattimore, Trans.), p. 164, lines 449-454.

[99] Jung, The psychology of the transference, para. 455

[100] Homer, The Odyssey. (Samuel Butler, Trans.). In *The Iliad and the Odyssey*, pp. 468-469.

[101] Homer, The Odyssey. (Samuel Butler, Trans.). In *The Iliad and the Odyssey*, pp. 556-557.

[102] Jung, C. G. (1967). Symbols of transformation (R. F. C. Hull, Trans.) (H. Read et al., Eds.), *The collected works of C. G. Jung* (Vol. 5, 2nd ed.). Princeton, NJ: Princeton University Press. (Original work published 1952), para. 671.

[103] Homer, The Odyssey. (Samuel Butler, Trans.). In *The Iliad and the Odyssey*, p. 559.

[104] Campbell, *The masks of God: Occidental mythology*, pp. 171-172.

[105] Jung, Symbols of transformation, para. 553.

[106] Houston, J. (2009). *The hero and the goddess: The Odyssey as pathway to personal transformation.* Wheaton, IL: Quest Books, p. 206.

[107] Homer, The Odyssey. (Samuel Butler, Trans.). In *The Iliad and the Odyssey*, pp. 567-568.

[108] Houston, *The hero and the goddess,* p. 206.

[109] Homer, The Odyssey. (Samuel Butler, Trans.). In *The Iliad and the Odyssey*, p. 571.

[110] Jung, The relations between the ego and the unconscious, para. 308.

[111] Homer, The Odyssey. (Samuel Butler, Trans.). In *The Iliad and the Odyssey*, p. 571.

[112] Jung, C. G. (1969). On psychic energy (R. F. C. Hull, Trans.). In H. Read et al. (Eds.), *The collected works of C. G. Jung* (Vol. 8, 2nd ed.). Princeton, NJ: Princeton University Press. (Original work published 1928), paras. 63-69.

[113] Homer, The Odyssey. (Samuel Butler, Trans.). In *The Iliad and the Odyssey*, p. 573.

[114] Homer, The Odyssey. (Samuel Butler, Trans.). In *The Iliad and the Odyssey*, p. 575

[115] Kalsched, *Trauma and the soul*, p. 229.

[116] van der Kolk, *The body keeps the score.*

[117] Homer, The Odyssey. (Samuel Butler, Trans.). In *The Iliad and the Odyssey*, p. 575.

[118] Kerven, *Viking myths & sagas: Retold from ancient Norse texts*, pp. 43-45.

[119] Perrera, S. (1981) *Descent to the goddess*. New York: Inner City Books.

[120] Campbell, J. (2013). *Goddesses: Mysteries of the feminine divine.* Novato, CA: New World Library. pp. 93-98.

[121] Homer, The Odyssey. (Samuel Butler, Trans.). In *The Iliad and the Odyssey*, p. 484.

[122] Homer, The Odyssey. (Samuel Butler, Trans.). In *The Iliad and the Odyssey*, p. 508.

[123] Homer, The Odyssey. (Samuel Butler, Trans.). In *The Iliad and the Odyssey*, p. 484.

[124] Jung, On psychic energy, para. 69.

[125] Tick, *War and the soul*, p. 5.

[126] Tick, *Warrior's return*, p. 145.

[127] Bremner, J. D. (2006). Traumatic stress: Effects on the brain. *Dialogues in Clinical Neuroscience.* December 2006 8(4): pp. 445-461. Retrieved from https://www.ncbi.nlm.nih.gov/pmc/articles/PMC3181836/

[128] van der Kolk, *The body keeps the score.*

[129] McWilliams, *Psychoanalytic diagnosis.*

[130] Jung, C. G. (1966). On the psychology of the unconscious (R. F. C. Hull, Trans.). In H. Read et al. (Eds.), *The collected works of C. G. Jung* (Vol. 7, 2nd ed., pp. 1–119). Princeton, NJ: Princeton University Press. (Original work published 1943), paras. 67-68.

[131] Jung, The aims of psychotherapy, paras. 84-85.

[132] Jung, C. G. (1970). *Mysterium coniunctionis* (R. F. C. Hull, Trans.) (H. Read et al., Eds.), *The collected works of C. G. Jung* (Vol. 14, 2nd ed.). Princeton, NJ: Princeton University Press. (Original work published 1955-56), para. 778.

[133] Homer, The Odyssey. (Samuel Butler, Trans.). In *The Iliad and the Odyssey*, p. 488.

[134] Shay, *Odysseus in America*, pp. 65-66.

[135] Homer, The Odyssey. (Samuel Butler, Trans.). In *The Iliad and the Odyssey*, p. 491.

[136] Singer, *Boundaries of the soul*, pp. 210-211.

[137] Jung, C. G. (1969). Psychotherapists or the clergy (R. F. C. Hull, Trans.). In H. Read et al. (Eds.), *The collected works of C. G. Jung* (Vol. 11, 2nd ed., pp. 327-347). Princeton, NJ: Princeton University Press. (Original work published 1932), para. 534.

[138] Homer, The Odyssey. (Samuel Butler, Trans.). In *The Iliad and the Odyssey*, p. 492.

[139] Homer, The Odyssey. (Samuel Butler, Trans.). In *The Iliad and the Odyssey*, pp. 496.

[140] Von Franz, M. L. (1980). *Projection and re-collection in Jungian psychology.* Peru, Illinois: Open Court Publishing, p. 16.

[141] Homer, The Odyssey. (Samuel Butler, Trans.). In *The Iliad and the Odyssey*, 497-501.

[142] Campbell, J. (2015). *Romance of the grail: The magic and mystery of Arthurian myth.* Novato, CA: New World Library. pp. 35-93.

[143] Johnson, R. A. (1989). *He: Understanding Masculine Psychology.* New York, NY: Harper and Row, pp. 70-71.

[144] Homer, The Odyssey. (Samuel Butler, Trans.). In *The Iliad and the Odyssey*, pp. 505-506.

[145] Homer, The Odyssey. (Samuel Butler, Trans.). In *The Iliad and the Odyssey*, p. 513.

[146] Homer, The Odyssey. (Samuel Butler, Trans.). In *The Iliad and the Odyssey*, p. 515.

[147] Homer, The Odyssey. (Samuel Butler, Trans.). In *The Iliad and the Odyssey*, p. 515.

[148] Campbell, J. (2004). *Pathways to bliss: Mythology and personal transformation.* Novato, CA: New World Library, pp. 32-33.

[149] Homer, The Odyssey. (Samuel Butler, Trans.). In *The Iliad and the Odyssey*, p. 516.

[150] Homer, The Odyssey. (Samuel Butler, Trans.). In *The Iliad and the Odyssey*, p. 519.

[151] Campbell, *Romance of the grail*, pp. 42, 50-51.

[152] Campbell, *Romance of the grail*, pp. 167-168.

[153] Homer, The Odyssey. (Samuel Butler, Trans.). In *The Iliad and the Odyssey*, pp. 523-524.

[154] Marlantes, *What it is like to go to war*, pp. 206-207.

[155] Homer, The Odyssey. (Samuel Butler, Trans.). In *The Iliad and the Odyssey*, p. 586.

[156] Homer, The Odyssey. (Samuel Butler, Trans.). In *The Iliad and the Odyssey*, p. 524.

[157] Smith, *Jung and shamanism in dialogue.*

[158] Leader, C. (2009). The odyssey—a Jungian perspective: Individuation and the meeting with the archetypes of the collective unconscious. *British Journal of Psychotherapy.* Vol. 25, Issue 4, p. 513.

[159] Kalsched, *Trauma and the soul.*

[160] Homer, The Odyssey. (Samuel Butler, Trans.). In *The Iliad and the Odyssey*, pp. 617-618.

[161] Cline, E. H. (2013). *The Trojan war: A very short introduction.* New York, NY: Oxford University Press, p. 12.

[162] Levine, P. A. (2008). *Healing trauma: A pioneering program for restoring the wisdom of your body.* Boulder, CO: Sounds True, p. 21-22.

[163] Campbell, *Goddesses: Mysteries of the feminine divine*, p. 144.

[164] Homer, The Odyssey. (Samuel Butler, Trans.). In *The Iliad and the Odyssey*, pp. 626-627.

[165] Kalsched, *Trauma and the soul.*

[166] Homer, The Odyssey. (Samuel Butler, Trans.). In *The Iliad and the Odyssey*, p. 674.

[167] Homer, The Odyssey. (Samuel Butler, Trans.). In *The Iliad and the Odyssey*, p. 697.

[168] Homer, The Odyssey. (Samuel Butler, Trans.). In *The Iliad and the Odyssey*, p. 713.

[169] Homer, The Odyssey. (Samuel Butler, Trans.). In *The Iliad and the Odyssey*, p. 714.

[170] Homer, The Odyssey. (Samuel Butler, Trans.). In *The Iliad and the Odyssey*, pp. 730-731.

[171] Edinger, E. (1972). *Ego and archetype.* New York, NY: Penguin Books.

[172] Kalsched, D. (1996). *The inner world of trauma: Archetypal defenses of the personal spirit.* London, England: Routledge; and Kalsched, D. (2013). *Trauma and the soul: A psycho-spiritual approach to human development and its interruption.* Hove, East Sussex, England: Routledge.

[173] Kalsched, *Trauma and the soul.*

[174] Kalsched, *Trauma and the soul*, pp. 19-20.

[175] Kalsched, *Trauma and the soul*, p. 242.

[176] Kalsched, *Trauma and the soul.*

[177] Wilmer, Combat nightmares: Toward a therapy of violence, pp. 135-136.

[178] Kalsched, *Trauma and the soul*, p. 143-144.

[179] Whitmont, *The symbolic quest.*

[180] Whitmont, *The symbolic quest*, p. 86.

[181] Kalsched, *Trauma and the soul*, pp. 141-141.

[182] Jung, Archetypes of the collective unconscious, p. 122.

[183] Jung, Archetypes of the collective unconscious, pp. 125-126.

[184] Jung, Archetypes of the collective unconscious, p. 128.

[185] Rank, O. (2004). *The myth of the birth of the hero: A psychological exploration of myth* (G. C. Richter & E. J. Lieberman, Trans.). Baltimore, MD: Johns Hopkins University Press. (Original work published 1909).

[186] Singer, *Boundaries of the soul*, pp. 98-99.

[187] Wilmer, H. A. (1986b). The healing nightmare: A study of the war dreams of Vietnam combat veterans. *Quadrant*, Vol. 19, Issue 1, p. 55.

[188] Homer, The Odyssey. (Samuel Butler, Trans.). In *The Iliad and the Odyssey*, p. 559.

[189] Shay, *Odysseus in America*, p. 120.

[190] Hillman, J. (1996). *The Soul's Code: In Search of Character and Calling*. New York, NY: Random House, Inc., pp. 81-82.

[191] Hillman, *The Soul's Code*, p. 80.

[192] Jung, Commentary on The secret of the golden flower, para. 54.

[193] Jung, *Memories, dreams, reflections*, p. 4.

[194] Jung, Archetypes of the collective unconscious, para. 271.

[195] Cline, *The Trojan war*, pp. 18-26.

[196] Cline, *The Trojan war*.

[197] Cline, *The Trojan war*.

[198] Graziosi, B. (2019). *Homer: A very short introduction*. New York, NY: Oxford University Press.

[199] Graziosi, *Homer: A very short introduction*, p. 18.

[200] Gómez, C., ed. (2019). *The encyclopedia of ancient Greece*. London, UK: Amber Books, p. 46.

[201] Graziosi, *Homer: A very short introduction*, p. 23.

[202] Gómez, *The encyclopedia of ancient Greece*, p. 28.

[203] Graziosi, *Homer: A very short introduction*, p. 26.

[204] Graziosi, *Homer: A very short introduction*, p. 24.

[205] Cline, *The Trojan war*.

[206] Graziosi, *Homer: A very short introduction*.

[207] Cline, *The Trojan war*, pp. 18-26.

[208] Apollodorus. *The Library Epitome*. Translated by J. G. Frazer. Retrieved from https://www.theoi.com/Text/ApollodorusE.html#3

[209] Jung, Psychological types, para. 837.

[210] Jung, Psychological types, para. 808.

[211] Downing, *The Goddess*.

[212] Jung, Psychological types, para. 808.

[213] Jung, Psychological types, para. 808.

[214] Jung, The relations between the ego and the unconscious, paras. 303-304.

[215] Hillman, *Anima: An Anatomy of a Personified Notion*, pp. 11-13.

[216] Hillman, *Anima: An Anatomy of a Personified Notion*, p. 61.

[217] Downing, *The Goddess*, pp. 66, 105.

[218] Jung, The relations between the ego and the unconscious, pp. 188-211.

[219] Jung, A review of the complex theory.

[220] Jung, Psychological types, para. 797.

[221] Jung, C. G. (2009). *The red book: Liber novus* (S. Shamdasani, Ed.) (S. Shamdasani, M. Kyburz, & J. Peck, Trans.). New York, NY: Norton, p. 59.

[222] Hopcke, R. H. (1999). *A guided tour of the collected works of C. G. Jung*. Boston, MA: Shambhala Publications, Inc., p. 96.